MEMOIRS

Illustrating the

HISTORY OF JACOBINISM

written in French by

AUGUSTIN BARRUEL

and translated into English by

THE HON. ROBERT CLIFFORD, F.R.S. AND A.S.

*Princes and nations shall disappear from
the face of the earth . . . and this* REVOLUTION
shall be the WORK OF SECRET SOCIETIES.
—Adam Weishaupt's *Discourse for the Mysteries*

Part III

THE ANTISOCIAL CONSPIRACY

London
Spradabach Publishing
2021

SPRADABACH PUBLISHING
BM Box Spradabach
London WC1N 3XX

*Memoirs Illustrating the History of Jacobinism,
Part III: The Antisocial Conspiracy*
originally published in English in 1798
© Spradabach Publishing 2021

First Spradabach edition published 2021

ISBN 978-1-9993573-3-7

Table of Contents.

TABLE OF CONTENTS

Preliminary Observations.

On the Illuminées and on the Different Works whereon These *Memoirs* Are Grounded.

he third conspiracy, which I am now about to investigate, is that of the *Atheistical Illuminées*, which at my outset[1] I denominated *the conspiracy of the Sophisters of Impiety and Anarchy against every religion natural or revealed; not only against kings, but against every government, against all civil society, even against all property whatsoever.*

The name of Illuminée which this Sect (the most disastrous in its principles, the most extensive in its views, the most atrociously cunning in its means)

---

1   Vol. I., page xxix.

has chosen, is of ancient standing in the annals of disorganizing Sophistry. It was the name which Manes and his disciples first affected, *gloriantur Manichæi se de cœlo illuminates.*[2] The first Rosicrucians also, who appeared in Germany, called themselves Illuminées. And later, in our time, the Martinists (with many other sects) have pretended to Illuminism. As an outline for history I distinguish them by their plots and tenets, and will reduce them into two classes, the *Atheistical* and the *Theosophical* Illuminées. These latter more particularly comprehend the *I*, whom I have already mentioned in my second volume, and the *Swedenbourgians*, whom I shall mention in thier proper place, where also I shall give what information I have been able to collect relating to them. The *Atheistical* Illuminées are the objects of the present volume, and it is their conspiracy that I mean to disclose.[3]

The very numerous letters, books, and manuscripts, which I have received since the publication

---

2   Gaultier, *Verbo Manichæi*, sect. 3.

3   The Translator thinks it proper to inform the Reader, that, considering how much the abuse of terms, such as of *Philosophy, Reason,* &c. &c. has contributed to diffuse the new-fangled doctrines, he has adopted in the present volume (which may be said to be the first methodical work published on the subject of which it treats) the words *Illuminée, Illuminize,* and *Illuminization,* though Illuminate and Illumination might perhaps be more correct expressions. Every reader will feel, that the illumination of the world, and to illuminate mankind, are objects worthy of the true philosopher. But may the man be ever accurst who shall attempt to illuminize his countrymen, or aim at the *illuminization* of the world! —Tr.

of my proposals, has rendered it impossible for me to comprise the proposed investigation in one volume. The baleful projects of the Sect and the laws for their execution are so strangely combined, that I thought it necessary to begin by making my reader perfectly acquainted with its code; that is to say, with the regular progression of its degrees, mysteries, and government.

This alone requiring an entire volume, I am reduced to the necessity of giving a *fourth*, in which I shall develope the history of Illuminism, and make an application of the triple conspiracy to the French Revolution. I have more particularly applied myself to the investigation of the legislative part of this conspiring Sect, as no work has yet been published in which the whole of their code is to be found. Detached parts only were to be met with scattered throughout the papers which had been seized by the public authority. These I have collected and digested; thus enabling the reader more easily to judge what has been and what must have been the result of such laws. In such an undertaking, I feel myself bound to lay before the public an account of the documents on which I ground my proofs. The following then is a list of the principal works, with a few observations on each, that the reader may form his own judgment as to their authenticity.

I. The first is a collection entitled "Some of the *Original Writings*[4] of the Sect of Illuminées, which

---

4   *Einige Originalschriften des Illuminatenordens, welche bey*

were discovered on the 11th and 12th of October, 1786, at Landshut, on a search made in the House of the Sieur Zwack, heretofore Counsellor of the Regency; and printed by Order of His Highness the Elector.—Munich, by Ant. Franz, Printer to the Court."[5]

II. The second is a supplement to the *Original Writings*, chiefly containing those which were found on a search made at the castle of Sandersdorf, *a famous haunt of the Illuminées*, by order of His Highness the Elector. Munich, 1787.[6]

These two volues contain irrefragable proofs of the most detestable conspiracy. They disclose the principles, the object, and the means of the Sect; the essential parts of their code, the diligent correspondence of the adepts, particularly that of their chief, and a statement of their progress and future hopes. The editors indeed have carried their attention so far, as to mention by whose hand the principal documents or letters were written. At the beginning of the first volume,

---

dem gewesenen Regierungsrath Zwack durch vorgenommene Hausvisitation zu Landshut den 11. und 12. Octob. ec. 1786 vorgefunden worden (Munich: Anton Franz, 1786). — Ed.

5   Einige Originalschriften des Illuminaten Ordens, welche bey dem gewesenen regierungsrath Zwack, durch vorgennommene haus-visitation zu Landshut den 11 und 12 Octob. 1786, vorgefunden worden. Auf höchsten Befehl Seiner Churfürstlichen Durchleucht zum Druck befördert. München. Gedruckt bey Ant. Franz Churfl. Hofbuchdrucker.

6   Nachrichten von weitern Originalschriften, etc.

and on the frontispiece of the second, is seen the following *remarkable advertisement* by order of the Elector:—"Those who may harbour any doubt as to the authenticity of this collection, have only to apply to the office where the secret archives are kept at Munich, and where orders are left to show the originals."[7]

I entreat that my readers will recollect this advertisement whenever they shall see the *Original Writings* cited.

III. "*The True Illuminée*, or the real and perfect *Ritual* of the Illuminée; of the Illuminée; comprehending the Preparation, the Noviciate, the Minerval Degree, that of the Minor and Major Illuminée, all without addition or omission."—With respect to the authenticity of this work, we need only quote the testimony of the Baron Knigge, surnamed *Philo*, the most famous of the Illuminées after the Founder of the Sect; and who was actually the chief compiler of its Code, as he tells us himself: "All these degrees (says he), such as I composed them, have been printed this year at *Edesse* (Frankfort on the Mein) under the title of the *True Illuminée*. I am ignorant of the author; but *they appear exactly as they flowed from my pen;* that is to say, as I compiled them."[8] This certainly is an

---

7   *Wer an der aechtheit dieser versammlung einen zweifel tragt, mag sich nur bey den hiesigen geheimen archiv melden, allwo man ihm die urschrifften selbst vorzulegen befehligen ist. München 26 Marz 1787.*

8   *Philo's Endliche erklarung,* &c., page 96.

authenticated document on the Sect, and recognized by the compiler himself.

IV. I now proceed to a work which was published by this same Philo,—under the title of *"Last Observations, or Last Words of Philo,* and Answers to divers Questions on my connections with the Illuminées."[9] In this work Philo-Knigge gives us an account of himself and of his Illuminism, of his agreements with the chiefs of the Sect, and of his labours for it. His vanity, however, makes this narrative fulsome. The reader will observe in his writings one of those pretended Philosophers who treat all religious objects with that contempt which they themselves deserve. This is of no consequence; he attempts to justify his own conduct; his avowals may therefore be received in testimony against the Sect.

V. "The last Works of Spartacus and Philo," *Die neusten Arbeiten des Spartacus und Philo.* Except the *Original Writings*, this is the most intelligent and important work that has been published on the Illuminées. It contains the two degrees of the greatest consideration both on account of the mysteries revealed in them by the Sect, and of the laws laid down for the adepts.—Not a shadow of doubt can be maintained as to the authenticity of this work. These degrees and laws are published with a certificate of Philo attesting their conformity with

---

9   The English translation, translated by Jeva Singh-Anand, published in 2012, bears the title *Philo's Reply to Questions Concerning His Association With the Illuminati.*

the original, and under the seal of the Order. This certificate was scarcely necessary. *Whoever can read* must easily perceive that these degrees and these laws are no other than a compilation, and often (in the most essential parts) but a copy of the discourses, precepts, and principles, contained in the *Original Writings*. The publisher is a man who has passed through all the degrees of Illuminism. More dexterous than Philo, he makes himself master of his secret, and of that of the whole Sect. The better to unmask Illuminism, he becomes an Illuminée; and he has so well succeeded, that no member of the Order was better acquainted with it than himself.

VI. The same writer has published *A Critical History of the Degrees of Illuminism*, a valuable work, in which every thing is proved from the very letters of the grand adepts.

VII. The *Directing Illuminée*, or the Scotch Knight. This may be said to be the counterpart of the *Last Works of Philo and Spartacus*. It is a description of the most important intermediary degree of Illuminism. The Editor does not indeed publish it under the signet of the Order; but when the reader has compared it with the *Original Writings*, and even with the criticism on it by the chief, who was not much pleased with the compiler, he will soon decide that the grand seal of the Order is not necessary to authenticate it.

VIII. *Remarkable Depositions respecting the Illuminées*. These are three juridical depositions on oath, and signed 1st by Mr. *Cosandey*, Canon and Professor at Munich; 2dly by Mr. *Renner*, Priest and Professor of the same Academy; 3dly by Mr. *Utzschneider*, Counsellor of the Electoral Chamber; 4thly by Mr. *George Grümberg*, a member of the Academy of Sciences, and Professor of Mathematics. As every thing is juridical in these depositions, it would be useless for me to insist on the weight they must carry with them. These were four pupils, who did not wait to be initiated in the grand mysteries of the Sect to form their judgement on, and to quit the Sect. They were cited at a tribunal to declare all they knew, and they answered with moderation and truth. Their depositions will find a place in the historical part of this work.

IX. The *Apologies* published by some of the leaders of the Sect are also to be classed among the incontrovertible evidence which we have acquired. These gentlemen will not be expected to have aggravated their own wickedness.

X. The list would be endless were I to subjoin all the works that have been written against the Sect. But I must distinguish in this place the works of Mr. *Hoffman*, Professor at the University of Vienna. I am but little acquainted with those of Doctor *Zimmerman*, though I have been informed by letter, that he furnished many valuable articles in a journal published at Vienna, and chiefly directed against the Sect. I often find Mr. *Stark*'s name mentioned as a strenuous opponent of the Sect. I have seen no publication with his name to it, except an Apology in Answer to the Calumnies of the Sect, which it continues to repeat, notwithstanding the victorious manner in which he has answered them.

Among the anonymous writings I find an excellent work entitled the *Ultimate fate of the Free-masons (Endliches schicksal des Freymaurer Ordens).*[10] It is a discourse pronounced at the breaking-up of a Freemason's Lodge. The writer of this discourse gives an excellent statement of the reasons why the Lodges should suspend their labours since Illuminism had intruded itself into Masonry.—I believe he would have pronounced this discourse much sooner, had he known that all Lodges were not so pure as his own.

I have also perused the *Biographical Fragments* of the Sieur *Bode*, a famous Illuminée; these will be very useful in our Historical Volume. As to numberless other works which I have read on the same subject, it will suffice to give the titles of them when quoted. I have said more than enough to show that I am not in the dark with respect to the subject on which I am writing.

I could wish to express my gratitude to those virtuous men who, by their correspondence, and the memorials which they have sent me, have greatly advanced my undertaking. But open expressions of such a gratitude would prove fatal to them. To have contributed to the public utility is a sufficient reward for their virtue; and if my work is

---

10   This work has since been credited to Ludwig Adolf Christian von Grolmann. —Ed.

not so perfect as it ought to be, it arises not from any want of energy in their endeavours.

I find myself much against my will obliged to answer certain objections which my Translator has made, and which will, doubtless, be repeated by many other readers, grounded on the work of Mr. Robison, entitled *Proof of a Conspiracy against all the Religions and Governments of Europe*, &c. &c. That work was published just as this Third Volume was going to the press. Its author had not then met with my two first Volumes; but in a second Edition he is pleased to mention them in his Appendix. I am much flattered by his approbation, heartily congratulate him on the zeal he has himself shown in combating the public enemy, and am happy to see that he has wrought on the best materials. Without knowing it, we have fought for the same cause with the same arms, and pursued the same course; but the public are on the eve of seeing our respective quotations, and will observe a remarkable difference between them. I fear lest we should be put in competition with each other, and the cause of truth suffer in the conflict. I entreat the reader to observe, that these differences arise from the different methods followed by him and myself. Mr. Robison has adopted the easiest, though the most hazardous method. He combines together in one paragraph what his memory may have compiled from many, and sometimes makes use of the expressions of the German author when he thinks it necessary. Beside, he has seen much, and read much, and relates it all together in the paragraphs marked by *inverted Commas*. The warning he has given in his preface will not suffice to remove the objections of some readers. In some passages he has even adopted as truth certain assertions which the correspondence of the Illuminées evidently demonstrate to have been invented by them against their adversaries, and which in my Historical Volume I shall be obliged to treat in an opposite sense. Nor will I pretend to say, that Illuminism drew its origin from Masonry; for it is a fact demonstrated beyond all doubt, that the founder of Illuminism only became a Mason in 1777, and that two years later than that he was wholly unacquainted with the mysteries of Masonry.[11]

I know perfectly well, that this will not make Illuminism less disastrous; nevertheless I am obliged to differ from Mr. Robison when treating on that subject, as well as on some other articles.—So much for objections; here is my reply.

In the first place Mr. Robison and I always agree as to the essential facts and the Conspiracy of the Illuminized Lodges; we also agree on their maxims and degrees; and this must be sufficient to convince the reader.

In the next place, in his general view of the Sect he has observed its detestable and most dangerous principles. Like a traveller he has seen the

---

11   *Original Writings*, vol. I., let. 6, to Ajax.—*Ibid*. Let. 36 to M. C. Porcius—and the first pages of the *Critical History of the Degrees*.

Monstrum horrendum, informe, ingens . . .

But he has not described its forms, its manners, and its habits. Nor would it be very prudent to reject his narrative because some few circumstances are not perfectly authenticated, or because here and there some want of order may be observable.

In short, if we except one or two letters, which may be said to be translations, all the other quotations (though in the form of letters) cannot be called so, for they are not to be found in the letters of the Illuminées. They are Extracts from different parts, all brought together under one head; Mr. Robison has given them to the public in his own stile, and sometimes makes the Illuminées speak in clearer terms than is done in the Originals. His addition in the Translation of the famous letter from Spartacus to Marius, page 165-6,[12] has given rise to numberless questions, how the—*even d—*. was expressed in the German text. A parenthesis follows (*can this mean death?*). I was obliged to answer that the even *d—*, as well as the parenthesis, were additions; but at the same time that they were not additions contrary to the sense of the letter. I could willingly have attributed these deviations to a difference in the editions of the *Original Writings*; but a new work must be supposed, as well as new letters, to justify the quotations, and all Germany must have noticed such changes. In the first place, the Court of Bavaria would have protested against

---

12   See page 4 of this Volume.

such a supposition; as the *Original Writings* could not have coincided with an edition so dissimilar; next, the Illuminées who have not spoken in such clear language, though clear enough in their letters; in fine, the authors who have combated Illuminism, and whose quotations all exactly agree with the Edition of Munich. The Pages may change in different Editions; but whole Letters and Discourses cannot, especially when the public may, as we have seen above, have access to the Originals.

As for myself, whose name cannot be expected to have such authority as Mr. Robison's, I have taken all the precautions of which I felt myself to stand in need.[13] I never make a quotation but with the Original before me; and when I translate any passage which may stagger the reader, I subjoin the original, that each may explain and verify the text. I follow the same line of conduct when I compare the different testimonies. I never mention a

---

13 I am also afraid that the difference that exists between the degrees of Rosicrucian, of which Mr. Robison is in possession, and those which I have mentioned, may give rise to argument. I answer, 1st. That I am acquainted with three degrees of Rosicrucians, very different in themselves; 2dly. That the Cathechisms, Questions, and Rituals for the same degree gready differ in different countries: 3dly. That I have followed the works of *Mr. L'Abbe Le Franc*, which Mr. Robison has quoted: 4thly. That Mr. Robison allows the degree of *Knights of the Sun* as described by me to be similar to that which he is in possession of. Since the publication of my Second Volume, I have received an account of the same degree which coincides with what I had said, and this degree is a sufficient ground for all that Mr. Robison or myself have asserted on the attack carried on by Masonry against Religion and Governments.

single law in the code without having the original before me, or the practice of it to vouch for my assertion. Hence it will be perceived, that we are not to be put in competition with each other; Mr. Robison taking a general view while I have attempted to descend into particulars: as to the substance we agree. I heartily congratulate him on his zeal in combating the monster; and though we do not agree in certain particularities, we both evince the monstrous nature of the Sect, and the certainty of its horrible Conspiracies.

CHAPTER I.

Spartacus-Weishaupt,
Founder of the Illuminées.

here sometimes appear men formed with such unhappy dispositions, that we are led to consider them in no other view than as emanations from the evil genius, bereft by the avenging God of the power of doing good. Imbecil in the sphere of wisdom, such men are only efficient in the arts of vice and destruction; they are ingenious in those conceptions, skilful in that cunning, and fruitful in those resources which enable them despotically to reign in the schools of falsehood, depravity, and wickedness. In competition with the Sophisters, these men will surpass them in the arts of exhibiting error in false and delusive col-

Spartacus-Weishaupt.

1

ours; of disguising the vicious passions under the mask of virtue; and of clothing impiety in the garb of Philosophy. In the den of conspirators they are pre-eminent by the atrocity of their deeds; they excel in the arts of preparing revolutions, and of combining the downfal of the Altar with that of Empires. If their career be ever impeded, it is only when they approach the paths of virtue and of real science. When Heaven in its wrath permits a being of this species to appear on the earth, it has only to put nations within the sphere of his activity, and it will be awfully avenged.

With such qualities, and under such auspices, was born in Bavaria, about the year 1748, ADAM WEISHAUPT, better known in the annals of the sect by the name of SPARTACUS. To the eternal shame of his Serene protector, this impious man, heretofore Professor of Law at the University of Ingolstadt, but now banished from his country as a traitor to his Prince and to the whole universe, peacefully at the court of Ernest Lewis, Duke of Saxe Gotha,[1] enjoys an asylum, receives a pension from the public treasury, and is dignified with the title of Honorary Counsellor to that Prince.

An odious phenomenon in nature, an Atheist void of remorse, a profound hypocrite, destitute of those superior talents which lead to the vindication of truth, he is possessed of all that energy and ardour in vice which generates conspirators for

---

1   Ernst II. Lewis, Duke of Saxe-Gotha-Altenburg (1745 - 1804; reigned 1772 - 1804). —Ed.

impiety and anarchy. Shunning, like the ill-boding owl, the genial rays of the sun, he wraps around him the mantle of darkness; and history shall record of him, as of the evil spirit, only the black deeds which he planned or executed. Of mean birth, his youth was passed in obscurity, and but a single trait of his private life has pierced the cloud in which he had enveloped himself—but it is one of hateful depravity and of the most consummate villany.—Incestuous Sophister! it was the widow of his brother whom he seduced.—Atrocious father! it was for the murder of his offspring that he solicited poison and the dagger.—Execrable hypocrite! he implored, he conjured both art and friendship to destroy the innocent victim, the child whose birth must betray the morals of his father. The scandal from which he shrinks is not that of his crime; it is (he says and writes it himself) the scandal which, publishing of the depravity of his heart, would deprive him of that authority by which, under the cloak of virtue, he plunged youth into vice and error.—Monstrous Sophister! he accuses the devils of not having skreened him from this scandal by those abominations which called the vengeance of the God of Nature on the son of Judah.— Then, impudently daring, he perjures himself; he calls every thing that is sacred to witness, that neither he nor his friends ever knew of the existence of those poisons or secret means of skreening him from infamy, much less that they had ever proposed, sought, or employed them. He challenges, and at length forces, the magistrates to prove the accusation; they produce the letters of the perjured Sophister, and therein we behold him entreating a first, a second, and even a third confidant, to seek, or cause to be sought, and to communicate to him, these horrid arts. We see him recalling promises of three years standing with respect to these means. He complains of the little success of his attempts, he accuses the agents of timidity or of ignorance; he entreats and conjures them to renew their attempts, telling them, that it was not yet too late, but that expedition was necessary. Who can paint the depravity of this single trait. How monstrous the being who could have combined such depravity! That the God who humiliates the Sophister should have permitted this single trait to have been brought to light, will suffice to show how far wickedness may be carried by the man who, with virtue on his tongue, and under the shade of that sacred name, was forming and fanaticising the blood-thirsty legions of a Robespierre.

After so shocking an accusation the reader will naturally expect us to produce incontrovertible proofs. We will, therefore, first lay before him the letter of *Weishaupt* to his adept *Hertel*; it is the Third Letter in the Second Volume of the *Original Writings* of the *Illuminées* in Bavaria.

"Now," says Weishaupt to this adept,

> let me, under the most profound secrecy, lay open the situation of my heart. It destroys my

rest, it render me incapable of every thing. I am almost desperate. My honour is in danger, and I am on the eve of losing *that reputation which gave me so great an authority over our people. My sister-in-law is with child.* I have sent her to Athens (Munich) to Euriphon, to solicit a marriage licence from Rome. You see how necessary it is that she should succeed, and that without loss of time; every moment is precious. But should she fail, what shall I do?—How shall I restore the honour of a person who is the victim of a crime that is wholly mine? *We have already made several attempts to destroy the child*; she was determined to undergo all; but Euriphon is too timid. Yet I scarcely see any other expedient. Could I depend on Celse's secrecy (the professor Bader at Munich), he could be of great service to me; *he had promised me his aid three years ago.* Mention it to him if you think proper. See what can be done. I should be sorry that Cato knew any thing of it, lest he should tell all his friends. If you could extricate me from this unfortunate step, you would restore me to life, to honour, to rest, and to authority (that is over his people) . If you cannot, I forewarn you of it, I will hazard a desperate blow, for I neither can nor will lose my honour. I know not what devil.

. . . [Here decency obliges us to be silent; but he continues]

As yet nobody knows any thing of it but Euriphore, it is not too late to make an attempt, for she is only in her fourth month, and the worst of it is, that it is a criminal case, and that alone makes the greatest efforts and the most extreme (or boldest) resolution necesssary. Be well and live happier than I do, and do think of some means which can extricate me from this affair. I am yours, &c. SPARTACUS.

Notwithstanding his repugnance to let Cato into the secret, Weishaupt is at length obliged to write to him on the subject, and, after repeating that which through decency we have omitted above, this monster of hypocrisy says, "what vexes me the most in all this is, *that my authority over our people will be greatly diminished*—that I have exposed a weak side, of which they will not fail to advantage themselves whenever I may preach morality, and exhort them to virtue and modesty."[2]

Now let us observe the same Weishaupt barefacedly saying in his apology,

> I think and declare before God (and I wish this writing to be looked upon as a most solemn declaration), that in all my life I have never heard of those secret means (of abortion) nor of those poisons; that I have never seen nor had knowledge of any occasion when I or my friends could even have thought of advising, administering, or making any use whatever of them. *And this I say in testimony and affirmation of the truth*[3]

---

2   *Original Writings*, vol.I. Let. 61, to Cato.

3   Introduction to his Apology, p. 6.

It is thus that by the most abominable hypocrisy he sustains a barefaced and detestable perjury.

So much for the moral virtue of this man; but our chief object is, to consider him in his character of a Conspirator. Let us then descend into that baleful abyss, and observe him in the schools of impiety, rebellion, and anarchy. Here again he appears to have been ignorant of the gradations of crime, of the space that lies between the slightest deviation from rectitude and the most profound wickedness. Here, scarcely have the magistrates cast their eyes upon him when they find him at the head of a conspiracy which, when compared with those of the clubs of Voltaire and d'Alembert, or with the secret committees of d'Orléans, make these latter appear like the faint imitations of puerility, and show the Sophister and the Brigand as mere novices in the arts of revolution. It is not known, and it would be difficult to discover, whether *Weishaupt* ever had a master, or whether he is himself the great original of those monstrous doctrines on which he founded his school. There exists, however, a tradition which on the authority of some of his adepts we shall lay before the reader.

According to this tradition, a Jutland merchant, who had lived some time in Egypt, began in the year 1771 to overrun Europe, pretending to initiate adepts in the antient mysteries of Memphis. But from more exact information I have learned that he stopped for some time at Malta, where the only mysteries which he taught were the disorganiz-

Tradition as to his master.

ing tenets of the antient Illuminées, of the adopted slave; and these he sedulously infused into the
minds of the people. These principles began to
expand, and the island was already threatened
with revolutionary confusion, when the Knights
very wisely obliged our modern Illuminée to seek
his safety in flight. The famous Count (or rather
mountebank) Cagliostro is said to have been a dis-
ciple of his, as well as some other adepts famous
for their Illuminism in the county of Avignon and
at Lyons. In his peregrinations, it is said, he met
with Weishaupt, and initiated him in his mysteries. If impiety and secrecy could entitle a person
to such an initiation, never had any man better
claims than Weishaupt. More artful and wicked than Cagliostro, he knew how to direct them
among his disciples to very different ends.

Whatever may have been the fact with respect to
this first master, it is very certain that Weishaupt
needed none. In an age when every kind of error had
taken root, he did what is naturally to be expected
from men who, guided by their unhappy bias, both
in religious and political opinions, always select
the most abominable. He must have had some no-
tion of the ancient Illuminées, for he adopted their
name, and the disorganizing principles of their
horrid system. These notions were then strenght-
ened, without doubt, by his favorite application to
the disorganizing mysteries of *Manichæism*, since
we may observe him recommending the study of
them to his disciples as a preparatory step for,

He makes
choice
of his
systems.

8

and as having a close connection with, those for which he was preparing them.[4] But perfect Atheist as he was, and scorning every idea of a God, he soon despised the twofold God of Antient Illuminism, and adopted the doctrines of Manes only in as much as they threatened every government, and led to universal anarchy. He was acquainted with the systems of the modern Sophisters; but, notwithstanding all their democracy, he did not think they had given sufficient latitude to their systems of Liberty and Equality. He only adopted their hatred for God, or pure Atheism. One class led to the destruction of all civil and political laws, the other to the overthrow of all religion; he combined them both, and formed a monstrous digest, whose object was the most absolute, the most ardent, the most frantic vow to overthrow, without exception, every religion, every government, and *all property whatsoever*. He pleased himself with the idea of a distant possibility that he might infuse the same wish throughout the world; he even assured himself of success.

With the talents of a vulgar Sophister such a hope would have been the summit of folly; but with a genius like that of Weishaupt, formed for great

---

4   See the degree of *Directing Illuminée*, oder Scottischer Ritter (Scotch Knight) page 72. [Full title in German: *Illuminatus Dirigens, oder Scottischer Ritter, Ein Pendant zu der nicht unwichtigen Schrift: Die neuesten Arbeiten des Spartacus und Philo in den Illuminaten Orden, jetzt zum erstenmal gedruckt, und zur Beherzigung bei gegenwärtigen Zeitläuften herausgegeben* (Munich, 1794). —Ed.]

crimes, it was the confidence of unlimited wickedness. The Bavarian Sophister knew his powers;
he believed no crime impossible; he only sought
to combine them all to reduce his systems to practice. The mediocrity of his fortune had obliged him
to consecrate the latter years of his education to
the study of the laws. Whether by dissimulation
he concealed the plans fostered in his breast, or
whether he had not as yet digested them all, he
however found means of getting himself named to
the chair of Laws in the University of Ingolstadt,
before he had attained his twenty-eighth year. On
the 10th of March, 1778, he writes to *Zwack* that
he was not yet thirty years of age; and in the same
letter he informs him, under secrecy, of his future
projects on Illuminism, which he had founded two
years before.

Origin
and first
idea of the
sect.

He must have known himself possessed of profound dissimulation; he must have been master
of strange resources, to ground his plans for the
subversion of all laws throughout all empires, on
the very function of public interpreter of the law.
It was nevertheless at the college of Ingolstadt
that Weishaupt, affecting the greatest zeal for his
duty, conceived himself to be admirably situated
for forming and conducting by invisible means the
great revolution which he had planned. He justly
estimated the influence which his office of teacher
gave him over his scholars, and he had the courage
to supply in private the *deficiency* of those lessons
which he was obliged to give to them in public.

But it would have been too poor a conquest for Anarchy or Impiety to have gained only those who were under the eye of the founder. Weishaupt beheld mankind subject to religious and political laws from pole to pole, and his jealous zeal weighed the means which the saints had employed to extend the faith of Christ. There still existed the scattered remnants of an Order which the imprudent policy of Kings had obliged the Sovereign Pontiff to sacrifice to the machinations of a Philosophism, the professed enemy of both Kings and Pontiffs. Weishaupt knew how to appreciate the support which the laws had acquired from men who were heretofore spread throughout all Catholic countries, and who, in the towns and villages, publicly taught youth, thundered from the pulpit against vice, directed Christians toward the path of virtue, and went to preach the faith of Christ to idolatrous and barbarous nations. He well knew how much empires were indebted to religious Orders, that in preaching the duty which each man owed to his God, strengthened the ties that bound him to his neighbour and to his Prince. Though he in his heart detested the children of Benedict, Francis, or Ignatius, he admired the institutions of these holy founders, and was particularly charmed with those of Ignatius, whose laws directed so many zealous men dispersed throughout the world toward the same object and under one head: he conceived that the same forms might be adopted, *though to operate in a sense diametrically opposite,*[5]

---

5   Mirabeau, *De la Monarchie Prussienne*, vol. V., p. 97.

> What these men have done for the Altar and
> the Throne (said he to himself) why would not
> I do in opposition to the Altar and the Throne?
> With legions of adepts subject to my laws, and
> by the lure of mysteries, why may not I destroy
> under the cover of darkness, what they edified
> in broad day? What Christ even did for God
> and for Cæsar, why shall not I do against God
> and Cæsar, by means of adepts now become my
> apostles?

In attributing such a wicked emulation to
Weishaupt, I will not leave the historian to fruitless conjectures. No, these very wishes in plain
language are contained in his confidential letters
to his disciples; and he even reproaches them with
not imitating the submission of the followers of
those holy founders.[6] His most celebrated adepts
have declared, that they had observed him copying
them throughout his code;[7] they must also have remarked, that Weishaupt, in planning his systems
according to the forms adopted by those religious
founders, had reserved it to himself to add all the
artifices which the most infernal policy could suggest. At the actual period when this conspirator
formed his plans, he was ignorant of the object of
Freemasonry:[8] He only knew that the fraternity

---

6   *Vid. Original Writings*, vol. I., let 27, to Cato.

7   See the *Original Writings*, vol. I, *Instructio pro recipientibus*,
     art. B—Let. 2, to Ajax.—Divers letters to Cato.—*Last Observa-
     tion of Philo.*

8   See hereafter the chapter on *Masonry illuminized*, vol. IV.

held secret meetings: he observed that they were bound by mysterious ties, and recognized each other for brethren by certain signs and words, whatever might be their country or religion. In his mind, therefore, he combined the plan of a society, which was at once to partake as much as convenient of the government of the Jesuits, and of the mysterious silence and secret conduct of Masonry. Its object was, the propagation of the most Antisocial Systems of ancient Illuminism, and of the most Antireligious Systems of modern Philosophism.

Brooding over this disastrous project, Weishaupt cast his eyes on the young pupils whom government had entrusted to his care to form them for magistrates of their country, and defenders of the laws, and he resolved to begin his warfare against both by the perversion of these youths. He beheld in distant succession his first disciples seducing others, those again, subject to his laws, forming further adepts; and thus by degrees he came complacently to view his legions multiplying and spreading from the towns to the country, and resident even in the courts of Princes. He already heard those oaths which, under the secrecy of the Lodges, were to bind the minds and hearts of those new legions who, replete with his disorganizing spirit, were silently to undermine the Altar and the Throne. He calculated the time necesssary, and smiled to think that he would one day have only to give the signal for the general explosion.

He founds
his Illumi-
nism.

Scarcely had this modern Eratostratus attained his eight-and-twentieth year, ere he had laid the foundations of those laws which he meant to give to his disorganizing Sect. Though he had not actually written his code, he had arranged it in his mind, and he made his first essay on two of his pupils, one named *Massenhausen* (whom he sumamed *Ajax*), about twenty years of age, and afterwards a Counsellor at Burkhausen; the other called *Merz* (whom he sumamed *Tiberius*)[9] nearly of the same age, but whose morals and character proved so abominable, that they made even his vile seducer blush. These two disciples soon vying with their master in impiety, he judged them worthy of being admitted to his mysteries, and conferred on them the highest degree that he had as yet invented. He called them *Areopagi*, installed himself their chief, and called this monstrous association THE ORDER OF ILLUMINÉES.[10]

It was on the first of May, 1776, that the inauguration was celebrated. Let the reader well observe this epoch. It indicates a feeble beginning; it preceded the French Revolution but by a few years; that however was the time when that abominable Sect first started into existence, which was to com-

9   Weishaupt, in a letter to Zwack, says, "My three first colleagues were *Ajax, you*, and Merz." (*Let.* 15, *Feb.* 1778). This clearly states, that *Merz* was the Tiberius who was illuminated with *Ajax*; for it is clear that *Zwack* was only initiated ten months after the two adepts *Ajax* and *Tiberius*. (*See Orig. Writ., vol. I. Sect. IV.*)

10   *Orig. Writ.* Vol. I. Sect. IV.—Let. 2, to Philip Strozzi.

bine all the errors, all the conspiracies, and all the crimes of the adepts of Impiety, Rebellion, or Anarchy, and which, under the name of Jacobin, was to consummate the dreadful Revolution. Such was the origin of that Sect which I had in view when I proclaimed to all nations, and unfortunately with too much truth,

> That whatever their government or religion might be, to whatever rank they might belong in civil society, if Jacobinism triumphed all would be overthrown; that should the plans and wishes of the Jacobins be accomplished, their religion with its Pontiffs, their government with its laws, their magistrates *and their property*, all would be swept away in the common mass of ruin! Their riches and their fields, their houses and their cottages, their very wives and children would be torn from them. You have looked upon Jacobinical faction as exhausting itself in France, when it was only making a sportive essay of its strength.[11]

According to the wishes and intentions of this terrible and formidable Sect, nations, astonished, have yet only seen the first part of the plans formed for that general Revolution which is to beat down every Throne—overturn every Altar—*destroy all property*—blot out every law—and conclude by the total dissolution of all society!

The omen is fatal;—but (more fatal still!) I have numberless proofs to demonstrate the truth of

Plan of this volume.

---

11   Vol. I, page 23.

this assertion. With respect to the Conspiracies of Illuminism, I shall draw my proofs from their own code and their archives. I will begin with their code; it will lay open the object, the extent, the manner, the means and inconceivable depth of the Conspiracies of the Sect. This First Part will comprehend the plan of their conspiracies, the extract and analysis of the code of laws which they had constructed for attaining their ends. The Second Part will show their progress and their successes from their first origin, till that period when, powerful in Revolutionary Legions, without leaving their secret dens, they unite and confound themselves with the Jacobins, and in unison with them prosecute that war of desolation which menaces with total ruin the Altar of every God—the Throne of every Monarch—The Law of every Society—and the Property of every Citizen. O! that I could in delineating what the Sect has done, what it is doing, and what it still meditates to do—that I could but teach nations and the chiefs of nations what they themselves ought to do, to avert the impending danger; those, I say, who have mistaken these disasters for a sudden explosion, while they are in fact but an essay of the strength of the Sect, and the commencement of their general plan.

CHAPTER II.

Code of the Illuminées.—
General System, and Division
of the Code.

B y the code of the sect of Illuminées I mean the principles and systems which it had formed to itself on Religion and Civil Society, or rather against all Religion and Civil Society whatever; I mean the government and the laws which it has adopted to realize its plans, and to guide the adepts in bringing the whole universe into its systems. This was not so much a code springing from an ardent mind, and an enthusiastic zeal for a great revolution, as the offspring of reflection on the means of rendering it infallible; for no sooner had Weishaupt conceived a plan, than he foresaw the obstacles which might thwart

Weishaupt prepares the code of the Illuminées.

17

its success. Though he decorated the first pupils whom he had seduced with the title of his profound adepts, yet he did not dare unfold to them the vast extent of his plans. Pleased with having laid the foundation, he did not hurry the elevation of that edifice, which might have been exposed to fall for want of the proper precautions; no, he wished it to be as durable as time itself. For five whole years he meditated; and he foresaw that he should still have to pause for many a tedious day on the means of securing the success of his plans. His plodding head silently ruminated and slowly combined that code of laws or rather of cunning, of artifice, of snares and ambushees by which he was to regulate the preparation of candidates, the duties of the initiated, the functions, the rights, the conduct of the chiefs, and even his own. He watched every means of seduction, weighed and compared those means, tried them one after the other; and when he had adopted any of them would still reserve the power of changing them, in case he should happen to fall upon any that would be more disastrous.

Meanwhile his first disciples, now his apostles, gained him many partizans; he seduced many himself, and directed their conduct by letter. His advice was adapted to circumstances, and, artfully husbanding his promises, he kept the minds of his disciples perpetually in suspense as to the last mysteries. To his trusty adepts he promises *systems of morality, of education, and of polity, all entirely new*; and they might easily surmise that this future code would be no other than that of a morality without restraint, of a religion without a God, and of a polity without laws or any dependence whatsoever;[1] though he did not dare entirely to throw away the mask. But his laws appeared imperfect, his snares were not sufficiently concealed; and he was convinced that time and experience alone could perfect the work on which he had so long meditated. Such are the colours, at least, in which we see him representing himself when his adepts, impatient to be initiated in the last mysteries, reproach him with the slowness of the proceedings: "It is from time and experience," says he,

> that we are to learn. I daily put to the test what I made last year, and I find that my performances of this year are far superior. Give me then time to reflect on what may forward and on what may delay the execution of our plans; to weigh what may be expected of our people left to themselves or led and conducted by us.— Remember that what is done in haste, speedily falls to ruin. Leave me then to myself, let me act alone; and believe me, *time and I are worth any other two.*[2]

Let not the reader imagine that these meditations of Weishaupt alluded to the objecct of his views; that never varied; the destruction of Reli-

His alarms.

---

1   *Original Writings*, vol.I., let. to Marius and Cato.
2   *Original Writings*, vol, I., letters 3, 4, 47, 60 &c. to Marius and Cato.

gion, the destruction of Society and the civil Laws, the destruction of property,—that was the point at which he always aimed; and this impious man too well knew his crime, not to be alarmed; we see him writing to his confident,

> You know the situation in which I stand. I must direct the whole by means of five or six persons. It is absolutely necessary that I should during my life remain unknown to the greater part of the adepts themselves.—I am often overwhelmed with the idea that all my meditations, all my services and toils are perhaps only twisting a rope or planting a gallows for myself; that the indiscretion or imprudence of a single individual may overturn the most beautiful edifice that ever was reared.[3]

At other times wishing to appear above such fears, but still reproaching the adepts with want of caution, he says,

> If our affairs already go on so ill, the whole will soon be undone: the fault will be thrown upon me, and, as author of every thing, I shall be the first sacrificed. Yet that is not what frightens me; I know how to take every thing on my own score; but if the imprudence of the Brethren is to cost me my life, let me at least not have to blush before men of reflection, nor to reproach myself with an inconsiderate and rash conduct.[4]

---

3   *Original Writings*, vol. I., lett. 11 and 25, to Cato.

4   Let. 22, to Cato.

Thus does every motive stimulate this famous Conspirator to transfuse into his code every precaution that could at the same time skreen him from condign punishment, and secure the success of his plots. At length, after five years meditation on his side, and numerous consultations with his trusty adepts, particularly with *Philo*, or the Baron *Knigge*, who acts a very exalted part in *Illuminism*, Weishaupt had regulated the mode of his mysteries, and had digested the code of his Sect, that is to say, the principles, the laws, and government adopted by the Illuminées to accomplish the grand object of their Conspiracy. Before we lead our readers through the immense labyrinth of this code, let us give a general idea of the system which stimulated its author to the formation of those laws.

Terminates his code.

The more we meditate on that part of the code which we shall lay before our readers when we come to treat of the mysteries of Illuminism, the more clearly we observe Weishaupt adopting the principles of *Equality* and of *Liberty*, (propagated by modern Philosophism) in order to present them in a new light, and to lead his disciples to the ultimate consequences of the most absolute Impiety and Anarchy.

General plan of his system.

The modern Sophisters, some following Voltaire, others Rousseau, had begun by saying, that all men were equal and free; and they had concluded *with respect to Religion*, that nobody, though speaking in the name of a God who reveals himself, had the right of prescribing rules to their faith. The authority of revelation being cast aside, they left no other basis for Religion to rest upon, than the Sophistry of a reason the perpetual prey of our passions. They had annihilated Christianity in the minds of their adepts. *With respect to Governments* they had also asserted, that all men were equal and free, and they had concluded that every citizen had an equal right to form the laws, or to the title of Sovereign; this consequence abandoning all authority to the capricious fluctuations of the multitude, no government could be legitimate but that founded on Chaos, or the volcanic explosions of the democratic and sovereign populace.

Weishaupt, reasoning on the same principles, believed both the Sophisters and the Democratic Populace to be too timid in drawing their inferences, and the following may be said to be the essence of all his mysteries.

> Liberty and Equality are the essential rights that man in his original and primitive perfection received from nature. *Property* struck the first blow at *Equality*; political Society, or Governments, were the first oppressors of *Liberty*; *the supporters of Governments and property are the religious and civil laws*; therefore, to reinstate man in his primitive rights of Equality and Liberty, we must begin by destroying all Religion, all civil society, and finish by the destruction of all property.

Had true Philosophy but gained admittance to these lodges of Illuminism, how clearly would she have demonstrated the absurdity of each and all of these principles, and the extravagance and wickedness of such consequences, both to the master and his adepts! She would have shewn, that the rights and laws of primitive man alone upon earth, or parent of a scanty generation, neither were nor ought to be the rights and laws of man living on an inhabited globe. She would have proved, that Nature, when she ordained that man should increase and multiply on this earth, and that he should cultivate it, clearly announced that his posterity were hereafter to live under the empire of social laws. She would have observed, that without property this earth would have remained uncultivated and uninhabited; that without religious and civil laws the same earth would have only nurtured straggling hordes of vagabonds and savages. Then would our Bavarian Illuminée have concluded, that his Equality and Liberty, far from being the essential rights of man in the state of perfection, would only be the instruments of his degradation, and assimilate him to the beasts of the earth, if they were to be incompatible with Property, Religion, and Society. But true Philosophy was an alien to his school; and Weishaupt, with his detestable genius formed for error, applauds the sophism, makes it the basis of his system, and the ultimate secret of his mysteries.

I am not simply to prove that such is the grand object of the Conspiracy, and of the ultimate revolution which he is preparing with all his adepts. Its danger.

23

Were that my only task, I should cite the blessings which the hierophant of Illuminism pours out on those hordes that roam without laws or society, and the curses which he vents against those men who, fixing their abodes, name chiefs and constituted states. The very menaces of the teacher unfold the whole of the Conspiracy. *"Yes, princes and nations shall disappear from off the face of the earth; yes, a time shall come when man shall acknowledge no other law but the great book of nature: This revolution shall be the work of the* SECRET SOCIETIES, *and that is one of our grand mysteries,"*[5] This single passage of the code is sufficient to demonstrate both the object of the Conspiracy and the extent of the projects of the sect; but though the Conspiracy should be clearly proved, still that would be doing little for the public good. Instead of a terrible and formidable Sect, nations and chiefs of nations might mistake the Illuminées for a band of senseless madmen, plodding without means a chimerical Revolution; therefore little to be feared, and too despicable to deserve notice. Thus would wickedness find a cloak in its excesses; the Sect would prosecute its hellish plots more actively, more confidently, and more successfully, merely because their object was supposed impossible. Society would be dissolved; our laws, our religion, and our property, would be wrested from us, because we believed them proof against any attempt. Nations would tranquilly slumber on the brink of the prec-

---

5   See hereafter the *Discourse on the Mysteries.*

24

ipice, and be plunged into destruction while they considered the fatal cause as the delusion of delirium, and smiled on the plots of Illuminism. And its founder foresaw this: for he says to his adepts, "*Let the laughers laugh, let the scoffers scoff; he that compares the past with the present, will see that nature continues its course without the possibility of diverting it. Its progress is imperceptible to the man who is not formed to observe it; but it does not escape the attention of the Philosopher.*"[6]

Society then calls upon me to develop more than the existence, or even the extent of the plots of the Sect—I say, it calls on me loudly to proclaim the dangers which threaten us; yes, the evils which threaten all society must be clearly shown. A manner of proceeding and an artful cunning big with crime, which will speedily plunge nations into those disasters which they may believe chimerical, is to be clearly ascertained. I have to unfold the whole of a system, an entire code, in which each institute, each maxim, each regulation, is a new step towards a universal revolution which shall strike society a mortal blow. I am not then about to inform each citizen that his religion, his country, *his property*, that every society, people, or nation, are menaced; unfortunately that would be a task too easily performed. But I am bound to say, "In this horrible plot, such are the dangers which threaten your country, and such the perils that hang over your persons." I must show extensive resources

---

6   See hereafter the *Discourse on the Mysteries*.

combined with consummate villainy, where you imagined that nothing existed but the delirium of modern Philosophism, destitute of means.

Weishaupt, like yourselves, had foreseen numerous obstacles to his conspiracy; and it appears that he had even exaggerated them. That for which his most famous adepts seem to despise their countrymen, should be mentioned here as redounding to their honour. Weishaupt, surrounded by the faithful Bavarians, faithful to their God and to their country (rather speculating on the human heart from his books, than closely observing men in the common intercourse of life), was not aware of how very much Philosophism had forwarded his systems.[7] The generation which had attained the age of manhood appeared too much infected with the antiquated ideas on religion and government. But, unfortunately, facts soon undeceived him; and this error only served, by deferring his hopes, to turn his mind to farther precautions and meditations, which sooner or later were to render his success infallible. He would say to himself, he would say to his trusty brethren, "*According to my views, I cannot employ men as they are; I must form them*; each class of my Order must be a preparatory school for the next; and all this must necessarily be the work of time."[8] But to accelerate the time he cast his eyes on that class of young men, which, just entering the world, easily fall a prey to error, because at that age they

---

7   See the *Last Observations of Philo.*

8   *Original Writings*, vol.I., let. to Cato.

are under the influence of their passions. I shall hereafter show what it was that both shortened the time, and abridged their education, in presenting him with whole legions of adepts ready formed to his mysteries. It is first necessary, however, that the reader should be acquainted with the profundity of his system; because, had the French Revolution not taken place, that system would alone have sufficed to render it certain and infallible; for, could the French Revolution be done away at the present moment, and the ancient regimen be restored, this code would furnish Illuminism with all the means of effectuating one that should be still more disastrous. Let us then study it, let us dissipate the cloud in which it is enveloped. Reader, your own interest requires that you should follow our steps; and observe all the snares that have been laid for you; see with what art its disciples are beguiled, with what precaution it chooses, calls, and disposes its adepts. Its proceedings appear indeed to be slow, but they are nevertheless sure. It seems to exhaust all its art to acquire a single proselyte, but the same allurements attract whole legions. Its springs are secret, but the reader must know their power and with what constancy they move toward and direct the common ruin. He has seen the people agitated, animated, and even misled to ferocity; but he must also be informed how those adepts were created who fanaticised the people and rendered them ferocious.

Weishaupt lays down as an invariable and infallible principle, that

the grand art of rendering any revolution whatsoever certain—is to enlighten the people;—and
to enlighten them is, insensibly to turn the public opinion to the adoption of those changes
which are the given object of the intended revolution.

When that object cannot be promulged without exposing him that has conceived it to public
vengeance, he must know how to propagate his
opinion IN SECRET SOCIETIES.

When the object is an universal Revolution,
all the members of these societies, aiming at
the same point, and aiding each other, must
find means *of governing invisibly, and without any appearance of violent measures, not
only the higher and more distinguished class
of any particular state, but men of all stations,
of all nations, and of every religion—Insinuate the same spirit every where—In silence,
but with the greatest activity possible, direct
the scattered inhabitants of the earth toward
the same point.*

This is what he calls the grand problem on the
polity of states, on which he grounds *the force of
secret societies*, and on which the empire of his Illuminism was to rest.[9]

"This empire once established by means of the
union and multitude of the adepts, let force succeed to the invisible power. *Tie the hands of those
who resist; subdue and stifle wickedness in the
germ*;" that is to say, crush those whom you have

---

9   See the *Discourse on the Mysteries*.

28

not been able to convince.[10] He that teaches such doctrines is not to be looked on as a weak enemy. When Weishaupt reserved them for his mysteries, as well as the revelation of his ultimate object, he knew too well that they were only fitted for men who had long been trained to view them as the lessons of nature and of Philosophy, and should he meet with any who had anticipated them, it would only abridge their novitiate. But he needed nothing less than a whole generation. It was therefore to multiply the number of adepts, to dispose them by insensible degrees to receive his doctrines; by an invisible hand to direct their ideas, their wishes, their actions, and their combined efforts, that the code of laws which he framed for Illuminism constantly tended.

According to these laws, the sect is divided into two grand classes, and each of these again subdivided into lesser degrees proportionate to the progress of the adepts. *Its division.*

The *first class* is that of PREPARATION. It contains four degrees, those of *Novice,* of *Minerval,* of *Minor Illuminée* or *Illuminatus Minor,* and of *Major Illuminée* or *Illuminatus Major.*

Some intermediary degrees belong to the *class of* PREPARATION, which may be called of Intrusion; such are those which the sect have borrowed from *Freemasonry* as a means of *propagation.* Of these masonic degrees the code of *Illuminées admit the three first without any alteration*: it adapts more

---

10   *Ibid.*

particularly to the views of the sect the degree of *Scotch Knight* as an ultimate preparation for its mysteries, and it is stiled the degree of *Directing Illuminée* or *Illuminatus Dirigens*.

The *second class* is that of the MYSTERIES, and this is subdivided into the *lesser* and *greater mysteries*. The lesser comprehend the priesthood and administration of the sect, or the degrees of Priests and of *Regents* or *Princes*.

In the *greater mysteries* are comprized the two degrees of Magi or Philosopher, and of the Man King. The *Elect* of the latter compose *the council and the degree of Areopagites*.[11]

In all these classes, and in every degree, there is a part of the utmost consequence, and which is common to all the Brethren. It is that employment known in the code by the appellation of Brother *Insinuator or Recruiter*,[12] The whole strength of the Sect depends on this part; it is that which furnishes members to the different degrees; and Weishaupt, well knowing the importance of the task, turned all his genius toward it. Let us therefore begin by directing our attention to the discovery of it.

---

11 See the *Original Writings*, Chap., II., Part II. page 8. and the last Observations of Philo, page 89, See. &c.

12 This is not a term of my invention; it really is to be found in the code. Insinuator or *Anwerber* (signifying Recruiter) are the two words generally made use of to express this character.

CHAPTER III.

First Part of the Code of the Illuminées.—Of the Brother Insinuator, or the Recruiter.

B y the appellation of *Brother Insin-* *uator*, is to be understood the *Illu-* *minée* whose peculiar office is to make proselytes for the Sect. Some brethren were more particularly instructed for that end; they might, indeed, be called the Apostles or Missionaries of the Order, being those whom the superiors sent to the different towns and provinces, and even into distant countries, to propagate its doctrines and to establish new Lodges. These had received, in addition to the common rules, farther instructions peculiar to the higher degrees. "These (as Weishaupt writes) may sometimes be the most *imbecile*, and

Object of the Insinuator.

at other times the most ingenious of the Brotherhood." From the former he can depend on a blind obedience to the rules he lays down, which are never to be deviated from; and with respect to the latter, provided they be zealous and punctual, should they even transgress any of the laws, it would not be in such a manner as to commit either their own safety or that of the Order; and they would soon make amends for their indiscretion by some new artifice. But, whatever may be the sense of the Illuminée, he is obliged once or twice in his life to act the part of Brother Insinuator, and that with a certain success, by the acquisition of two or three proselytes, under pain of perpetually remaining in the lower degrees. Some Brethren of high rank may have been dispensed from this formality; but as to the generality of them there exists a positive law on that point.[1] To stimulate the zeal of the Brethren, the Insinuator is by the laws of the code established superior over every novice that he has gained to the Order: It is expressed as follows: "Every Illuminée may form to himself a petty empire; *and from his littleness, emerge to greatness and power.*"[2]

Such then is the first duty imposed upon every Illuminée for the propagation of the Sect; and this is the part which first claims our attention, in order that we may be able to form an idea of the immensurable powers of Weishaupt for seduction.

---

1   *Original Writings.* The Statutes reformed, Art. 18.
2   *Ibid.*

This part may be said to be subdivided into three. The rules laid down are, first, those which are to guide the Brother *Insinuator* in the choice of persons to be admitted or excluded; then follow those which are to teach him how to entice into the order those persons whom he has judged proper for it; and lastly come those rules and arts by which novices are to be formed, and even involved in Illuminism before they are officially admitted.

In order to judge of the qualifications of the persons whom he may enlist, every Illuminée is to begin by procuring tablets, which he is to keep in the form of a Journal; and this is *his Diary*. Assiduously prying into every thing that surrounds him, he must vigilantly observe all persons with whom he becomes acquainted, or whom he meets in company, without exception of relations, friends, enemies, or entire strangers; he must endeavour to discover their strong and their weak side; their passions and prejudices; their intimacies, and above all, their actions, interests, and fortune; in a word, every thing relating to them: and the remarks of every day he must enter in his Diary.

A twofold advantage is to be reaped from these particulars of information; first, by the Order in general and its superiors; secondly, by the adept himself. Twice every month he will make a general statement of his observations, and he will transmit it to his superiors. By these means the Order will be informed what men, in every town or village, are friendly or inimical to it. The means of gaining

Part I. of his mission. The choice of Candidates.

33

over the one or destroying the other will naturally occur. With respect to the *Insinuator*, he will learn how to judge of those who are proper persons to be received or rejected, and he will carefully insert his reasons for the admission or rejection of those persons in his monthly statements.[3]

The Recruiting Brother will carefully guard against giving the most distant hint that he is an Il-luminée. This law is peremptory for the Brethren, but more particularly for all the *Insinuators*, whose success may often essentially depend on it. It is to them that the legislator so strongly recommends all that exterior of virtue and of perfection, that care of shunning all public scandals which might deprive them of their ascendancy over the minds of those whom they seek to entice into the Order.[4] The law expressly says, "*Apply yourselves to the acquiring of interior and exterior perfection;*" but lest they should conceive that this perfection even hinted at the mastering of their passions, and at renouncing the pleasures of the world, he adds, "Attend particularly to the art of dissembling and of disguising your actions, the better to observe those of others, and to penetrate into their inmost thoughts." *Die kunst zu erlemen sich zu verstellen, andere zu beobachten, und aus zu forschen.* "It is for that reason that these three great precepts are

---

3   *Original Writings.*—The Statutes reformed, Art. 9, 13, and fol-
     lowing.—Instructions for the Insinuators, Sect. XI, No. I.—for
     the Insinuated Nos. 1, 3, 5, &c.—Let. the 4th to Ajax.

4   See *Original Writings*, vol.II., lett. 1, and 9.

to be found in the summary of the Code: HOLD THY
TONGUE—BE PERFECT—DISGUISE THYSELF—almost
following each other in the same page, and serving
as an explanation of each other."[5]

Having made himself perfect master of these
precepts, and particularly of the last, the *Insinuator* is next to turn his attention to those persons
whom he may admit or ought to reject. He is not
to admit into the Order either Pagans or Jews; but
he is equally to reject *all religious*; and above all to
*shun the Ex-Jesuits as he would the plague. Or-
dens geistliche dürfen nie aufgenommen werden,
und die Ex-Jesuiten soll man wie die pest fliehen.*[6]

The cause of such exclusions is obvious. To
speak of religion, and admit, without any precaution, Jews, Turks, and Pagans, would be too open
a manifestation of what their religion was; and not
to reject religious, would be exposing themselves
to be betrayed by their own adepts.

Unless they gave evident signs of a sincere
amendment, all indiscreet talkers were to be rejected; and also those men whose pride, or headstrong,
interested, and inconstant minds denoted that it
would be impossible to infuse into them that zeal
so necessary for the order; all those again, whose
drunken excesses might injure that reputation of
virtue which the Order was to acquire; all those, in

Who are to be excluded.

---

5   *Original Writings*, vol. I., p. 40. Nos. 4, 6, and 8.

6   *The Last Works of Spartacus and Philo.*—Instruction for the
    Stationary Prefects and Superiors, Page 153, Let. the 2d.—And
    Original Writings, Instructio pro Recipientibus, Nos. 1, and 5.

short, whose meanness and grossness of manners would render them too untractable to give hope for their ever becoming pliant and useful.[7]

"Leave those brutes, those clownish and thick-headed fellows!" he exclaims in his Chapter on Exclusions; but, though he excluded these thick-headed fellows, Weishaupt was aware that there existed a good sort of being which some might call stupid, but who are not to be told so, as advantage may be taken of their stupidity. Such were, for example, a Baron *d'Ert*, and many others, who holding a certain rank in the world, though destitute of common sense, have at least their riches to recommend them. *"These are a good sort of beings,"* says our illuminizing legislator;

> they are necessary beings. They augment our number and fill our coffers, *augent numerum et ærarium.* Courage then! and make these gentry swallow the bait; but beware of comunicating to them our secrets; *For this species of adept must always be persuaded that the degree they are in is the highest.*[8]

Indeed, there is a sort of half exclusion for princes. The Code ordains that they shall seldom be admitted, and even when they are, shall scarcely ever rise beyond the degree of Scotch Knight; or, in other words, they are never to pass the threshold

---

7   Instructio pro Recipientibus, page 94, and Weishaupt's Letters, *passim.*

8   *Original Writings.* See the first Letters to Ajax and Cato.

of the mysteries. Hereafter we shall see the Legislator finding an expedient for introducing them beyond that degree, but still without giving them any further insight into the mysteries;[9] and being particuarly careful to hide from them certain Laws of the Order.[10]

I cannot take upon myself to say, whether a similar expedient had been found as an exception to the general rule which excluded women; but it is certain, that this law was, during a long time at least, only provisional; and many of the brethren sought to revoke it. Freemasonry had its female adepts, and the Illuminées wished to have theirs. The plan is written in *Zwack*'s own hand-writing, and he was the most intimate friend and confidant of Weishaupt, in short, his *incomparable* man. It is couched in the following terms:

Plan for an Order of Women.—This Order shall be subdivided into two classes, each forming a separate society, and having a different secret. The first shall be composed of virtuous women; the second, of the wild, the giddy, and the voluptuous, *auschweifenden*.[11]

Both classes are to be ignorant that they are under the direction of men. The two superiors are to be persuaded that they are under a mother Lodge of the same sex, which transmits its

Plan for the admission of women.

---

9   See Degree of Regent, page 154, Letter N.
10   See Instructions for the Provincial, No. 16.
11   Erroneously *Ausschveifenden* in the English; correctly spelt in the French. Meaning: dissipated, wild. —Ed.

orders; though in reality these orders are to be transmitted by men.

The Brethren who are intrusted with this superintendance shall forward their instructions without making themselves known. They shall conduct the first, by promoting the reading of good books, but shall form the latter to the arts of *secretly gratifying their passions, durch begnügung ihrer leidenschaften im verborgenen.*

A preliminary discourse prefixed to this plan points out the object and future services of these illuminized sisters.

The advantages which the real Order would reap from this female Order would be, first, the money which the sisterhood would pay at their initiation; and, secondly, a heavy tax upon their curiosity, under the supposition of secrets that are to be learned. *And this association might moreover serve to gratify those brethren who had a turn for sensual pleasure.*[12]

A list and description of eighty-five young ladies of Manheim accompanied this project of Zwack, very properly surnamed the Cato of Illuminism; from among whom, in all probability, the founders of these two classes were to be chosen. Circumstances not having favoured our modern Cato's views, we observe several other adepts proposing similar plans. An assessor of the Imperial Chamber

---

12   *Original Writings*, vol.I., sect. V.

at Wetzlaar of the name of *Distfurt*, known among the Illuminées by that of *Minos*, and who rose to the degree of *Regent*, and to the dignity of Provincial, seemed to dispute the honor of this invention, both with Brother Hercules and even with Cato himself: We must allow, at least, that nobody was more anxious for the execution of the project than he was. He had already submitted his ideas to the Baron Knigge, and he applies anew to Weishaupt. He even despairs of ever bringing men to the grand object of the order without the support of the female adepts. Indeed, so ardent is his zeal, that he makes an offer of his own wife and his four daughters-in-law to be the first adepts. The eldest was exactly the person for the philosophized sisterhood; she was four-and-twenty years of age, *and with respect to religion her ideas were far above those of her sex*; they were modelled on her father's. He had attained to the degrees of *Regent* and *Prince* of the Illuminées, and she would have been *Regent* and *Princess*. In the higher mysteries, together with Ptolemy's wife, we should have seen the one corresponding with her father, the other with her husband. These illuminized Princesses would be the only two persons of the order who should know that they were all under the direction of men. They would preside over the trials and receptions of *Minervals*, and would initiate those whom they judged worthy into the grand projects of the sisterhood for the reform of governments and the happiness of mankind.[13]

---

13   *Original Writings*, vol. I., let. of Minos, p. 169.

But, notwithstanding all the plans and zeal of the Brethren, it does not appear that the legislator ever consented to the establishment of the Sisterhood. Yet he supplied the want of such an institution by secret instructions which he gave the *Regents* on the means of making the influence of women over men subservient to the order, without initiating them in any of the secrets. He says, that the fair sex having the greatest part of the world at their disposition, *"no study was more worthy of the adept* than the art of flattery in order to gain them; that they were all more or less led by vanity, curiosity, the pleasures or the love of novelty; that it was on that side they were to be attacked, and by that they were to be rendered serviceable to the order."[14] He nevertheless continued to exclude great talkers and women from all the degrees, nor was the sixth article of his instructions for the *Insinuator* rescinded.

Who are to be chosen.

Notwithstanding all these exclusions, the legislator leaves a sufficient scope wherein the Insinuator may exercise his zeal. He recommends generally young men of all stations from eighteen to thirty; but more particularly those whose educations were not completed, either because he thought they would more easily imbibe his principles, or would be more grateful and more zealous for doctrines for which they were indebted solely to him.[15]

---

14 See the New Works of Spartacus and Philo, and Instructions for the degree of Regent, no. 6.

15 *Orig. Writ.* Instructiones pro Recipientibus, page 54, no. 4;

But this preference is not an exclusion for men of a certan age, provided they are not past service, and are already imbued with the principles of Illuminism.[16] This, however, chiefly regards those persons whose rank in life can give *consequence* and afford *protection* to the order. The Recruiters are particularly instructed to insinuate themselves into the good opinion of such persons, and if possible to entice them into the Order.

There is yet another species of men, who have speech as it were at command; such are attornies, counsellors, and even physicians. "Those are worth having," says Weishaupt; "but *they are sometimes real devils, so difficult are they to be led; they however are worth having when they can be gained over.*"[17]

The *Insinuator* is also to admit artists, mechanics of all professions, painters, engravers, whitesmiths and black-smiths; but above all booksellers, those who keep post-horses, and school-masters. Hereafter the reader will see the use for which these men were intended.[18]

To yet another class of men our legislator often calls the attention of the *Insinuator*: "*Seek me out, for example,*" says Weishaupt,

---

and page 55, no. 18.

16   *Ibid.*, vol. II. Part the 2d, Section and Degree of Regent.

17   *Orig. Writ.* Vol. I. let. to Ajax.

18   See Instructions for the Insinuator, no. 4.—Weishaupt's Letters, *passim*—and the Degree of Regent.

the dexterous and dashing youths. We must have adepts who are insinuating, intriguing, full of resource, bold and enterprising; they must also be flexible and tractable, obedient, docile, and sociable. Seek out also those who are distinguished by their *power, nobility, riches, or learning, nobiles, potentes, divites, doctos, quærite*—Spare no pains, spare nothing in the acquisition of such adepts. If heaven refuse its aidance, conjure hell.

Flectere si nequeas superos, Acheronta moveto.[19]

With respect to religions, he prefers the disciples of Luther and Calvin to the Roman Catholics, and greatly prefers the former to the latter. This distinction should alone suffice to open the eyes of many who wish to persuade themselves that the whole of the revolutionary fury is aimed at the Roman Catholic religion. This motley crew certainly did the Catholics the honour of directing their shafts more pointedly at them, as strenuous opponents of their impiety and of their religious and civil anarchy; but was it to preserve the Protestant religion that Weishaupt gives them such a preference, in hopes of making them subservient to his plots? That he did give such a preference cannot be doubted, when we see him expressly writing to an adept whom he had commissioned to look out for a person proper to be received into

---

19   *Ibid.*, let. 3d to Ajax.

the higher mysteries and to found a new colony of Illuminées—*were this man a Protestant I should like him much better.—Wäre es ein Protestant, so wäre es mir um so lieber.*[20] Weishaupt's most famous adept constantly manifests the same predilection; he even wishes to retrench certain parts of the mysteries that he may not alarm the Catholics, and seems always to hint at Frederic the IId's saying, *We Protestants go on brisker.*[21] Most certainly this proves beyond a possibility of doubt, that the destruction of all Protestant laws, whether civil or religious, had place in their plans. Nor were the Protestants of Germany the dupes of such a policy, as many of the most determined antagonists of Illuminism were of that religion.

Further, he wishes to entice men into his order who have fixed residences in towns, such as *merchants* and *canons*, who might assiduously propagate his doctrines, and establish them in their neighbourhoods.[22]

The Recruiter must use every art (for an obvious reason) to engage *schoolmasters*, and to insinuate his doctrines into, and gain adepts in the military *academies*, and other places of education; he is even to attempt the seduction of the *superiors of ecclesiastical seminaries.*[23]

---

20   *Orig. Writ.*, vol. I., let. to Tiberius, p. 223.

21   See vol. I., page 32.

22   Instructions for the Provincial and *Orig. Writ.*, vol. I., part II, No. 3, page 26.

23   *Ibid.*, nos. 11 and 13.

"He will spare no trouble to gain the Prince's officers, whether presiding over provinces, or attending him in his councils. He that has succeeded in this has done *more*," says the code, "than if *he had engaged the Prince himself.*[24] In fine, the Provincial, or the chief Insinuator, is *to recruit* every thing that can be tainted with Illuminism, or can be serviceable to its cause."[25]

The following extraordinary instructions are also given by Weishaupt respecting the choice of adepts:

> Above all things (he says to his Insinuators) pay attention to the figure, and select the well-made men and handsome young fellows. They are generally of engaging manners and nice feelings. When properly formed, they are the best adapted for negotiations; for first appearances prepossess in their favour. It is true, they have not the depth that men of more gloomy countenances often have. They are *not the persons to be entrusted with a revolt, or the care of stirring up the people*; but it is for that very reason that we must know how to chuse our agents. I am particularly fond of those men whose very soul is painted in their eyes, whose foreheads are high, and whose countenances are open. Above all, examine well the eyes, for they are the very mirrors of the heart and soul. Observe the look, the gait, the voice. Every external appearance

---

24   *Ibid.,* no. 15.
25   *Ibid.,* no. 18.

leads us to distinguish those who are fit for our school.[26]

Select *those in particular who have met until misfortunes, not from accidents,* but by some act of injustice; that is to say, in other words, the DISCONTENTED; *for such are the men to be called into the bosom of Illuminism, as into their proper asylum.*[27]

Let not the reader already exclaim, How deep are the views of this illuminizing Sophister? How has he foreseen every point! With what discernment does he lay his snares to entrap those who are to be the future agents of his plots! The reader has as yet seen merely a schedule of those persons who may be admitted or rejected; but that does not sufficiendy secure the order with respect to the elections which the Insinuator may have made. Before he undertakes the initiation of any person whom he may have thought proper, he is to make a statement from his diary of every thing that he may have observed with respect to his morals, opinions, conduct, and even of his connections in life. He is to submit this statement to his superiors, who will compare it with the notes they are already in possession of, or may acquire from other adepts, respecting the candidate, or even with a new statement, in case they judge the last to be insufficient. Even when the choice made by the Insinuator is approved of, all is not settled; the superiors have

26   Let. 11th to Marius and Cato.

27   Instruction for the Local Superiors, Letter H.

to determine which of the Insinuators is to be entrusted with the care of enticing the approved person into the Order: for all this is foreseen in the code. It is not allowed to all the brethren to exercise promiscuously so important a trust among the prophane, though they may have pointed out the person proper for reception. The young adept is not to measure his strength with the man who has the advantage over him in years and experience, nor is the tradesman to undertake the magistrate. The superior is to name the most proper Insinuator, judging from the circumstances, age, merits, dignities, or talents of the future candidate.[28] At length, when the mission is given, the Insinuator begins to lay his snares.—Such is the second part of this extraordinary functionary, and all his subsequent steps are regulated by the code.

Part II. How to entice the Candidate.

Candidate, in the ordinary acceptation of the word, means a person who has shown a desire or taken some steps into some order, or to acquire some dignity. In Illuminism it means the person on whom the Order has fixed its attention. It often happens, that the candidate is ignorant of the very existence of the sect. It is the Insinuator's business to inspire him with the wish of entering it. To accomplish this grand object, two different methods are inculcated. The first is for the Insinuator who has some candidate in view remarkable for his science or of a certain age. The second, for him who

---

28   Instructiones pro Recipientibus. *Orig. Writ.,* vol. I., nos. 1 and 7, page 54.

is entrusted with young men from eighteen to thirty, and who are susceptible of a second education.
A third method was proposed for workmen, and
those clownish fellows whose education had been
but little attended to. We may observe Weishaupt
consulting with his confidant Zwack on this part
of the code; but whether it was never digested, or
that he saw the Insinuators could easily supply
the defect, no further mention is made of the third
method. Let us then examine the essence of the
first two.

To exemplify the first method, let us suppose
one of those men who have gone through a complete course of modern Philosophism, who, should
they not scoff at Christianity, would at least hesitate at every thing which is called religion; for
the code forewarns the Insinuator, that his efforts
would be vain should he attempt to seduce Philo-
sphers of another stamp, men of sound judgment,
and who would never be partizans of doctrines
which could not endure the light of broad day. But
when he shall have discovered one of the former
who has already pretty well imbibed the principles
of the sect, he will assume the character of a Philosopher well versed in the mysteries of antiquity.
He will have little difficulty in acting such a part,
as he will find ample instructions in the code. To
follow those instructions faithfully, he must begin

by descanting on the supreme felicity of being
versed in sciences which few can approach, of

walking in the paths of light while the vulgar are groping in darkness. He must remark, that there exist doctrines solely transmitted by secret traditions, because they are above the comprehension of common minds. In proof of his assertions he will cite the Gymnosophists in the Indies, the Priests of Isis in Egypt, and those of Eleusis and the Pythagorean school in Greece.

He will select certain sentences from Cicero, Seneca, Aristides, and Isocrates; and, lest he should ever be taken unawares, he will learn those by heart which the legislator has carefully inserted in the code. Though it would be very easy to demonstrate from those very authors, that the ancient mysteries laid down no fixed principles on the important points of the *Providence of God*, and of the origin and order of the universe, the Insinuator is nevertheless to quote those texts to prove that there exists a secret doctrine on these objects, and above all a doctrine calculated *to render life more agreeable, and pain more supportable; and to enlarge our ideas on the majesty of God.*

Let him add, that all the sages of antiquity were acquainted with these doctrines; let him insist on the uncertainty that man is in with respect *to the nature of the soul, its immortality, and its future destiny.* He will then sound his candidate, to know whether he would not rejoice at having some satisfactory answers on objects of such great importance. At the same time he will hint that he has had the happiness of being initiated into these doctrines, and that, should the candidate wish it, he would do his best to procure him the same felicity; but that it was a science gradually imparted, and that certain men possessed the talent of guiding him from a distance, of leading him to the discovery of this new world, and that without being ever in his presence.[29]

When the Insinuator has by such language succeeded in exciting the curiosity of his candidate, he must then ascertain his opinions on some particular articles. He will propose the discussion of certain questions in writing, and of certain principles, as the groundwork on which they are in future to proceed. The code does not determine what these questions are to be, because they vary according to the political and religious dispositions which the Insinuator may have observed in the candidate. Should these dissertations noway agree with the principles of the sect, the Insinuator will abandon his prey. Should the sophisticated candidate, or the man of importance, be found properly disposed, he will be admitted to the very threshold of the mysteries. The Insinuator will simply explain the inferior degrees to him, and mention the divers trials which the order has dispensed with in consideration of his merit.[30]

Notwithstanding the artifice observable in this method, it is still reserved for those who need only

29 *Original Writings*, vol. II., part II., sect. I.
30 *Original Writings*, vol. II., part II., sect. I.

to be acquainted with Illuminism to adopt its tenets. But should the Insinuator be entrusted with a young candidate, or with one whose principles noway coincide with those of the sect, and who is yet to be formed; it is then that Weishaupt developes that immense theory of art and cunning by which he is insensibly to ensnare his victims. "Let your first care," he says to the Insinuators,

> be to gain the affection, the confidence, and the esteem of those persons whom you are to entice into the Order—let your whole conduct be such, that they shall surmise something more in you than you wish to show—hint that you belong to some secret and powerful society—excite little by little, and not at once, a wish in your candidate to belong to a similar society—Certain arguments and certain books which the Insinuator must have, will greatly contribute to raise such a wish; such are, for example, those which treat of the union and strength of associations.

The Legislator then carefully adds a list of those books, and the Order charges itself with the care of furnishing a certain number of them to the adepts. The works ot *Meiners*, and particularly of *Bassadows*, are frequently recommended by Weishaupt, as the best fitted to inspire their readers with the love and principles of secret societies. But nothing can equal the art with which he himself has drawn up the reasons, by the help of which the Insinuator is to persuade his young candidate of the pretended necessity for these mysterious associations.

"One represents, for example," says the code,

> a child in the cradle; one speaks of its cries, its
> tears, its weakness—One remarks how this child,
> abandoned to itself, is entirely helpless; but that
> by the help of others it acquires strength—One
> shows how the greatness of Princes is derived
> from the union of their subjects—One exalts the
> advantages of the state of society over the state
> of nature—Then one touches on the art of know-
> ing and directing mankind—How easily, you will
> say, could one man of parts lead hundreds, even
> thousands, if he but knew his own advantages.
> This is evidently proved by the organization of
> armies, and the amazing power which princes
> derive from the union of their subjects.

After having descanted on the advantages of
society in general, touch upon *the defects of civil
society, and say how little relief is to be obtained
even from one's best friends,—and how very necessary it would be to support each other in these
days. Add, that men would triumph even over
heaven were they but united—That it is their dis-
union which subjects them to the yoke.*—This is to
be explained by the fable of the wolf and the two
dogs, the latter of whom could only be vanquished
by the former after he had parted them; and by
many other examples of the same kind which the
Insinuator will collect.[31]

As a proof of what great and important things
secret societies can effectuate, he will adduce the

31 Extract of the Instructions for the Brethren charged to enroll

examples of the Freemasons, of the mysterious societies of antiquity, and even of the Jesuits. He will
assert, that all the great events of this world are dependent on hidden causes, which these secret societies powerfully influence; *he will awake in the
breast of his pupil the desire of secretly reigning,
of preparing in his closet a new constitution for
the world, and of governing those who think they
govern us.*[32]

"When you shall have got thus far," says the code,

> begin to show (as it were unguardedly) that you
> are not entirely ignorant of those secrets; throw
> out some half sentences which may denote it.
> Should your candidate take the hint, press him,
> and return to the charge, until you see him be-
> tray symptoms of a desire instantaneously to
> unite with such a society.
>
> The Insinuator, however, who has thus far
> succeeded in inspiring his pupil with such a
> wish, has not played off every engine with which
> the code has furnished him. To sound the very
> bottom of his mind, he will pretend to consult
> him as if he had been entrusted with certain
> secrets, he will make objections on the secre-
> cy of these societies; but should they make too
> much impression he will resolve them himself.
> At other times, to stimulate the curiosity of his
> pupil, he will hold a letter in his hand written in

and receive the candidates—*Original Writings*, vol. I., sec. IX.
and XII.—Also in the degree of Illuminatus Major; instructions on the same object. Document A.

32 *Original Writings, Ibid.*, no 11 and 12.—Illuminatus Major,
Document A, and letters K, L.

cypher, or he will leave it half open on his table, giving his candidate sufficient time to observe the cypher, and then shut it up with all the air of a man who has important correspondences to keep secret. At other times studying the connections and actions of his pupil, he will tell him of certain circumstances which the young man will think he has learned by means of these secret societies, from whom nothing is hidden, though *they* are concealed from all the rest of the world.[33]

These artifices may be greatly abridged, according as the friendship or communicative disposition of the candidate shall have laid him more open; but on the other hand, should they not suffice, the Insinuator is not on that account to abandon his purpose; let him try to accomplish by others what he has failed in himself.—Let him examine his own conduct, and see if he has not neglected some one or more of the rules prescribed in the code; let him redouble his attention and his complaisance. Should it be necesssary to humble himself in order to command, let not the Insinuator forget the formal precept of his legislator, "Learn also to act the valet in order to become master." *Auch zu weilen den knecht gemacht, um dereinst herr zu werden.*[34]

After such a long series of condescensions and discussions the candidate at length must pro-

33   *Original Writings, Ibid.*, no. 17 to 22.
34   *Ibid.*, let 3d, to Ajax.

nounce. If he submit to all these insinuations, he is admitted among the novices of the order; but should he persist in his refusal, let him learn the fate which awaits him from those who have experienced it.

The fate of indocile candidates.

Unhappy, supremely wretched is the youth whom the Illuminées have sought in vain to entice into their sect. Should he even escape their snares, do not let him flatter himself with being proof against their hatred; and let him take care. *The vengeance of* SECRET SOCIETIES *is not a common vengeance; it is the hidden fire of wrath. It is irreconcilable, and scarcely ever does it cease the pursuit of its victims until it has seen them immolated.*[35]

Such at least is the account which history gives us of those who have been guarded enough to withstand the insinuations of the Sect, and particularly of those who, after having gone the first steps with the Insinuator, have refused to proceed any farther with him.

I could cite divers examples; though I once thought that I had met with one of a quite opposite nature, in the person of *Camille de Jourdan*, the same deputy who was to have been involved in the sentence of transportation against Barthelemy and Pichegru after the revolution of the 4th of September, but who luckly escaped from the grasp of the triumvirate. I hear him speaking in the highest

---

35   Important Advice, &c. by Hoffmann. Preface to vol. II.

terms of one of these Insinuators, who had for a
long time endeavoured to entice him into the order. He was much astonished at hearing me speak
of these men as consummate in all the artifices of
the most villanous hypocrisy. He maintained that
his Illuminée was mild, modest, and moderate;
full ot respect for the Gospel, in a word, one of the
most virtuous men he had ever known. In reply, I
enumerated all the proceedings of the Insinuator,
and the artifices he had played off before he quit-
ted his prey. To all that Mr. Camille answered, "It
is true; such was his behaviour; but it was his zeal
for the sect which blinded him, and made him have
recourse to such expedients in order to work what
he called my conversion; yet, with all that, it was
impossible for any body to speak of virtue and religion in so impressive a manner as he did without
being at least an honest man."—"Well," said I, "I
will venture to assert, that the last attempt of your
Insinuator was as follows. He proposed to you to
give your thoughts in writing on certain questions;
you did so; your opinions proved directly opposite
to his; he never saw you after, became your implac-
able enemy, and has never since ceased calumniat-
ing you." "All that again," answered Mr. Camille,
"is very true; nor was it his fault that I did not lose
both friends and fortune. Before that affair he used
to praise me; afterwards, however, he represented
me as a most dangerous man. You cannot conceive
what lies he invented about me, and I was unfortunate enough to observe that they had made impres-

sion."—Is it possible to be believed? Mr. Camille could not yet be persuaded but that his Insinuator was a virtuous man; so profound are the arts of hypocrisy which are to be imbibed from Weishaupt's laws! I was acquainted with two bishops, who had as completely mistaken the characters of their Insinuators as Mr. Camille de Jourdan.

But I will cite the example of Mr. Stark. I never could conceive what this Mr. Stark was whom I saw perpetually abused by the Illuminées. Nicolai and Mirabeau spared no pains to render him odious to the Protestants in Germany; they said he had received the Catholic orders of priesthood privately,[36] though every thing seemed to denote that he was a Protestant. I took some pains to inform myself who this Mr. Stark was, and I found him one of the most learned Protestant ministers in Germany; that his zeal for his religion had acquired him the degree of Doctor, and had preferred him to be Grand Almoner and Counsellor to the Landgrave of Hesse Darmstadt; but that in common with several other learned men, such as Hoffman and Zimmerman, he had had the misfortune of being sought after by the Illuminées; that he would not hearken to them; that the Illuminées had expressed a wish to have an Adept near the person of the prince, and that he had been bold enough to answer his Insinuator, "*If you seek support, I am too little and my prince too great to protect you.*"—And every candidate who will make the

---

36 Mirabeau, *Monarchie Prussienne*, vol. V., art. Religion.

same resolute stand against the agents of the order must expect to be repaid with similar calumnies. The law of the order is invariable and precise, particularly with respect to those whose talents may be obnoxious to Illuminism. *They must he gained over, or ruined in the public opinion.* Such is the text, *so soll man den schrift steller zu gewinnen suchen, oder verschreyen.*[37] But it is now time to follow the candidate who has shown himself more docile through the various preparatory degrees.

---

37 Instructions for the Regent, no. 15.

CHAPTER IV.

Second Part of the Code of the Illuminées.—First Preparatory Degree, of the Novice and of His Teacher.

n the early stages of Illuminism the duration of the time of trial for the Novice was three years for those who were not eighteen years of age; two years for those between eighteen and twenty-four; and one year for those who were near thirty.[1] Circumstances have since occasionally caused the time to be abridged; but, whatever may be the dispositions of the Novice, though the time may be dispensed with, he must go through the different trials, or have got the start of them before he is admitted into the other degrees. Dur-

Length of the novitiate.

---

1   The Statutes reformed, no. 7.

ing the interval he has no other superior but the Insinuator to whom he is indebted for his vocation, and during the whole time of the noviciate, the Insinuator is expressly forbidden to inform his pupil of any other member of the Order. This law was made to skreen the order from the dangers which might result rom an indiscretion of the Novice, and to render the Insinuator alone responsible in such cases; for, should the Novice unfortunately be an indiscreet talker, the code expressly says, his imprudence would at most betray only one of the brethren.[2] The first lessons of the Insinuator (in future his teacher) treat entirely on the importance and the inviolability of the secrecy which is to be observed in Illuminism. He will begin by telling his Novice,

I.
Study
of the
Noivce.
Secresy.

> Silence *and secresy are the very soul of the order*, and you will carefully observe this silence as well with those whom you may have only reason to suppose are already initiated, as with those whom you may hereafter know really to belong to the Order. You will remember, that it is a constant principle among us, *that ingenuousness is only a virtue with respect to our superiors, but that distrust and reserve are the fundamental principles.* You will never reveal to any person, at present or hereafter, the slightest circumstance relative to your admission into the order, the degree you have received, nor the time when admitted; in a word, you will never speak of any object relating to

---

2   The Statutes reformed, no. 16.

the order even before Brethren, without the strongest necessity.[3]

Under the restrictions of this severe law, one Illuminée will often be a stranger to another; and the Novice will see in this no more than a measure of safety for the order, which might be ruined by the least indiscretion.[4]

More certainly to assure himself of the discretion of the Novice, the Insinuator will give him no further insight, nor entrust him with any writing relative to the order, until he has obtained the following declaration:

> I, the undersigned, promise upon my honour, and without any reservation, never to reveal either by words, signs, or actions, or in any possible manner, to any person whatever, either relations, allies, or most intimate friends, any thing that shall be entrusted to me by my Introducer relative to my entrance into a *secret society*; and this whether my reception shall take place or not. I subject myself the more willingly to this secresy, as my *Introducer assures me that nothing is ever transacted in this society hurtful to religion, morals, or the state.* With respect to all writings which I may be entrusted with, any letters which I may receive concerning the same object, I engage myself to return them, after

---

3   *Original Writings*, Statutes, No. 20. Statutes reformed, No. 27. True Illuminism, General Statutes, No. 31, 32.

4   Summary of the Statutes, no. 15., B.

having made for my sole use the necessary extracts.[5]

These writings or books relative to the order are only lent to the Novice at first in small numbers, and for a short time; and then he must promise to keep them out of the reach of the prophane; but as he is promoted in rank, he may preserve them for a longer time, and is intrusted with a larger quantity; though not without having informed the Order of the precautions he shall have taken, lest in case of his death any of these writings should fall into prophane hands.[6] He will afterwards learn, that the Brotherhood take many other precautions for secresy, not only respecting the statutes, but even with regard to the very existence of the Order. He will see, for example, in its laws, that should any of the brotherhood fall sick, the other brethren are assiduously to visit him, in the first place *to fortify* him, that is to say, to hinder him from making any declarations at the hour of his death; and secondly, to carry away whatever writings relative to the Order the sick man may have had in his possession, as soon as any symptoms of danger appear.[7]

II.
Study.

He will at length learn, that to frustrate all attempts to trace even their very existence, the *order*

5   *Original Writings*, and the true Ilium. Art. *Reverse*.

6   Institutes of the Insinuated, No 8. *Orig. Writ.*, the real Illuminée no. 7

7   Statutes of the Minerval, no. 12.

does not exist every where UNDER THE SAME NAME,
but that they are to assume the name of *some other order*, perhaps even of a literary society, or meet
without any name which can attract the attention
of the public.

The first writing delivered to the Novice, to ac- Diction-
custom him to profound secrecy, is what may be ary of the
called the Dictionary of Illuminism. He must be- Order.
gin by learning the language of the Sect, that is to
say, the art of communicating with the superiors
and other adepts without the possibility of being
understood by the prophane. By means of this language, the Illuminées are to be able to correspond
with each other, without running the risk of its being discovered of what Brother they speak; from
what place, in what language, at what period, and
to whom, or by whom the letter is written.

To avoid the discovery of persons, the Novice Charac-
will learn, that no Brother bears the same name in teristic
the Order which he does in the world; indeed, had names of
he been initiated in the higher degrees of Mason- its Mem-
ry, he would have seen the same precaution tak- bers.
en, where the Rosicrucians receive what they call
their Characteristic or their adoptive name. The
Novice will receive the characteristic immediately on his admission, and it will in some measure
imply the parts which he is in future to act in the
general conspiracy. It will be his task hereafter to
study and write the history of his new patron; he
will by this method recognize in the qualities and
actions of his hero the particular services which

the order will expect from him.[8] This name will be chosen as conformably as possible to the dispositions observed in him. Has he shown any propensity to repeat the impieties of Philosophism against the Gospel, he will be classed with the Celsi and Porphirii, or with the Tindals and Shaftsburys; should his turn be toward the hatred of Kings, or should his talents be judged useful for the polity of the Order, then his characteristic will be of the Brutus, Cato, or Machiavel tribe. He will not be told what he is to do to deserve his name, but they will contrive that it shall occur to him. Neither will he be told why Weishaupt assumed the name of Spartacus (a name so famous in Rome because he waged the war of the slaves against their masters); but should he ever be admitted to the higher mysteries, he will easily recognize the reason.[9]

Its Geography.

The place from whence they write, as well as the persons of whom or to whom they write, is in like manner to be kept secret; a new Geography is therefore taught the Novice. He will thence learn, that Bavaria, the country of their founder, is denominated *Achaia*; *Swabia, Pannotia*; *Franconia, Austria, and Tyrol* are denoted by *Illyria, Egypt, and Peloponnesus*; *Munich* is called *Athens*; *Bamberg, Antioch*; *Inspruck, Samos*; *Vienna* in Austria, *Rome*; *Wurtzburg, Carthage*;

---

8   *Original Writings*, vol.I. Instructions for the Insinuated, no. 7, and vol. II., let 13.

9   *Original Writings*, vol. I., sec. 4.

Frankfort on the Mein becomes *Thebes*; and *Heidelberg Utica*. *Ingolstadt*, the natal soil of the Order, was not sufficiently denoted by *Ephesus*; this privileged town was to be decorated with a more mysterious name, and the profound adepts bestowed on it that of *Eleusis*.

Should the Novice ever be sent on a mission out of his own country, or to distant shores, he will then receive further instructions in the Geography of the Sect.[10]

He must also learn how to date his letters, and be conversant with the Illuminized Hegira or Calendar; for all letters which he will receive in future will be dated according to the Persian era, called *Jezdegert* and beginning A.D. 630. The year begins with the Illuminées on the first of *Pharavardin*, which answer to the 21st of March. Their first month has no less than forty-one days; the following months, instead of being called May, June, July, August, September, and October, are *Adarpahascht, Chardad, Thirmeh, Merdedmeh, Shaharimeh, Meharmeh*: November and December are *Abenmeh, Adameh*: January and February, *Dimeh*, and *Benmeh*: The month of March only has twenty days, and is called *Asphandar*.[11]

The Novice must next learn how to decypher the letters he may receive; in order to which, he must make himself master of that cypher, which is to serve him until initiated into the higher degrees,

Its Calendar.

Its Cypher.

---

10   *Original Writings*, sect. 2 and 3.

11   See the real Illuminée first degree.

when he will be entrusted with the hieroglyphics of the Order.[12]

He will also remember, that he is never to write the name of his Order; so venerable a word cannot be exposed to prophane eyes, and a circle ☉ with a point in the middle of it will supply this sacred word, and a long square or parallelogram ☐ will denote the word Lodge.

III.
Study of
the stat-
utes.

After these preliminary studies, the young brother receives a part of the code, under the title of *Statutes of the Illuminées*. But these first statutes are nothing more than a snare, and the young Novice, with pleasure no doubt, sees them begin with the following words:

> For the tranquillity and security of all the Brethren, whether Novices or active Members of the Society, and to prevent all ill-grounded suspicions, or disagreeable doubts, the venerable Order declares, that it absolutely *has in view no project, enterprize, or undertaking hurtful to*

---

12   The common cypher of the Illuminées consist in numbers corresponding to letters in the following:

12.	11.	10.	9.	8.	7.	6.	5.	4.	3.	2.	1.
a.	b.	c.	d.	e.	f.	g.	h.	i.	k.	l.	m.
13.	14.	15.	16.	17.	18.	19.	20.	21.	22.	23.	24.
n.	o.	p.	q.	r.	s.	t.	u.	w.	x.	y.	z.

The hieroglyphics are contained in the opposite Plate, and are copied from those published at the end of the degree of Scotch Knight or Directing Illuminée. There is a third cypher, but that has never been published.

a	⊕	⊓	t	⊢	⊕
b	✡	⊔	u	⊣	⊶
c	⌐	☾	v	4	≡
d	↓	⌐	w	⊠	♄
e	⌐	✳	x	⊥	⊓
f	♂	⊏	y	⋮	⊟
g	⊐	⊥	z	∿	⊠
h	•	▬			
i	+	△	1	∴	
k	☿	⧺	2	◡	
l	∟	♀	3	◡	
m	I	⟩	4	⊡—⊡	
n	H	◿	5	√3	
o	⊤	♂	6	✗	
p	⋮	▭	7	✗	
q	⊥	☿	8	✗	
r	✕	⊖	9	✗	
s	◇	☉	0	⋮	

,	⋈	;	3	:	3
.	6	!	9	?	69

the state, to religion, or to good morals; and that it favours nothing of that nature in any of its members. Its designs, all its toils, solely tend to inspire men with a zeal for the perfection of their moral characters, to impregnate them with humane and sociable sentiments, to counteract the plans of the wicked, to succour oppressed and suffering virtue, to favour the advancement of men of merit, and to render those sciences universal which are as yet hidden from the generality of men. Such is not the *coloured* pretext, but the real object of the order.[13]

Even should the Novice not have entirely laid aside all suspicions respecting the intentions of the Order, still so positive a declaration he must think would guarantee him as to all obligations which might be imposed upon him. His grand aim is to be, to *form his heart* in such a maner as to gain not only the affection of his friends but even of his enemies. He is positively ordered to endeavour *with all his might to acquire both interior and exterior perfection*. It is true, he is soon after as positively ordered *to study the arts of dissimulation and disguise*; but then the Brother Insinuator is at his elbow to explain to him how that art coincides with true perfection, and thus suppress any suspicions which might arise from a comparison of these two injunctions. Beside, the Novice has many other duties to fulfil, which will deprive him of opportunity for such reflections.

13   The True Illuminée, General Statutes—*Original Writings*, vol. 1., sect. 8.

He is next told, that the Brethren must have
but one mind, one will, and similar sentiments;
that, to effectuate this, the Order has made choice
of certain works, to which he must apply with the
greatest attention. Should the Novice be one of
those men whom an attachment to the Gospel
rendered more circumspect as to the snares laid
for his belief, the very choice of the books would
suffice to show him, that the first object of the Insinuator was to persuade him, that it is not even
necessary to be a Christian to acquire the perfection enjoined by the statutes. The *Morality* he is
taught is that of *Epictetus, Seneca, Antoninus,*
and *Plutarch,* all foreign to Christianity. He will
also receive the works of modern Sophisters, such
as *Wieland, Meiners,* and *Bassadows,* who by no
means make perfection to consist in Christianity. Under the soothing and mellifluous language
of a moderate and specious Philosophy, he will
be led to lubricity and impiety, traced by the sophisticated pen of Helvétius in his celebrated
work *De L'Esprit.*[14] But the Insinuator must previously have sufficiently studied the dispositions
of his pupil to know whether such propositions
would any longer startle him. Beside, nothing is
better calculated to dissipate all such fears, than
the constant application that is required to those
books which are put into the hands of the Novice, added to the care taken to deprive him of all

IV.
Study the
morality
of the
Order.

---

14   See the list of these works in the *Original Writings* in the Statutes reformed, no. 25.

such as might inspire him with contrary ideas. The Teacher is carefully to attend to all the rules laid down in the code on this subject, and to see that his Novices fulfil the intentions of the Order in this respect. He is frequently to converse with them; he is to mark out their occupations for them; he is even to make them unexpected visits to surprize them, and thus to see in what manner they apply to the code and other writings with which the Order has entrusted them. He is to require an account of what they have read, and extracts from the different works; he will assist them by his explanations; in short, nothing is to be neglected which can secure their progress in the spirit and morals of the Order.[15]

V.
Study the knowl-edge of mankind.

An object of far greater importance next attracts the attention of the Novice; it is that which the code calls *the greatest of all*; it is, *the knowledge of men*. The teacher will represent this to his pupil *as the most interesting of all sciences*.[16] To make himself master of this science, the Novice receives the model of a journal in the form of tablets, and his teacher shows him how they are to be used. Provided with this journal, he is to make his observations on every body he finds himself in company with; he is to trace their characters, and account to himself every thing he has seen or heard. Lest his memory should fail him, he

---

15   *See* Instructiones pro Insinuantibus et Recipientibus.

16   The true Illuminée. Instructions on the Art of forming Pupils, No. 12.

must always be provided with a loose paper or small tablets, on which he may at all hours note his observations, which he is afterwards carefully to digest in his journal. To be certain of the Novice's attention to this point, the Brother Teacher will examine his tablets and his journal from time to time. To render him more expert in the art of drawing the characters of the living, he will exercise the Novices on ancient authors, and on the heroes of antiquity. No study or custom is so frequendy recommended as this in all the code of Illuminism. It is to be the grand study of the Novice, and the prime occupation of every degree.[17]

It is by his assiduity in this great art that the Novice will learn how to distinguish those whom he may hereafter judge proper to be admitted into or rejected from the Order; and it is with that view that the Preceptor perpetually presses him *to propose those whom he may think fit for the order.*[18] By this means a double object is attained; first, the propagation of the Order; and, secondly, a knowledge of its friends or enemies; the dangers it may be threatened with; and the means to be adopted, or the persons to be gained or courted, to avert the impending storm; in fine, of extending its conquests. Whether the Illuminée be a Novice, or in any other degree, he is bound by the laws of the

17   See *Ibid.* No. 13,—*Original Writings*, the Statutes reformed, No. 9, 10, 13, 14.—Instructiones pro Insinuantibus, No. 5, pro Recipientibus, No. 16, &c. &c.

18   Instructiones pro Recipientibus, no 13.

Order to make his report in the prescribed forms at least once a month.[19]

The Bonds of the Novice. While the Novice is perpetually making researches of this nature, he is not aware that he is as carefully watched by his Insinuator, who on his side notes and writes down every thing that he observes either as to the failings or the progress, the strong or weak side of his pupil, and these he as regularly transmits to the superiors.[20]

The pupil little suspects that the grand object of his Insinutor is *to bind him* in such a maner to Illuminism, *even long before he is acquainted with its secrets*, that it shall be impossible for him to break those bonds which fear and terror shall have imposed upon him, should he ever wish to shrink from the horrid plots and systems which he might thereafter discover.

His blind obedience. This profound policy of binding the Novices to Illuminism consists, first, in giving them a magnificent idea of the grandeur of the projects of the Sect, and, secondly, in a vow *of blind obedience* to the superiors in every thing which they judge conducive to the ends of the Order, which vow the Insinuator is to find means of extorting from his pupil.

It is here particularly that Weishaupt appears to wish to assimilate the government of his Sect to

---

19 Instructions for the Insinuated, no. 5. C. and *Original Writings*, &c.

20 Instructions for the Insinuator, no. 3 and 4.—The real Illuminée, Instructions on the Art of forming the Brethren, no. 1, 2.

that of the religious orders, and especially to that of the Jesuits, by a total sacrifice of their own will and judgment, which he exacts of the adepts; and to the exercising of the Novices in this point, he expressly adverts in his instructions to the Insinuators.[21] But this is precisely the place to remark on the amazing difference between the illuminized and the religious obedience. Of that immense number of religious who follow the institutes of St. Basil, St. Benedict, St. Dominic, or St. Francis, there is not one who is not thoroughly convinced that there exists a voice far more imperious than that of his superior, the voice of his conscience, of the Gospel, and of his God. There is not one of them who, should his superior command any thing contrary to the duties of a Christian, or of an honest man, would not immediately see that such a command was a release from his vow of obedience. This is frequently repeated and clearly expressed in all religious institutes, and no where more explicitly or positively than in those of the Jesuits. They are ordered to obey their superior, but in cases only where such obedience is not sinful, *ubi non cerneretur peccatum*.[22] It is only in cases where such obedience can have no sinful tendency whatever, *ubi definiri non possit aliquod peccati genus*

21 Mirabeau, Monarchic Prussienne, vol. V., and Essay on the Illuminées, Chap. III. Last Observations by Philo, page 61.

22 Constitution of the Jesuits, part. III., chap. I., parag. 2, vol. I., Edition of Prague.

intercedere.[23] And, as if this were not sufficiently expressed, we hear their founder, at the very time when he recommends obedience to his religious, expressly saying, *but remember that your vow is binding only when the commands of man are not contrary to those of God, ubi Deo contraria non prcecipit homo.*[24] All those person therefore who, like Mirabeau, surmised certain coincidences, or as he calls them *points of contact,* between the religious institutes and the code of the Illuminées, should have begun by observing, that religious obedience is in its very essence an obligation of doing all the good which may be prescribed without the least taint of harm. It was easy for them on the contrary to demonstrate, that the obedience sought for by Weishaupt's code was a dispositon to obey every order received from the superior in spite of conscience, and unheedful of the most iniquitous guilt, provided it tended to the good of the Order.

> Our society (for such are the expressions of the code) exacts from its members the sacrifice of their liberty, not only with respect to all things, *but absolutely with respect to* EVERY MEANS *of attaining its end.* Yet the presumption on the goodness of the *means prescribed is always in favour of the orders given by the superiors.* They are clearer-sighted on this object; they are better acquainted with it; and it is on this very

---

23 *Ibid.*, part VI., chap. I.

24 *Epist. Ignatii De Obedientia.*

account that they are nominated superiors—It is their business to lead you through the labyrinth of errors and darkness; and in such a case obedience is not only a duty, but an object for grateful acknowledgment.[25]

Such is the obedience of the Illuminées; nor is there a single exception to be found in all their code. We shall see the Novice, before he terminates his trials, obliged to explain himself explicitly with respect to orders which he may receive from his superiors, and which he may think contrary to his conscience. In the first place his teacher is to intangle him, and make himself perfectly master of his most secret thoughts. Under the pretence of knowing himself better, while studying the art of knowing others, the Novice is to draw a faithful picture of himself, to unfold his interests and connections, as well as those of his family.

His secrets discovered.

Here again the Insinuator furnishes him with the tablets in the requisite form, that he may give this new proof of confidence to the Order; but this will neither be the last nor the most important one for which he will be called upon.

On these tablets, the Novice is to write down his name, age, functions, country, and abode; the species of study in which he occupies himself, *the books of which his library is composed*, and the secret writings of which he may be in possession;

---

25 Statutes reformed, no. 1, 4, and 25.—The true Illuminée, General Statutes, no. 11, 12 .

his revenue, his friends, his enemies, and the reason of his enmities; in fine, his acquaintances and his protectors.

To this table he is to subjoin a second, explaining the same objects with respect to his father, his mother, and all their other children. He is to be very explicit with respect *to the education they received, to their passions and prejudices, to their strong and weak sides.*

We will exemplify this second table by an extract from the *Original Writings,* by which the reader will perceive that parents are not very much favoured—

> The Novice, Francis Antony St. . . . . . .
> aged 22, represents his father as *violent, and of soldierlike manners*; his mother as *a little avaricious*; the weak side of both to be flattery and interest; both living after the old fashion, and with an antiquated frankness; in their devotion, headstrong, arrogant; with difficulty abandoning an ill-conceived project, and still more unforgiving to their enemies; that they nevertheless were little hated, because little feared; and hardly in the way of doing any body any harm.

While the Novice is thus occupied in revealing all his secrets, and those of his family, the Insinuator on his side is drawing up a new statement of every thing he has been able to discover during the whole time of his pupil's trial, either with respect to him or to his relations.

On comparing the two statements, should the superior approve of the admission of the Novice to the last proofs, he is then to answer the grand questions. It is by these questions that the Novice is to judge of the extent of the sacrifice he is about to make, and of the awful subjection of his whole will, conscience, and person, to Illuminism, if he wishes to gain admittance.

The Questions are twenty-four in number, and couched in the following terms: Questions he is to answer.

I. Are you still desirous of being received into the Order of the Illuminées?

II. Have you seriously reflected on the importance of the step you take, *in binding yourself by engagements that are unknown to you?*

III. What hopes do you entertain, or, by what reasons are you induced to enter among us?

IV. Would you still persevere in that wish, though you should find that we had no other object or advantage whatever in view but the perfection of mankind?

V. What would be your conduct should the Order be of new invention?

VI. *Should you ever discover in the Order any thing wicked, or unjust to be done, what part would you take*; Wenn unanstandige, ungerechte sachen vorkamen, wie er sich verhalten wurde?

VII. *Can you and will you look upon the welfare of the Order as your own?*

VIII. We cannot conceal from you, that Members, entering into our Order without any other motive than to acquire power, greatness, and consideration, are not those whom we prefer. In many cases one must know how to lose in order to gain. Are you aware of all this?

IX. Can you love all the Members of the Order, even such of your enemies as may be members of it?

X. Should it so happen that you should be obliged to do good to your enemies who are of the Order, to recommend them, for example, or extol them; would you be disposed to do so?

XI. *Do you, moreover, grant the* POWER OF LIFE AND DEATH *to our Order or Society?* On what grounds would you refuse, or recognize in it such a right; *Ober dieser geselschaft, oder order auch das* JUS VITÆ ET NECIS, *aus was grnden, oder nich zugestehe?*

XII. *Are you disposed on all occasions to give the preference to men of our Order, over all other men?*

XIII. How would you wish to revenge yourself of any injustice, either great or small, which you may have received from strangers or from any one of our Brethren?

XIV. What would be your conduct should you ever repent of having joined our Order?

XV. Are you willing to share with us happiness and misfortune?

XVI. Do you renounce the idea of ever making your birth, employment, station, or power, serve to the prejudice or contempt of any one of the Brethren?

XVII. Are you, or have you any idea of becoming a Member of any other society?

XVIII. Is it from levity, or in hopes of soon being acquainted with our constitution, that you so easily make these promises?

XIX. Are you fully determined to observe our laws?

XX. *Do you subject yourself to a* BLIND OBEDIENCE WITHOUT ANY RESTRICTION WHATEVER? *And do you know the strength of such an engagement?* Ober unbedingten gehorsam angelobe, und wisse was das sey?

XXI. Is there no consideration that can deter you from entering into our Order?

XXII. *Will you, in case it is required, assist in the propagation of the Order, support it by your counsels, by your money, and by all other means?*

XXIII. Had you any expectation that you would have to answer any of these questions; and if so, which question was it?

XXIV. What security can you give us that you will keep these promises; and to what punishment will you subject yourself in case you should break any of them?[26]

In order to judge of the nature of the answers written and signed by the Novice, and confirmed by his oath, it will be sufficient to cast our eyes on the account of the reception of two Brethren, as it is contained in the archives of the Sect. To the VIth

26 *Original Writings.* The account of the reception of two Novices, vol. I., sect. 17.

questrion, *should you ever discover in the Order any thing wicked, or unjust to be done, what part would you take?* The first of these two Novices, aged 22, and named *Francis Anthony St . . . .* *answers, swears, and signs,*

> I would certainly execute those things, if so commanded by the Order, because it may be very possible that I am not capable of judging of what is just or unjust. Besides, should they be unjust under one aspect, *they would cease to be so as soon as they became a means of attaining happiness, the general end.*

The Novice Francis Xaverius B . . . . answers, swears, and signs, in like manner, "I would not refuse to execute those things (wicked and unjust) provided they contributed to the general good."

To the XIth question, *on life and death*, the first Novice answers with the same formalities,

> Yes, I acknowledge this right in the Order of Illuminées; and why should I refuse it to the Order, should it ever find itself necessitated to exercise it, as perhaps without such a right it might have to fear *its awful ruin. The state would lose little by it, since the dead man would be replaced by so many others.* Besides, I refer to my answer to question VI.;

that is to say, where he promised to execute whatever was just or unjust, provided it was with the approbation or by order of the Superiors.

CHAPTER IV

The second answers, swears, and signs to the same question,

> The same reason which makes me recognize the right of life and death in the governors of nations, leads me to recognize most willingly the same power in my Order, which really contributes to the happiness of mankind as much as governors of nations ought to do.

On the XXth question, on *blind obedience without restriction*, one answers, "Yes, without doubt, *the promise is of the utmost importance; nevertheless I look upon it as the only possible means by which the Order can gain its ends.*" The second is less precise:

> When I consider our Order as of modern invention and as little extended, I have a sort of repugnance in binding myself by so formidable a promise; because in that case I am justified in doubting whether a want of knowledge or even some domineering passion might not sometimes occasion things to be commanded totally opposite to the proposed object of the general welfare. But when I suppose the order to be more univerally spread, I then believe, that in a society comprehending men of such different stations, from the higher to the lower, those men are best enabled to know the course of the world, and how to distinguish the. means of accomplishing the laudable projects of the Order.

This doubt of the Novice as to the antiquity of the Order must have displeased Weishaupt, who spared no pains to make it appear that Illuminism was of ancient date, the better to excite the curiosity and the veneration of the pupils; being content to enjoy the glory of his invention with his profound adepts, to whom only he revealed the secret of the invention of the highest degrees and the last mysteries. But our Novice went on to say, that on the whole he rather believed the Order to be of ancient than of modern invention; and, like his fellow Novice, he "promises to be faithful to all the laws of his Order, to support it with his counsels, his fortune, and all other means; and he finishes by *subjecting himself to forfeit his honour, and even his* LIFE, *should he ever break his promise.*"[27]

When the Insinuator has found means of binding the Novice to the Order by such oaths, and especially when the young candidate shall have recognized without hesitation that strange and awful right which subjects the life of every citizen to the satellites of Illuminism, should any be unfortunate enough to displease its Superiors; when the Novice is blinded to such a degree as not to perceive that this pretended right, far from implying a society of sages, only denotes a band of ruffians and a federation of assassins like the emissaries of the Old Man of the Mountain; when, in short, he shall have submitted himself to this terrible power, the oath of the modern Seyde is sent to the archives of the Order.

---

27   See the two accounts.

His dispositions then prove to be such as the superiors required to confer on him the second degree of the preparatory class; and the Insinuator concludes his mission by the introduction of his pupil.

At the appointed time in the dead of the night, the Novice is led to a gloomy apartment, where two men are waiting for him, and, excepting his Insinuator, these are the first two of the Sect with whom the Novice is made acquainted. The Superior or his Delegate holds a lamp in his hand half covered with a shade; his attitude is severe and imperious; and a naked sword lies near him on the table. The other man, who serves as Secretary, is prepared to draw up the act of initiation. No mortal is introduced but the Novice and his Insinuator, nor can any one else be present. A question is first asked him, whether he still perseveres in the intention of entering the Order. On his answering in the affirmative, he is sent by himself into a room perfectly dark, there to meditate again on his resolution. Recalled from thence, he is questioned again and again on his firm determination blindly to obey all the laws of the Order. The Introducer answers for the dispositions of his pupil, and in return requests the protection of the Order for him.

"Your request is just," replies the Superior to the Novice. "In the name of the most Serene Order from which I hold my powers, and in the name of all its Members, I promise you protection, justice, and help. Moreover, I protest to you once more, *that you will find nothing among us hurtful to Re-*

The promotion of the Novice.

ligion, to Morals, or to the State;"—here the Initiator takes in his hand the naked sword which lay upon the table, and, pointing it at the heart of the Novice, continues,

> but should you ever be a traitor or a perjurer, assure yourself that every Brother will be called upon to arm against you. Do not flatter yourself with the possibility of escaping, or of finding a place of security.—Wherever thou mayst be, the rage of the Brethren, shame and remorse shall follow thee, and prey upon thy very entrails.

—He lays down the sword.—"But if you persist in the design of being admitted into our Order, take this oath:"

The oath is conceived in the following terms:

> In presence of all powerful God, and of you Plenipotentiaries of the most high and most excellent Order into which I ask admittance, I acknowledge my natural weakness, and all the insufficiency of my strength. I confess that, notwithstanding all the privileges of rank, honours, titles, or riches which I may possess in civil society, I am but a man like other men; that I may lose them all by other mortals, as they have been acquired through them; that I am in absolute want of their approbation and of their esteem; and that I must do my utmost to deserve them both. I never will employ either the power or consequence that I may possess to the prejudice of the general welfare. I will, on the contrary, resist with all

my might the enemies of human nature, and
of civil society.

Let the reader observe these last words; let him
remember them when reading of the mysteries of
Illuminism; he will then be able to conceive how,
by means of this oath, *to maintain civil society,*
Weishaupt leads the adepts to the oath of eradicating even the last vestige of society. "I promise,"
continues the adept,

> ardently to seize every opportunity of serving
> humanity, of improving my mind and my will,
> of employing all my useful accomplishments for
> the general good, *in as much as the welfare and
> the statutes of the society shall require it of me.*
>
> *I vow* (ich gelobe) *an eternal silence, an
> inviolable obedience and fidelity to all my su-
> periors and to the statutes of the Order.* WITH
> RESPECT TO WHAT MAY BE THE OBJECT OF THE
> ORDER *I fully and absolutely renounce my own
> penetration and my own judgment.*
>
> I promise to look upon the interests of the
> Order as my own; and as long as I shall be a
> Member of it, *I promise to serve it with my
> life, my honour, and my estates.* Should I ever,
> through imprudence, passion, or wickedness,
> act contrary to the laws or to the welfare of the
> Serene Order, *I then subject myself to whatever
> punishment it may please to inflict upon me.*
>
> I also promise to help the Order, to the best
> of my power, and according to my conscience,
> with my counsels and my actions, and without
> the least attention to my personal interest; also,
> to look upon all friends and enemies of the Or-

der as my own, and to behave to them as the Order shall direct. I am equally disposed to labour with all my might and all my means at the propagation and advancement of the Order.

In these promises I renounce every secret reservation, and engage to fulfill them all, according to the true purport of the words, and according to the signification attached to them by the Order when it prescribed the Oath—

So help me God. N. N.

The oath being signed by the Novice, and enregistered in the minutes of the Order, the Initiator declares his admission, telling him at the same time that he is not to expect to know all the members, but those only who, being of the same degree, are under the same Superior.—From that moment advanced to the degree of *Minerval*, he is instructed in the signs of his new degree, which are much of the same nature as those of Masonry. He is then enjoined to give an exact *list of all his books*, particularly of those which might be precious or useful to the Order. He also receives the following questions which he is to answer in writing.

I. What should you wish to be the object of our Order?

II. What means, either primary or secondary, do you think most conducive to the attainment of that object?

III. What other things would you wish to find among us?

IV. What men do you either hope to meet, or not to meet, among us?[28]

The answers given to these questions will enable the Superiors to judge how far the young adept has imbibed the principles of the Order. But other helps are preparing for him, that he may be able to demonstrate by his answers both the progress he has made and that which he may be expected to make.

Thus admitted to the degree of *Minerval*, he will find himself in future a Member of the Academy of the Sect. Let us then observe well both the Scholars and their Masters; for they still belong to the class of preparation.

---

28 True Illuminée, 1st initiation, page 51 and following. *Original Writings*, vol. I., sect. 15.

CHAPTER V.

Third Part of the Code of the Illuminées.—Second Preparatory Degree.— The Academy of Illuminism, or the Brethren of Minerva.

eishaupt, ruminating on what turn he should give to his Code of Illuminism, that its progress might be more subtile and infallible, expresses himself in the following terms, on the preparatory degrees which were to succeed to the novitiate of his pupils.

Object of this Degree.

I am thinking of establishing, in the next degree, a sort of an academy of Literati. My design would include the study of the Ancients, and an application to the art of observing and drawing characters (even those of the living); and treatises and questions, proposed for public compositions, should form the occupations

89

of our pupils.—*I should wish, more especially, to make them spies over each other in particular, and over all in general.* It is from this class that I would select those who have shown the greatest aptness for the Mysteries. My determination, in short, is, that in this degree they shall labour at the discovery and extirpation of prejudices. Every pupil (for example) shall declare, at least once a month, all those which he may have discovered in himself; which may have been his principal one, and how far he has been able to get the better of it.

Ever influenced by a bitter hatred against the Jesuits, he does not blush to say—"I mean that this declaration shall be among us, what confession was among them." He was, however, unfortunate in his application; for in the Order of the Jesuits, no superior could ever hear the confessions of the Inferiors; and thus their very institutes rendered impossible the horrid abuse, under which Weishaupt affected to cloak the abominable breach of confidence with respect to his pupils, when he says, "by these means I shall discern those who show dispositions *for certain special Doctrines relative to Government or to Religion.*"[1]

The statutes of their Minerval degree are drawn up with a little more circumspection, and simply declare, "that the Order in that degree wishes to be considered only as a learned society or academy, consecrating its toils to form the hearts and minds

---

1   *Orig. Writ.,* vol. I.—let. 4, to Cato.

of its young pupils both by example and precept."[2] These are called the Brethren of *Minerva*, and are under the direction of the *Major or Minor Illuminées*. The academy properly so called is composed of ten, twelve, and sometimes fifteen Minervals, under the direction and tuition of a *major Illuminée*.

In the kalendar of the Sect, the days on which the academy meets are called holy, and its sittings are generally held twice a month; always at the new moon. The place where they meet is called, in their language, *a Church*. It must always be preceded by an anti-chamber, with a strong door armed with bolts, which is to be shut during the time of the meeting; and the whole apartment is to be so disposed, that it shall be impossible for intruders either to see or hear any thing that is going forward.[3]

Of the Minerval academy. Its sittings.

At the commencement of each sitting, the President is always to read, and, after his fashion, comment on some chosen passages of the BIBLE, or *Seneca*, of *Epictetus, Marcus Aurelius*, or *Confucius*.[4] The care he takes to give to all these works the same weight and authority, will be sufficient to make the pupils view the *Bible* in a similar light with the works of the Pagan Philosophers.

This lecture over, each pupil is questioned "as to the books which he has read since the last meeting; on the observations or discoveries he may have

---

2   Statutes of the Minerval, no. 16.

3   See the Minerval Ritual.

4   *Ibid.*

made; and on his labours or services toward the progress of the Order."

Its Library,

Nor are the studies and the books of which the Brethren are to give an account, left to their own choice. To each of these academies there is appropriated a particular library, whenever circumstances will permit, calculated to insure the spirit of the Order; and this collection the Sect takes care to furnish. By three different means it is accomplished. First, by the money which the Brethren contribute; secondly, by the list of his own private Library, which is exacted from each candidate, who is obliged to furnish therefrom such books as may be required of him; the third means is derived from Weishaupt's grand principle, that EVERY THING WHICH IS USEFUL IS AN ACT OF VIRTUE. Now as it would be very useful for the Order to get possession of those rare books and precious manuscripts which Princes, Nobles, and Religious Orders keep shut up among their archives or in their libraries; all Illuminées acting as librarians or archive-keepers are admonished, exhorted, and seriously pressed not to make any scruple of secretly stealing such books or manuscripts, and putting them into the possession of the Sect. This is one of the most explicit lessons that Weishaupt gives to his adepts; at one time telling them not *to make a case of conscience* of giving to the Brethren what they may have belonging *to the library of the Court*; at another, sending a list of what should be stolen from that of the Carmes, he says, "*all these*

how procuted.

would be of much greater use if they were in our hands.—What do those rascals do with all those books?"[5]

Yet, notwithstanding the caution with which the founder as yet withholds certain books from the hands of the *Minerval*, it is clear from the very assortment of the libraries of the Order, that he does not hesitate at giving the pupils a certain number directly tending to the grand object, and particularly those which may create a contempt for religion. He wishes much to see an *impartial history of the Church*; and he even proposes hereafter to publish one himself, or at least to contribute many articles toward such a work. He calls the attention of the young adepts to Sarpi, to *Le Bret's arsenal of calumnies*, and in short to all that has been written against Religious Orders.[6] He had even put on the list those impious works which appeared under the name of *Fréret*. He seemed to have forgotten for a moment his ordinary prudence; but, warned of it by *Knigge*, he corrected his error.[7] Many other books, however, were to be comprehended in the Minerval library, which were to disguise the object of it; and it was one duty of the Presiding Illuminée to select such as would gradually direct his pupils to the grand object of the Sect; always remembering, that the most impious and seditious *were reserved for the higher degrees*. Should the Presi-

---

5   *Orig. Writ.,* vol. I., let. 4.

6   *Ibid.*

7   Letter of Philo to Cato

dent chance to find *the System of Nature, Natural Polity,* Helvétius' *On Man,* or other such books, in the hands of his pupil, *he was to avoid showing his pleasure or displeasure,* and leave them.[8] In short, it is in the Minerval schools that the teachers are in a particular manner to practise that great art of making the adepts rather as it were invent than learn the principles of the Order; because they will then, looking upon them as the offspring of their own genius, more strongly adhere to them.

Its occupations.

There is yet another scheme in these schools for attaching the young adepts to the Order.—Every brother is, at his first reception, to declare to what art or science he means principally to apply, unless his station, genius, or particular circumstances, debar him from the literary career; in which latter case, *pecuniary contributions* are to be an equivalent for those services which his talents cannot contribute.[9] If the Brethren adopt literary pursuits, then the Order enters into engagements to furnish them with all possible assistance to forward their undertakings in the art or science on which they shall have determined; unless they should have chosen *Theology* or *Jurisprudence,* two sciences which the Order absolutely excepts from any such agreement.[10]

Their succours for the Minerval have a two-fold tendency. On the one side, they serve to prove that

8 Letter 3, to Cato.

9 *Orig. Writ.,* vol. I.—Summary of the Institute, no. 9.

10 Statutes of the Minerval, no. 1.

the adept does not *neglect* the science he has determined on, as he is to give an annual account of the discoveries he has made, and of the authors from which he has made selections. On the other hand, the brethren following the same branches of study are desired to help him with all the means in their power. Should he meet with difficulties which he cannot solve, he may apply to his Superior, who will either solve them himself, or send them to other members of the Order, who, better versed in those sciences, and bound to enlighten their Brethren, will send the required solutions.[11]

That his degree of *Minerval* may have all the Its prizes. appearances of a literary society, the Superiors annually propose some question for a public composition. The answers or dissertations are judged as in academies, and the discourse which obtains the prize is printed at the expence of the Order. The same advantages are held out to all adepts who wish to publish their works, provided they are not foreign to the views of the Founder.[12]—They are sure to coincide with his intentions should they be of the nature of those which he calls *pasquils*, or such as would create mirth among the people at the expense of the priesthood, and of *religious truths; such as parodies on the Lamentations of Jeremiah, or burlesque imitations of the Prophets*; in a word, all such satires as dispose the people to the grand object of the Sect. The Minerval can

11 *Ibid.* No. 2.

12 Statutes of the Minerval n°6, and 10.

give no better proofs than these of his progress. The Sect has booksellers who put these works into circulation, and the profits are transmitted to the coffers of the Order.

Its profits. It is, however, to be observed, that should a Minerval, or any other of the Brethren, make a discovery in any art or lucrative science, he is obliged, under pain of being looked upon as a false Brother, to impart the secret to the Order, who will look upon itself as proprietor of such secrets should they have been discovered by a Brother after his admission among them.[13]

Lest he should be unobserved *when travelling*, the Minerval is never to undertake any journey without previously informing his superiors, who will send him letters of recommendation for different Brethren on the road. He, in return, must carefully report every thing that he shall discover during his travels, which may be to the advantage or disadvantage of the Order.[14]

Its reprimands. But we must not forget to mention, that during the academic sittings, the presiding Illuminée is at least once a month to take a review of the principal faults which he may have observed in any of his pupils. He is to interrogate them concerning those which they may have observed themselves; "and it would be unpardonable neglect," says the statutes, "should any pupil pretend that during the space of a whole month he had remarked nothing

---

13 Summary of the Institutes, no. 11.—The true Illuminée.

14 Statutes of the Minerval, no. 11.

reprehensible. This would be a proof of the *utmost negligence in the training of his mind to observation; and the Superior must not suffer it to pass without reprehension.* He must also make his observations in such a manner as to excite their serious attention, and effectually to impress them with proper notions, so that each on returning home shall be ready to put in practice his advice for the advantage of the Order.[15] Beside, the Superior is as much as possible to avoid letting a day pass without seeing his pupils, either he visiting them, or they him.[16]

But what can be the object of such vigilance, such unremitting attention to the Minerval Academy? A single word from the adept who, under the inspection of Weishaupt, organized its laws, will explain the enigma. It is, to adopt Knigge's expressions, by the works required ot the young Academicians that the Order will be able to judge whether they are of *that sort of stuff* (that is to say of that turn of mind, susceptible of all the principles of Impiety and Anarchy) which is necessary for the higher degrees. After all these labours, should the *Minerval adept* still retain any of what they call *religionist inclinations*, he will then receive the three first Masonic degrees, and in them he may moulder during the rest of his life *in the insignificant study of all their hieroglyphics.* He will indeed still continue under the inspection of the Superiors of the

The judgment of the Minerval.

---

15   Instructions for the Minerval, no. 4.

16   *Ibid.* no. 3.

Order; but he may rest assured, that he will always remain a Minerval, with a brevet of imbecility, on the registers of the Sect.[17] On the contrary, should he have shown a sufficient want of attachment to religion or to his Prince; should he enthusiastically imbibe the principles of Illuminism,—he will certainly be promoted to higher degrees. During his academical course the Sect has had unerring means of judging him; viz. by the questions he has solved (and which were put by the Order, not so much with a view of exercising his talents as of prying into his opinions), and by the statements delivered in by the *Scrutators*, of the impression made by the different principles which they had disseminated either in the shape of conversation, or by way of refutation, to try the young Minerval.

The questions which he has had to investigate during his course sometimes regarded the secret of the Sect; at others, the security of the adepts, and of the Superiors. To envelop the chiefs in impenetrable darkness, and that their asylum may be proof against all attempts, death itself is to be divested of its horrors. The Minerval must not finish his Academical course till he has shown how far such fears have lost their influence over him; he shall declare whether he is ready to submit to every torture, rather than give the least information concerning the Order; or even evade the temptation by poison or suicide. A dissertation upon Cato, for example, will be given him as a task, and his management of

17   Last Word from Philo, Page. 90.

it will show whether he is ready to fall by his own hand for the preservation of the Brethren. The *patet exitus*, or the *exit is free*, that is to say, that every man is free to leave this life at his pleasure, is one of those grand principles which must be advanced; it must be commented on and discussed by the young adept; and should any of those puerile ideas appear, which lead to believe in a God the avenger of suicide, he is not the man to be entrusted with the secret, and he shall be rejected.[18]

Many other questions are proposed in order to convince the Sect of the principles of the young Academician. It must sound his opinions on the means it employs, and on those in which he may hereafter be instrumental. He will be ordered to discuss Weishaupt's famous doctrine, that *the end sanctifies the means*; that is to say, that there are no means, not even theft, poison, homicide, or calumny, but are just and laudable when used for the attainment of objects which the Order may chuse to style just or holy.[19]

After all this, the Minerval shall furnish some dissertation from which his opinions on Kings and Priests may be ascertained;[20] but the presiding adept must carefully avoid compromising himself; he must not openly applaud the epigrams, sarcasms, or even blasphemies of his pupils; that must be left to the brethren visitors, who will insinuate

---

18 See hereafter the Chapter on Juridical Depositions, in vol. IV.

19 *Ibid.*

20 *Ibid.*

and encourage them without ever hinting that they are in perfect unison with the mysteries of the Order. He must not fail, however, to observe which of his pupils are the most zealous for such doctrines, and who complacently repeat these sarcasms or blasphemies; those, in short, who enthusiastically blend them in their Academical compositions. This accomplished, they have run their Academic career, and are next promoted to the degree of *Minor Illuminée.*

Chapter VI.

Fourth Part of the Code of Illuminées.— Third Preparatory Degree.— The Minor Illuminée.

he object of the degree of *Minor Il-luminée* is not only to dispose the Brethren more and more for the secrets which have not yet been revealed to them; but it has also in view their preparation for presiding over the Minerval Academies in which they have already shown their talents, and their zeal for the Sect. The means which are to produce this double effect are worthy of remark, on account of one of those artifices which Weishaupt alone could have invented.

Double object of this Degree.

The Minor Illuminées hold sittings similar to those of the Minerval Academy. The President must necessarily be one of those adepts who, initiated in the higher mysteries of Illuminism, have attained the degree of *Priest*. He, alone having any knowledge of these higher mysteries, is particularly enjoined to keep his pupils in the persuasion that beyond the degree in which he is there is no farther secret to impart to them. But he is to spare no pains to infuse those opinions into their minds, of which the last mysteries are but the development. The Minor Illuminées are imperceptibly to become as it were the inventors and authors of Weishaupt's principles; that, believing them to be the offspring of their own genius, they may more zealously defend and propagate them. "It is necessary," says the code, "that *the adept look upon himself as the founder of the new Order*," that hence he may conceive a natural ardor for its success. To effectuate this object, an exordium is appropriated to the initiation in this degree. It is one of those discourses which, replete with *voluntary obscurities*, presents the most monstrous errors to the mind, but expressly mentions none. The veil which is thrown over them is neither coarse enough to hide, nor fine enough clearly to shew them; all that the new adepts can observe at a first hearing is, that *the object of the Order* is worthy of admiration and zeal; that an ardent enthusiasm should inflame the mind of the young adept for the attainment of the grand object of all the labours of Illuminism; that the enjoyment of this happiness depended much more on the *actions than on the words* of the adepts. What then is this object, and what are the obstacles that are to be overcome? Of what species are those actions, those labours of the adept, which are to forward its views? It is in these points that enigma and obscurity veils the intent, and it is here that genius is to invent. That the errors of the Sect might be considered as originating with the adepts, it goes on to say, *the same discourse shall serve in future as a text for all those which the Brethren shall prepare for the meetings of the Order.* The President will select the obscure passages, which may lead to the development of those opinions which he wishes to instil into his pupils; such will the the *subjects chosen for their themes*, and he will carefully exact *practical conclusions.*[1] But to give the reader a better idea of what these themes or commentaries are to be, we shall quote a part of the original text.

> There certainly exist in the world *public crimes which every wife and honest man would wish to suppress.* When we consider that every man in this delightful world might be happy, but that their happiness is prevented by the misfortunes of some, *and by the crimes and errors of others; that the wicked have power over the good; that opposition or partial insurrection is useless*; that hardships generally fall upon men of worth;—then *naturally results the wish of seeing an association formed of men* of vigorous and noble minds, capable of resisting the wicked, of succouring the good, and of procuring for

---

1   The true Illuminée, Instructions for the Superiors of this degree.

> themselves rest, content and safety—of *produc-*
> *ing all these effects, by means drawn from the*
> *greatest degree of force of which human na-*
> *ture is capable.* Such views actuating a SECRET
> SOCIETY would not only be innocent, but most
> worthy of the wise and well-inclined man.[2]

What an ample field already opens itself to the commentating genius of the young adept! The Minor Illuminée will begin by investigating those general crimes to which the Sect wishes to put an end. And what are the *crimes*, who are the wicked persons that disturb the peace of mankind by means of *power exercised over the good?* What SECRET SOCIETIES are they which are destined to consummate the wishes of the sages, not by *partial insurrections, but by the greatest degree of force of which human nature is capable?* In a word, what is that new order of things, which are by such unheard of exertions to be substituted in place of existing institutions?

The greater progress the adept shall make, and the nearer his commentaries shall coincide with the spirit of the Order, so much the more worthy shall he be judged to fulfil the second object of this degree. He is not yet to preside over a Minerval Academy, he is too inexperienced in the arts of a Superior; and the Order only entrusts him with two or three of those pupils; but, as a consolation for the smallness of his flock, he reads in his in-

---

2   Discourse on this Degree.

structions, *that should he have only formed one or two men for the Order during his whole life he will have done a noble act.*

Small as this mission is, still the adept is not left to his own prudence in the execution of it; he receives instructions by which he is to be guided. I forewarned my reader, that in this part of my Memoirs on Jacobinism, my object was, not solely to prove the Conspiracy of the Illuminées, but to render conspicuous the dangers which threatened society, while I was unveiling the means adopted by the Sect. Among these means, the laws laid down by Weishaupt for the Minor Illuminées are to be eminently distinguished; as the authority given, and the manner in which it is to be exercised (at first over two or three adepts only), naturally prepare them for more extensive commands. These laws and these instructions seem to be traced with the venom of the prudent serpent, unfortunately so much more active and ingenious in the arts of vice and seduction than good men are in the cause of virtue. This part of Weishaupt's Code is called—*Instructions for forming useful labourers in Illuminism*, and from it I shall make a large extract. Let the reader meditate on the tendency and probable consequences of such precepts, such laws, and artifices, all designed to form adepts for the most general, most astonishing, and most dreadful Conspiracy that ever existed.

For the
second
object.

Assiduously observe (say these instructions) every Brother entrusted to your care; watch him particularly on all occasions where he may be tempted not to be what he ought to be; that is precisely the moment when he must show himself; it is then that the progress he has made is to be discovered. Observe him again at those times when he least suspects it, when neither the desire of being praised, the fear of being blamed, nor the shame of, or reflexion on the punishment, can actuate his conduct. Be exact on such occasions in making your notes and observations. You will gain much both with respect to yourself and to your pupil.

Be careful lest your own inclinations should bias your judgment. Do not think a man excellent because he has a brilliant quality, nor judge him to be wicked because he has some striking defect: for that is the grand failing of those who are captivated at first sight.

Above all, guard against believing your man to be a transcendant genius because his discourse is brilliant. We are to judge by facts alone, whether a man is deeply interested.

Have little confidence in rich or powerful men; their conversion is very slow.

Your chief object must be to form the heart. He that is not deaf to the cries of the unfortunate; he that is constant though in adversity, and unshaken in his plans; he that feels his soul glow for great enterprizes; and he, particularly, who has formed his mind to observation, is the man of whom we are in quest. Reject those feeble and narrow minds who know not how to quit their usual sphere.

Read with your pupils those books which are easy to be understood, which abound in the picturesque, and are calculated to elevate the mind. Speak to them often; but let your discourses proceed from the heart, and not from the head. Your auditors easily kindle when they see you full of fire. *Make them thirst after the moment when the grand object is to be accomplished.*

Above all, stimulate them to the love of the object. Let them view it as grand, important, and congenial to their interests and favourite passions. Paint in strong colours the miseries of the world; tell them what men are, and what they might be; what line of conduct they should adopt; how little they know their own interests; how anxiously our society labours for them; and desire them to judge what they may expect from it, by what we have already done in the first degrees.

Shun familiarity on all occasions where your weak side may be seen; always speak of Illuminism in a dignified style.

Inspire esteem and respect for our Superiors; and dwell strongly on the necessity of obedience in a well-organized society.

Kindle the ardour of your pupil by laying great stress on the utility of our labours; avoid dry and metaphysical discussions. Let what you require of your pupils be within their means. Study the peculiar habits of each; *for men may be turned to any thing by him who knows how to take advantage of their ruling passions.*

To infuse into them a spirit of observation, begin by slight essays in conversation. Ask some easy questions on the means of discovering the character of a man notwithstanding all his dissimulation. Affect to think the answer a better one than you could have given yourself; that gives confidence, and you will find some other opportunity of delivering your own sentiments. Inform them of what observations you may have made concerning their voice, gait, or physiognomy. Tell them also, that they have the best dispositions, and that they only want practice. Praise some in order to stimulate others.

Having thus become acquainted with the immense difficulty attending on the art of bringing men to the point whither you wished to lead them, neglect no occasion of disseminating the good principles wherever you can, and of inspiring your pupils with courage and resolution: but never forget, *that he who wishes to convert too many at once will convert nobody.* In the towns where you reside, divide the task with the other Illuminées of the same degree as yourself. Chuse one or two, at most three, Minervals among those over whom you have the greatest influence or authority; but spare neither labour nor pains. *You will have accomplished a great undertaking if, during your whole life, you form but two or three men. Let those whom you have selected be the constant object of all your observations. When one method does not succeed, seek out another; and so on, till you have found a proper one.* Study to find out what your pupil is best fitted for; *in what intermediary principles he may be deficient, and therefore inaccessible to the fundamental ones.* The grand art consists in profiting of the right moment; at one time it is warm, at another cool reasoning which will persuade.—Let your pupil always think that it is to himself, and not to you, that he is indebted for the progress he makes. *If he falls in a passion, never contradict; hearken to him though he be in the wrong. Never controvert the consequences, but always the principle. Wait for a favourable moment when you may explain your sentiments without appearing to contradict his. The best method is to agree with another person, whom you will pretend to attack on those subjects, while the Candidate whom you really wish to convince is only a stander-by and takes no part in the dispute: then support your arguments with all the vigour of which you are capable.*

Whatever failings you wish to correct in him, speak of them as if they were not his; tell the story as if somebody else had been guilty of them; then take his advice on the subject; and by these means he becomes his own judge.

All this, it is true, requires time: hurry nothing; it is solidity and *facility of action* that we want in our adepts. Often to read, meditate, hearken to, see the same thing, and then to act, is what gives that facility which soon becomes natural. . . .

Do you wish to draw forth his opinion? Propose a dissertation on certain questions relative to your object, as it were merely to exercise his genius. He thus learns how to meditate on the principles while you make a discovery of those which it is your object to eradicate from his mind.

Instruct, advise; but beware of cold declamations: drop a few words to the purpose when you shall perceive his mind to be in a proper state to receive them.

Never ask too much at once; let your conduct be provident, paternal, and solicitous.—Never despair; *for one may do what one pleases with men.*

Make yourself master of the motives of the principles your pupil has acquired from his education. If they be not consonant with our views, weaken them by insensible gradations, and substitute and strengthen others. But great prudence is necessary to operate this.

Observe what religions, sects, and politics, make men do.—One may enthusiastically wed them to follies; it is therefore in the manner of leading them that the whole art of giving the upper hand to virtue and truth consists. *Only employ the same means for a good purpose which impostors employ for evil,* and you will succeed. If the wicked are powerful, it is because the good are too timid and too indolent. *There may be circumstances also, under which it will become necesssary to show displeasure, and even anger, in defence of the rights of man.*

Tell your pupils, that they are only to attend to the purity of the views which actuate the Order; and that antiquity, power, or riches, should be perfectly indifferent to them.

Tell them, that should they find elsewhere a society which would lead them with greater speed or with more certainty to the desired end, the Order would eternally regret the not having been acquainted with it before—That in the mean time we obey the laws of our Superiors, labouring in peace, and persecuting no man.—- Follow these rules of conduct, and once more remember, that you will have rendered an essential service to the world, though you should form but two men according to our principles.

Carefully profit of those moments when your pupil is discontented with the world, and when every thing goes contrary to his wishes; those moments when the most powerful man feels the want of the support of others, to attain a better order of things. It is then that you must press the swelling heart, stimulate the sensibility, and demonstrate how *necessary secret societies are, for the attainment of a better order of things.*

But be not too easy in your belief with respect to the reality or constancy of such feelings. Indignation *may be the effect of fear, or of the fleeting hopes of some passion which one wishes to gratify.* Such feelings are not naturalized; men are not perfect in so short a time; *prepare for the worst, and then insist.* A heart which easily melts easily changes.

Never promise too much, that you may be able to perform more than you promise. Rekindle exhausted courage; repress excessive ardour; inspire hope in misfortune, and fear in success.

Such are the rules which will form you for a good preceptor and a leader of men. By an exact attention to them you will add to the number of the elect. If your own happiness be dear to you, labour (under our direction) at delivering many thousands of men, who wish to be good, from the dire necessity of being wicked.—Believe us, for it is the precept of experience, *bereave vice of its power*,—and every thing will go well in this world: for if vice be powerful, it is only because one part of the good is too indolent, while the other is too ardent; or else, that men suffer themselves to be divided, or leave the care of Revolutions to futurity; *the fact is, that in the mean time they had rather bend under the yoke*, than efficaciously resist vice. If they once became sensible that *virtue does not entirely consist in patience, but in action also*, they would start from their sleep.—For your part, unite with the Brethren; place your confidence in our Society; nothing is impossible to it, if we follow its laws. We labour to secure to merit its just rewards; to the weak support, to the wicked the fetters they deserve; and to man his dignity. Such is the new Canaan, the new land of Promise, the land of abundance and blessing; though as yet, alas! we discover it but from a distance.[3]

I was frequently tempted to interrupt the course of this extract by my reflexions; but what reader is there that will not ask himself, What zeal, what strange ardour is this, that can have led Weishaupt to combine and dictate means so powerful to captivate the minds of his pupils? Is there a parent, is

3   Extract from the Instruction C, and D, for the Minor Illuminées.

there a preceptor, whose love for his child or his
pupil ever suggested more efficacious rules? These,
however, are only a few of the lessons which the Minor Illuminée is always to have present to his mind
to direct him in the training of the young adepts.
He is not alone entrusted with the task. All the
Brethren of the same degree partake in the care of
watching over the lower ones, and each notes on his
tablets even the most insignificant circumstances.
Their several observations are compared, and of the
whole a general statement is formed, according to
which each pupil will be judged by his superiors.[4]
Meanwhile, it is natural to ask, what can these principles be for which the youth is so carefully trained?
What can be the *sublime virtue* that is to be the result of so much care? We shall soon discover them,
the principles of shameless villainy. This *sublime
virtue* is the combination of every art that can
plunge mankind into corruption, and immerse him
in all the horrors of universal anarchy. Yes, we shall
see the man who says to his disciples, *employ the
same means for a good purpose which impostors
employ for evil*, proved to be the arch-impostor,
training his disciples to every crime, and preparing
the most terrible disasters for society with more ardour and more artifice than ever the upright man
has been seen to employ zeal and wisdom in the
cause of virtue and the support of the laws.

The better to dispose the young adepts, the Minor Illuminée is assisted in his functions and over-

---

4   Instruction C., sect. II., A, 2.

looked by the Major Illuminée, that is to say, by the adepts of the highest degree among those of the preparatory class.

Fifth Part of the Code of Illuminées.—Fourth Preparatory Degree.—The Major Illuminée, or the Scotch Novice.

he degree which follows chat of *Minor Illuminée* is sometimes called *Major Illuminée*, at other times, *Scotch Novice*. Under this two-fold denomination a double object is comprized. As Scotch Novice, the adept is turned in upon Masonry; and it is only a snare for imposing upon the credulity of those, who have not given the requisite symptoms for being initiated in the higher mysteries of the Sect. It is an introduction to the degree of Scotch Knight, which terminates the career of the dupes. But as a degree of Illuminism, it will encompass the adept with new bonds, more extraordinary and more firm than

Object of this Degree.

the former; it is a more immediate preparation for the grand mysteries; in short, it is from this degree that the masters of the Minerval Academies are selected.

Let us begin by laying open the artifice of that strange bond which the adept will never dare to rend asunder, though he should wish to withdraw from Illuminism, or more particularly should he be tempted to reveal what he may have already discovered of the artifices, principles, or grand object of the Sect.

Prelim-
inary
questions.

Before the candidate is admitted to the new degree, he is informed that his reception is resolved on, provided he gives satisfactory answers to the following questions:

I. Are you acquainted with any society grounded on a better constitution, or more holy and solid than ours, and which tends with more certainty or expedition to the object of your wishes?

II. Was it to satisfy your curiosity that you entered our society? or, was it to concur with the chosen among men to universal happiness?

III. Are you satisfied with what you have seen of our laws? Will you labour according to our plan, or have you any objection to propose against it?

IV. As there will be no medium for you, declare at once, whether you wish to leave us, or whether you will remain attached to us for ever?

V. Are you a member of any other society?

VI. Does that society impose any thing detrimental to our interests; for example, the discovery of our secrets; or, does it require you to labour for itself exclusively?

VII. Should such things be ever required of you, tell us upon your honour, whether you would be disposed to acquiesce in them?

These questions answered, there still remains another proof of confidence which the Order expects from the candidate. This is nothing less than an exact and candid account *of his whole life, written without any reservation or dissimulation* whatever. The necesssary time is given him; and this is the famous bond, or rather snare, into which when Weishaupt has once brought the candidate he exultingly exclaims, *"Now I hold him; I defy him to hurt us; if he should wish to betray us, we have also his secrets."* It would be in vain for the adept to attempt to dissimulate. He will soon find that the most secret circumstances of his life, those which he would most anxiously wish to hide, are all known by the adepts. The arts which he has hitherto practised to pry into the most secret motions of the hearts of his pupils, into their tempers and passions, their connections, their means, their interests, their actions and opinions, their intrigues and faults, have all been more artfully employed by others in watching himself. Those who compose the lodge into which he is going to be received, are the very persons that have been scrutinizing his past life.

All the discoveries made by his Insinuator, all the statements he has been obliged to give of him-

Life of the Candidate by himself.

self as required by the Code, every thing which the *Brother Scrutators,* either known or unknown, have been able to discover concerning him during his degrees of Minerval or of Minor Illuminée, have been accurately transmitted to the Brethren of the new lodge. Long before his admission, they had accomplished themselves in the scrutinizing arts.

These wretches then will mimick even the canonization of the saints! The very precautions which Rome takes to discover the least taint in those whom it proposes to the veneration of the faithful, this illuminizing Sect will adopt, in order to satisfy itself that in its adepts no civil nor religious virtue can be traced. Yes, the villains in their dens wished to know each other, and smiled to see their accomplices as wicked as themselves.

The Scrutators, or perfect Spies.

I cannot conceive whence Weishaupt could have taken this part of his Code; but let the reader form an idea of a series of at least fifteen hundred questions on the life, the education, the body, the mind, the heart, the health, the passions, the inclinations, the acquaintances, the connections, the opinions, the abode, the habits, and even the favourite colours of the candidate; on his relations, his friends, his enemies, his conduct, his discourse, his gait, his gesture, his language, his prejudices, and his weaknesses. In a word, questions which relate to every thing that can denote the life or character, the political, moral, or religious sentiments, the interior or exterior of the man; every thing he has said, done, or thought, and even what he would say, do, or think under any given circumstances. Let the reader form an idea of twenty, thirty, and sometimes a hundred questions on each of these heads. Such will be the Catechism to which the *Major Illuminée* must be able to answer; such are the rules he is to follow in tracing the lives or characters of the young Brethren, or even of those prophane of whom the Sect wishes to have particular information. Such is the scrutinizing Code which has directed the researches made as to the life of the candidate antecedent to his admission to the degree of *Major Illuminée*. These statutes are called by the Order the *Nosce te ipsum* (know thyself). When one brother pronounces these words, the other answers *Nosce alios* (know others); and this answer denotes much better the object of the Code, which might very properly be styled the *perfect spy*. Let it be judged by the following questions:

> On the *Physiognomy* of the Candidate:—Is he of a florid complexion, or pale? Is he white, black, fair, or brown? Is his eye quick, piercing, dull, languishing, amorous, haughty, ardent, or dejected? In speaking, does he look full in the face and boldly, or does he look sideways? Can he endure being stared full in the face? Is his look crafty, or is it open and free; is it gloomy and pensive, or is it absent, light, insignificant, friendly, or serious? Is his eye hollow, or level with the head, or does it stare? His forehead, is it wrinkled, and how; perpendicularly, or horizontally?

&c.

His *Countenance*:—Is it noble or common, open, easy, or constrained? How does he carry his head; erect or inclined, before, behind, or on one side, firm or shaking, sunk between his shoulders, or turning from one side to the other?

&c.

His *Gait*:—Is it slow, quick, or firm? Are his steps long, short, dragging, lazy, or skipping?

&c.

His *Language*:—Is it regular, disorderly, or interrupted? In speaking, does he agitate his hands, his head, or his body, with vivacity? Does he close upon the person he is speaking to? Does he hold them by the arm, clothes, or button-hole? Is he a great talker, or is he taciturn? If so, why? Is it through prudence, ignorance, respect, or sloth?

&c.

His *Education*:—To whom does he owe it? Has he always been under the eyes of his parents? How has he been brought up, and by whom? Has he any esteem for his masters? To whom does he think himself indebted for his education? Has he travelled, and in what countries?

Let the reader, by these questions, judge of those which treat of the mind, the heart, or the passions of the Candidate. I will just note the following:

> When he finds himself with different parties, which does he adopt, the strongest or the weakest, the wittiest or the most stupid? Or does he form a third? Is he constant and firm in spite of all obstacles? How is he to be gained, by praise, flattery, or low courtship; or by women, money, or the entreaties of his friends?

&c.—"Whether he loves satire, and on what he exercises that talent; on religion, superstition, hypocrisy, intolerance, government, ministers, monks?" &c. &c.

This however is not all that the scrutators are to note in their statements. They are to elucidate each answer by a fact, and by *such facts as characterize the man at a moment when he least suspects it.*[1] They are to follow their prey to his bolster, *where they will learn whether he is a hard sleeper, whether he dreams, and whether he talks when dreaming; whether he is easily or with difficulty awakened; and should he be suddenly, forcibly, or unexpectedly awakened from his sleep, what impression would it make on him?*

Should any of these questions, or any part of the Candidate's life, not have been sufficiently investigated by the Lodge, divers of the brethren are ordered to direct all their enquiries toward

---

1   See Weishaupt's Letters.

that point. When at length the result of all their researches is found to coincide with the wishes of the Sect, the day for his reception is appointed. Neglecting all the insignificant particularities of the Masonic rites, we shall attend entirely to those circumstances which peculiarly belong to Illuminism.

Reception to the degree of Major Illuminée.

The adept, introduced into a gloomy apartment, reiterates his oath to keep secret whatever he may see or learn from the Order. He then deposits the history of his life (sealed up) in the hands of his introducer. It is read to the Lodge, and compared with the historical table which the Brethren had already formed respecting the Candidate. This done, the Introducer says to him,

Life of the Candidate by the Brethren.

You have given us a welcome and valuable proof of your confidence; but indeed we are not unworthy of it; and we hope that it will even increase in proportion as you become better acquainted with us. Among men whose sole object is to render themselves and others better, no dissimulation should subsist. Far be any reserve from us. We study the human heart— and do not hesitate or blush at revealing to each other our faults or errors.— Here then is the picture which the Lodge had drawn of your person. You must own that some features are not unlike. Read, and then answer, whether you still wish to belong to a society which (such as you are represented here) opens its arms to receive you.

Could indignation operate more powerfully on the mind of the Candidate at the sight of his having been so treacherously watched, than the fear of abjuring a society which henceforth possesses such arms against him, he would not hesitate at asking for his dismission; but he sees the consequences of such a step, and feels that it might cost him very dear. Beside, he is so familiarized with the scrutinizing system, that he can scarcely be offended with it, though operating on himself. He is left for a certain time to his meditations. The desire of acquiring a new degree works upon him and at length turns the scales; he is introduced to the Lodge of the Brethren; and there the veil which hides the secrets of the Sect is partly raised; or, rather, he is himself still more unveiled, that the Sect may discern whether all his views and wishes coincide with theirs.

After a suitable preamble, the Initiator tells him, "that he has still some few questions to answer, relative to objects on which it is absolutely necessary that the opinions of candidates should be known."

The reader is desired to pay particular attention to these questions; as it will enable him, when he shall come to read of the mysteries, more clearly to observe the succession and gradation with which such principles are infused into the mind of the adept, as if he had invented and conceived them all himself.

I. Do you find that, in the world we live in, virtue is rewarded and vice punished? Do you not on the contrary observe, that the wicked man is exteriorly more comfortable, more considered, and more powerful, than the honest man? In a word, are you content with the world in its present situation?

II. In order to change the present order of things, would you not, if you had it in your power, assemble the good and closely unite them, in order to render them more powerful than the wicked?

III. If you had your choice, in what country would you wish to have been born rather than your own?

IV. In what age would you wish to have lived?

V. Always premising the liberty of choice, what science and what state of life would you prefer?

VI. With respect to history, who is your favourite author or your master?

VII. Do you not think yourself in duty bound to procure all the exterior advantages possible for your tried friends, in order to recompense them for their probity, and to render life more agreeable to them? *Are you ready to do what the Order exacts of each member in this degree, when it ordains that each one shall bind himself to give advice every month to the Superiors, of the employments, support, benefic-*

es, or other such like dignities, of which he can dispose, or procure the possession by means of his recommendations; that the Superiors may present worthy subjects of our Order to all such employments?

The answers of the candidate are to be returned in writing, and inserted in the registers of the Lodge. It will naturally be expected, that the greatest dissatisfaction with the present order of things is to be expressed, as well as an ardent wish for a revolution which shall change the whole face of the Universe. He will also promise to support, by all the means in his power, the election of none but worthy brethren to offices of emolument and trust, or such as may augment the power or credit of Illuminism, whether about the court or among the people. On his declaring such to be his sentiments, the Initiator addresses him in the following discourse:

> Brother, you are a witness, that it is after having tried the best of men, that *we seek little by little to reward them, and to give them support, that we may insensibly succeed in new modelling the world.* Since you are convinced how imperfectly men have fulfilled their real destiny; *how every thing has degenerated in their civil institutions;* how little the teachers of wisdom and of truth have enhanced the value of virtue, or given a happier disposition to the world; you must be persuaded, that the error lies in the means which the sages have hither-

to employed. Those means, therefore, must be changed, in order to reinstate in its rights the empire of truth and wisdom. And this is the grand object of the labours of our Order. Oh, my friend! my brother! my son! when here convened, far from the prophane, we consider to what an extent the world is abandoned to the yoke of the wicked, how persecution and misfortune is the lot of the honest man, and how the better part of human nature is sacrificed to personal interest. *Can we at such a sight be silent, or content ourself with sighing? Shall we not attempt to shake off the yoke?—Yes, my brother, rely upon us.* Seek faithful co-operators, but seek them not in tumults and storms; *they are hidden in darkness. Protected by the shades of night, solitary and silent, or reunited in small numbers, they, docile children, pursue the grand work under the direction of their superiors.* They call aloud to the children of the world, who pass by in the intoxication of pleasure how few hearken to them! He alone who has the eye of the bird of Minerva, who has placed his labours under the protection of the star of night, is sure of finding them.

But, lest this discourse should not have given the Candidate a sufficient insight as to the object of the new degree, the Secretary opens the Code of the Lodge, entitled *A general view of the system of the Order.* Here the young Illuminée learns, that the object of the Order *is to diffuse the pure truth, and to make virtue triumph.* Nothing, however, is explicitly said on what is to be understood by *the pure truth.* He is only told, that in order to diffuse it, "he must begin by liberating men from their prejudices, and by enlightening their understandings; then reunite all the common forces for the refinement of all sciences from the dross of useless subtleties, and for the establishment of principles drawn from Nature.—"To attain this," continues the Secretary,

> we must trace the origin of all sciences; we must reward oppressed talents; we must raise from the dust the men of genius; *we must undertake the education of youth*; and, forming an indissoluble league among the most powerful geniuses, we must boldly, though with prudence, combat *superstition, incredulity, and folly*; and at length form our people to true, just, and uniform principles on all subjects.
>
> Such is the object of our Minerval Schools, and of the inferior degrees of Masonry, over which our Order wishes to acquire all the influence possible, in order to direct it towards our object. We also have our superior degrees, where the Brethren, after having passed through all the preparatory degrees, become acquainted with the ultimate result of the labours and of all the proceedings of the Order.

To obtain the completion of that result,

> it will be necesssary to divest vice of its power, that the honest man may find his recompense even in this world; but in this grand project, *we are counteracted by the Princes and the Priest-*

hood; the political constitutions of nations op-
pose our proceedings. In such a state of things
then what remains to be done? To instigate revolutions, overthrow every thing, oppose force to
force, and exchange tyranny for tyranny? Far be
from us such means. Every violent reform is to
be blamed, because it will not ameliorate things
as long as men remain as they are, a prey to
their passions; and because wisdom needeth
not the arm of violence.

The whole plan of the Order tends to form
men, not by declamation, but by the protection
and rewards which are due to virtue. *We must*
insensibly bind the hands of the protectors of
disorder, and govern them without appearing
to domineer.

In a word, we must establish an universal empire over the whole world, without destroying the civil ties. *Under this new empire,*
all other governments must be able to pursue
their usual process, and to exercise every pow-
er, excepting that of hindering the Order from
attaining its ends and rendering virtue trium-
phant over vice.

This victory of virtue over vice was formerly the object of Christ, when he established his
pure religion. He taught men, that the path to
wisdom consisted in letting themselvees be led
for their greater good by the best and wisest
men. At that time preaching might suffice; the
novelty made truth prevail; but at present, more
powerful means are necesssary. Man, a slave to
his senses, must see sensible attractions in vir-

tue. *The source of passions is pure; it is necessary that every one should be able to gratify his within the bounds of virtue, and that our Order should furnish him with the means.*

It consequently follows, that all our brethren, educated on the same principles, and strictly united to each other, should have but one object in view. *We must encompass the Power of the earth with a legion of indefatigable men, all directing their labours, according to the plan of the Order, towards the happiness of human nature*—but all that is to be done in silence; our brethren are mutually to support each other, to succour the good labouring under oppression, *and to seek to acquire those places which give power, for the good of the cause.*

Had we a certain number of such men in every country, each might form two others. Let them only be united, and nothing will be impossible to our Order; *it is thus that in silence it has already performed much for the good of humanity.*

You behold, Brother, an immense field opening to your activity; become our faithful and worthy co-operator, by seconding us with all your might; and remember, that no service will pass without its just reward.

After this lesson, two chapters directly treating on the functions of the *Major Illuminée* are read to him. With the first he is already acquainted: it is the Code of the *Insinuator* or *Brother Recruiter*.

He is also now entrusted with it, as it is part of his duty in future to judge of the pupils of all the Insinuators. The second treats of the duties of the *Scrutator*, this is also delivered into his care, because he must particularly exercise that art while presiding over the Minerval academies: and he must necessarily learn how his new brethren found means of tracing so exact an historical portrait of himself, and of penetrating even more successfully than he could into the interior recesses of his heart; he must also learn to distinguish such pupils as, with dispositions similar to his own, are worthy of being admitted to his new degree. He now has but one more degree to go through, before he is admitted into the class of the mysteries, and this is termed by the Sect *the Scotch Knight*.[2]

---

2   The whole of this chapter is nothing more than an extract from the *degree of Major Illuminée*, and from the instructions contained in the ritual of that code in *The True Illuminée*.

CHAPTER VIII.

Sixth Part of the Code of the Illuminées.—Intermediary Class.—The Scotch Knight of Illuminism; or Directing Illuminée.

nder the appellation of *Interme-* diary *Class* of Illuminism might be comprehended all the Degrees which Weishaupt had borrowed from Freemasonry. In that case we should comprize under this denomination the three degrees of *Apprentice, Fellow-Craft, and Master.* But it has been already said, that these degrees are simply a passport for the Sect into the Masonic Lodges; and that its object may be less conspicuous, it leaves them in their original Masonic state. This, however, is not the case with the higher degrees of Scotch Masonry. The Sect shrewdly surmised that the views of these degrees

Nature and object of this Degree.

coincided with their own: beside, it wanted some of these superior degrees, either for the direction of those Masonic Lodges which it composed of its own members, or who were to gain admittance, dominate, and preside over other Lodges which were not devoted to Illuminism.—The great veneration in which the *Scotch Knights* are generally held by Masons, more strongly determined the Baron Knigge to make himself master of this degree, and engraft it on Illuminism. The Sect has constituted this into both an *intermediary* and a *stationary* degree. It is stationary for those into whom it despairs of ever infusing the principles required for a futher admission to the mysteries; but it is only *intermediary* for those who have shown dispositions more accordant with the pursuits of the Sect.[1]

Its preliminaries. Whatever may be his destiny, no Brother is ever admitted into this new degree, until he has previously given proofs of the progress he has made in the arts of *Scrutator*, whose code must have been his chief study since his admission to the degree of Major Illuminée. The secret Chapter of the Knights has had the precaution to propose certain questions to him to ascertain how far he is capable of judging *of the state of the mind by exterior appearances*. He will have had to answer, for example, to the following ones:—"What is the character of a man whose eyes are perpetually in motion, and whose countenance is changeable? What

---

1   *Original Writings*, vol. II., part I., sect. 11.

features denote voluptuousness, melancholy, and pusillanimity?"[2]

As a further proof of the progress he has made, he is to transmit to his superiors another dissertation on the life of the hero whose name he bears for his characteristic. The history of his own life, which he had delivered in the antecedent degree, had laid open the whole of his existence, and all his actions through life. This new dissertation will show the Order what he admires or disapproves of in others, and will particularly demonstrate whether he has discovered those qualities in his patron which the Order wished he should imbibe and imitate when it gave him his characteristic.[3] Should any part of his life have escaped the vigilance of the Scrutators, he is still at liberty to give a new proof of his confidence in the Order; and this is described as a meritorious act; but he may reserve it for the cognizance of the Superior of the Order only.[4] He is then to declare under his hand-writing, that he looks upon the Superiors of Illuminism as the *secret* and *unknown* though *legitimate* Superiors of *Freemasonry*, that he adheres and always will adhere to the illuminized system of Masonry, as the best and most useful existing; that he utterly renounces every other association; that he is, in short, so persuaded of the excellence of Illuminism, that he fully adopts its principles, and firmly

---

2   See this degree, sect. 4, no. 2 and 3.

3   See second Instruction for this degree, no. 8.

4   *Ibid.*

believes himself bound to labour, under the direction of his superiors, *at the object and according to the intentions of the Order* for the happiness of mankind.[5]

After having received these numerous pledges, the Scotch Knights invite the new Brother to a *secret Chapter*, for such is the name given to the Lodges of this degree. It is hung with green, richly decorated and brilliantly lighted. The Prefect of the Knights, booted and spurred, is seated on a throne erected under a canopy all of the same colour. On his apron a green cross is seen, and on his breast the star of the Order; he wears the riband of St. Andrew in salter from right to left, and holds a mallet in his hand. On his right stands the brother sword-bearer, holding the sword of the Order; on his left the master of the ceremonies with a stick in one hand, and the ritual in the other. The Knights assembled are all booted and spurred, each girt with a sword, and all wear the cross suspended at their necks by a green riband. The Officers of the Order are to be distinguished by a plumage, and a priest of the Order compleats the Lodge. The Prefect then delivers himself as follows to the Candidate:

> You here behold a part of those unknown legions which are united by indissoluble bonds to combat for the cause of humanity. Are you willing to make yourself worthy of watching

---

5   *Ibid.* Reversal Letters.

with them for the sanctuary? Your heart must be pure, and a heavenly ardour for the dignity of nature must fire your breast. The step you are taking is the most important one of your life. Our games are not vainly ceremonial. In creating you a knight we expect of you that you will perform exploits grand, noble, and worthy of the title you receive. Long life to you, if you come to us to be faithful; if honest and good you answer our expectations. Should you prove a false Brother, be both cursed and unhappy, and may the grand Architect of the Universe hurl you into the bottomless pit! Now bend thy knee, and on this sword take the oath of the Order.

At these words the Prefect seats himself, the Knights are standing with their swords drawn, and the Candidate pronounces the following oath:—

I promise obedience to the excellent Superiors of the Order. In as much as it shall depend upon me, I engage—never to favour the admission of any unworthy member into these holy degrees—to labour at rendering the Ancient Masonry triumphant over the false systems which have crept into it—to succour, like a true Knight, innocence, poverty, or oppressed honesty—*Never to be the flatterer of the great, nor the slave of Princes*;—to combat courageously, though prudently, in the cause of *Virtue, Liberty, and Wisdom*—to resist boldly, both for the advantage of the Order and of the world, *Superstition and Despotism*. I never will prefer my own private interest to that of the Order. I will defend my Brethren against calumny. *I will*

> dedicate my life to the discovery of the true Re-
> ligion and real doctrines of Freemasonry, and
> I will impart my discoveries to my Superiors.
> I will disclose the secrets of my heart to my Su-
> periors as to my best friends. So long as I shall
> remain in the Order I shall look upon the be-
> ing a Member of it as a supreme felicity. I also
> engage to look upon all my domestic, civil, and
> social duties as most sacred. So help me God,
> both for the happiness of my life, and for the
> peace of my mind.

In return for this oath the Prefect declares to the Candidate that he is going to create him a Knight of St. Andrew, according to the ancient usage of the Scotch—"*Rise*," he says, "and in future beware of ever bending thy knee before him who is only man like thyself."[6]

To these ceremonies the adept Knigge added a certain number of others which were mere derisions of the rites of the Church. Such, for example, was the triple benediction which the Priest pronounced over the new Knight, such the atrocious mockery of the last supper, which terminated the ceremony. But, impious as is the imitation, Weishaupt declares it to be *disgusting* because it is still *religious, theosophical,* and *borrowed from superstition.*[7] But what perfectly coincided with the views of the Bavarian founder were, the instructions given to the new Knight. He is enraptured with that discourse, where one may observe

---

6   *Ibid.,* sect. 7.

7   See the Last Word of Philo, page 100.

the Illuminizing Orator selecting the most impious, artful, and disorganizing systems of Masonry,
to make them at once the mysteries of their Masonic Lodges, and an immediate preparation for
those of Illuminism.

Let the reader recal to mind what was said in
the Second Volume of these Memoirs[8] concerning the Apocalypse of the Martinists, entitled *Of
Errors and of Truth*. He will there have read of a
time when man, disengaged from the senses and
free from matter, was still more free from the yoke
of the laws and from political bondage, to which he
was only subjected by his fall. He will there have
seen, that the daily efforts of man should tend to
the overthrow of Governments, that he may recover his former purity and ancient liberty, and thus
retrieve his fall. I might there have demonstrated
that absurd *Idealism* reducing our senses to vain
fictions, that the prostitution of them might be but
a chimerical crime;[9] there, in short, I might have

---

8   Chap. XI.

9   When treating in the Second Volume of the religious and po-
     litical tenets of the Martinists, I did not extend my reseraches
     to their doctrine of *Idealism*, and I frankly confess that I did
     not sufficiently understand that part of their Apocalypse. Since
     the publication of that Volume, however, I have met with a
     Gentleman perfectly capable of comprehending any intelligi-
     ble system whatever; I mean the Abbé Bertin, residing at pres-
     ent at Oxford. He reproached me in terms similar to those in
     which some other people had reproached me respecting the
     Rosicrucians. *What you have written, said he, is ALL true, hut
     you have not told the WHOLE truth*. I had indeed said a great
     deal of those gentry, and I never will advance any point which I

cannot prove. The Abbé Bertin condescended to give me some little insight into the doctrines of this famous Saint-Martin. It fully confirmed every thing which I had advanced on the tenets of the Martinists, with respect to the nature of the soul, and to the pretended origin of that soul forming *a part of God, of the essence of God, and of the same substance*—But what I had not said was, that according to the same system matter has no real existence, or at least has such a separate existence, and is so entirely null with respect to the soul, that there neither is nor can be any relation whatever between it and the soul; in fine, that it is, with respect to us, as if *it were not.* I had surmised these consequences in a conversation which I had had with an estimable young man, the Vicomte de Maimbourg, whom the Martinists had endeavoured to taint with their erroneous doctrines. When they came to treat of the pleasure of the senses, *throw that to the fire,* they say in their treatise of morality; *to the fire: give to the fire all it asks; that is not the spirit, all that does not affect the soul; and this fire is matter; it is the senses, the body.* It is not in the same sense that the Martinist tells us, "It is in vain that the enemy pursues me with his illusions. Matter shall not have remembrance of me here below. Does man taste the pleasures of matter? When the senses feel pain or pleasure, is it not easy to perceive that it is not man that feels this pain or pleasure?" (No. 235, of the *Man of Desire, by the Author of a work On Errors and on Truth*). How frightful is this enigmatical language! If all the passions and senses are foreign to man, if he may gratify them with affecting his soul either for the better or for the worse, what monstrous consequences must ensue to morals! And indeed a Danish Martinist was consulted by the Viscount, who, more candid than the recruiting Brethren, answered, "Beware, dear Sir, of ever entering into our mysteries;—I am unfortunately engaged, and should in vain attempt to withdraw myself from them. I could not succeed; but, for your part, take care never to deliver yourself over to those men." The Viscount followed his advice. As to the Abbé Bertins, he was too much for Mr. de St. Martin, who had to argue with a man that perpetually objected—if my soul is part of God, and of the substance of God, shown, according to the Martinist, that in all ages this system of corruption and disorder has been the doctrine and secret of true Philosophy. This intermediary degree was destined by Weishaupt to serve as a point of union between the Masonic Lodges and Illuminism. It was but natural that the should have selected the most monstruous and most artful system of the Craft. Let not the reader therefore be astonished when he sees the Antitheosophist, the Atheist, the Materialist Weishaupt borrowing in this degree the doctrines of the Martinists on the twofold principle or double spirit. But let it be also remembered, that whenever, in consequence of this artifice, he is obliged to use the words *spirit* or *soul*, he informs the candidate, that such words are employed in the Code only to conform to the *vulgar expression*. This precaution taken, the Initiator may without apprehension repeat the sophisticated lessons on the twofold principle. And indeed one might be tempted to think, that the doctrines he lays down as the grand object of Free-Masonry had all been copied from the Martinist system. He begins by deploring a great Revolution which had in former ages deprived man of his primitive dignity. He then represents man as having had the faculty of recovering his an-

---

my soul must be God. After three months lessons, which the reader will readily suppose the Abbe Bertins only submitted to through curiosity, the learned teacher violently exclaimed, "*I see I never shall be able to convince a Divine*:" and thus Mr. de Saint-Martin took leave of a scholar far more fitted to teach him real knowledge than to receive his sophisticated lessons.

cient splendour; but that by the abuse of his faculties he had again immersed himself still deeper in his defiled and degraded station. The very senses are blunted, and said to lead him into error on the nature of things. Every thing that he beholds in its actual state is *falsehood, show,* and *illusion*; and he lays particular stress on those schools of sages which had, ever since the time of the grand Revolution, preserved the secret principles of the antique doctrines, or of true Masonry. Nor does the montrous Hierophant blush at placing JESUS OF NAZARETH among those sages, and blasphemously numbering the God of the Christians among the Grand Masters of Illuminism. But soon was the doctrine of Christ falsified, and Priests and Philosophers raised on these divine foundations an edifice of *folly, prejudice, and self-interest. Soon also does the tyranny of Priesthood and the Despotism of Princes coalesce in the oppression of suffering humanity.* Free Masonry opposes these disastrous attempts, and endeavors to preserve the true doctrine; but it has overbumed it with symbols, and its lodges gradually subside into seminaries of ignorance and error.—The Illuminées alone are in possession of the real secrets of Masonry; many of them are even still to be the objects of their researches; and the new Knight is to devote all his attention to their discovery. He is particularly recommended *to study the doctrines of the ancient Gnostics and Manichceans, which may lead him to many important discoveries on this real Ma-*

sonry. He is also told, that the great enemies which he will have to encounter during this investigation will be ambition and other vices which make humanity *groan under the oppression of Princes and of the Priesthood.*[10]

The obscurity which enwraps these lessons on the new and grand Revolution which is to counteract the ravages of the former, is not the slightest of Weishaupt's artifices. With respect to Princes, this is the last degree to which they are admitted. They are to be persuaded, that the antique Revolution was no other than the coalition of the powers of the earth with the Priesthood, in order to support the empire of religious prejudice and superstition; and that the new Revolution to be effected is the re-union of Princes with Philosophy, to overthrow that empire and ensure the triumph of reason. Should the serene adept be startled at his having sworn *never to flatter the great, nor to be a slave of Princes*, he will be reconciled again by the latter part of the oath, where he *engages to look upon his domestic, civil, and social duties as most sacred.* But let him form what opinion he may as to his initiation, he has nevertheless sworn, that he will protect the Brotherhood from superstition and despotism; *that he will obey the most excellent superiors of the Order*, that he will favour its progress with all his power, and that he beheves it alone to be in possession of the secrets of real Masonry.

---

10   See this degree, art. 8. Instruction on the Masonic Hieroglyphics.

In the less important class of adepts, should any still hanker after their *Theosophical* ideas, that is to say, should Weishaupt despair of ever infusing into them its Anarchical and Atheistical principles, they are condemned to become *stationary* in this degree; and he imposes on them as a task the explication of all the Hieroglyphics of Masonry, which they may set to the tune of the grand Revolution. Under pretence of discovering a more perfect religion, he persuaded them that Christianity was at this day nothing more than superstition and tyranny. He has infused into them his hatred for the Priesthood and the existing forms of Government. That will suffice to procure him agents of destruction; as to re-edifiction, he has not so much as mentioned it to them.

Its duties and laws. But should there be found among the number of Knights men who of themselves dive into the meaning of that great Revolution which only deprived man of his primitive dignity by subjecting him to the laws of civil society, should they have comprehended the meaning of this other Revolution, which is to restore every thing by re-establishing man in his primitive independence, such men will be pointed out by the Scrutators. It is at them that the Code particularly aims when it says, *Let the Scotch Knights seriously reflect, that they are presiding over a grand establishment, whose object is the happiness of mankind.* In short, these Knights have to act the parts of Superiors in the Order; they are the Inspectors or the Directors of all the preparatory class. They have on that account assemblies peculiar to themselves, called *Secret Chapters*. The first duty of these chapters is to watch over the interests of the Order within their district. "The Scotch Knights," says their first instruction,

> are to pay particular attention to the *discovery of any plans which may contribute to fill the coffers of the Order. It were much to be wished that they could devise means of putting the Order into possession of some considerable revenues in their province.—He that shall have rendered so signal a service must never hesitate at believing that these revenues are employed in the most noble purposes.—The whole must labour with all their might to consolidate the edifice little by little within their district, until the finances of the Order shall be found to be competent to its views.*[11]

The second part of the Code entrusts these Knights with the government of the preparatory class. Each Knight is to correspond with a certain number of Brethren who have the direction of the Minerval academies. The Code contains instructions which point out to them upon what objects they are permitted to decide; what Brethren they are to forward or thwart in their promotion; and what reports they are to make to their Superiors. In their correspondence with their Inferiors they

---

11   See First Instruction for this degree.

make use of the common cypher, but when they write to the chiefs they employ a peculiar character which may truly be called Hieroglyphic.

They are particularly charged with the inspection of the Major Illuminées. "The Scotch Knights," says the Code, "shall be particularly attentive that the Major Illuminées do not neglect to mention in their monthly letters such employments as they may have to dispose of."[12]

I have shown, in the foregoing chapter, how useful and indeed how necessary this precaution proved for recompensing the zeal of the Brethren. The adept Knigge wished to demonstrate that it might be equally useful for princes, when combined with the scrutinizing Code. "Let us suppose," says he, "that a Prince, having an Illuminée for his Minister, wishes to find a proper person to fill any vacant office; by means of the Scrutators, the Minister may immediately present the faithful portrait of divers personages, from among whom the Prince will only have to make his election."[13]—But every reader, I hope, will recollect, that in consequence of the oath that has been taken by the Minister to dispose of all places in favour of the Brethren, and that according to the direction of the Knights, he will only present such adepts for those offices as the Order shall have chosen; and thus will Illuminism soon dispose of all benefices, employments, and dignities, and have the entire direction of the whole power of the State.

---

12   Second Instruction, no. 12.

13   Last Observations of Philo, page 95.

Meanwhile, until the Sect shall exert this influence over Courts, the Scotch Knights are to acquire
an absolute sway in the Masonic Lodges. Their
laws on this head deserve particular attention. We
shall select the following:

Its in-
structions
relative to
Free-Ma-
sonry.

> In every town of any note situated within
> their district, the Secret Chapters shall establish
> Lodges for the three ordinary degrees, and shall
> cause men of sound morals, of good repute, and
> of easy circumstances, to be received in these
> Lodges. Such men are much to be sought after,
> and are to be made Masons, *even though they
> should not be of any service to Illuminism in its
> ulterior projects.*[14]

> If there already exists a Lodge in any giv-
> en town, the Knights of Illuminism must find
> means of establishing a more legitimate one; at
> least, they should spare no pains to gain the as-
> cendancy in those which they find established,
> *either to reform or to destroy them.*[15]

> They must strongly exhort the members of
> our lodges not to frequent (without leave of
> their Superiors) any of those pretended consti-
> tuted lodges, *who hold nothing of the English
> but their diplomas, and some few symbols and
> ceremonies which they do not understand.* All
> such Brethren are perfectly ignorant of true
> Masonry, of its grand object, and its real pa-
> trons. Though some of the greatest merit are to

14   Third Instruction for the same degree, no. 1.
15   Third Instruction for the same degree, no. 3.

be found in such lodges, we nevertheless have strong reasons for not readily allowing them to visit ours.[16]

Our Scotch Knights must pay great attention to the regularity of the subordinate lodges, *and must above all things attend to the preparation of candidates.* It is here that in a *private intercourse* they will show a man that they have probed him to the quick. *Surprise him by some ensnaring question* in order to observe whether he has any presence of mind. If he be not staunch to his principles, and should expose his weak side, make him feel how great his necessities are, and how necessary it is for him to be guided entirely by us.[17]

The Deputy Master of the Lodge (who is generally the auditor of the accounts) must also be a member of our Secret Chapter. *He will persuade the lodges that they alone dispose of their funds; but he will take care to employ them according to the views of the Order.* Should it at any time be necesssary to help one of our brethren, the proposition is made to the lodge; though the brother should not even be a Mason, *no matter, some expedient must be found to carry the point.*

No part of the capital, however, must in any case be alienated, *that hereafter we may find the necessary funds for the most important undertakings.* The tenth part of the subscrip-

16   *Ibid.* no. 5.
17   *Ibid.* no. 9.

tions of these lodges must be annually carried to the Secret Chapter. The treasurer to whom these funds must be transmitted, shall collect them, and endeavour *by all kinds of expedients to augment them.*[18]

But before any part of our own funds are appropriated to the help of any of our Brethren, every effort shall be made to procure the necessary succours from the funds belonging to lodges which do not pertain to our system.—*In general, the money which these lodges spend in a useless manner, should be converted to the advancement of our grand object.*[19]

Whenever a learned Mason shall enter our Order, he must be put under the immediate direction of our Scotch Knights.[20]

From what code can Weishaupt, or his compiler Knigge, have selected such laws as these for their Scotch Knights? Many readers will be ready to answer, that they must have learned them from a

---

18 Third Instruction for the same degree. no. 12.

19 *Ib.* 13.

20 Third Instruction for the same degree, no. 16.

Mandrin[21], a Cartouche,[22] or some hero of the gibbet. But it is no such thing:—their own ingenuity was sufficient to invent such doctrines. Weishaupt lays down as a principle, *that the end justifies the means*: he made the application of it when he taught his adepts to rob the libraries of Princes and Religious Orders; his compiler Knigge applies the same principle to the funds of the honest Masons; and we shall soon see what use they made of those funds. It will be in vain for the Illuminée (more zealous for the honour of his founder than for that of the compiler Knigge) to object, that Weishaupt never approved of the degree of *Scotch Knight*. It is true, he never much admired it. But it is not the system of theft (evidently deduced from his own principles) that he reprobates; not a single expression in any of his letters can denote that he did so; for Knigge might have answered, *what do those fools of Masons do with that money?* just as Weishaupt had written *what do those rascals of*

---

21 Louis Mandrin (1725 - 1755) was a smuggler and highwayman who targetted the tax collectors of the *ancien régime*. He organised a gang of 300 men like a military regiment and operated in the Cantons of Switzerland, France, and Savoy, buying goods in Switzerland and selling them in France without paying the Ferme Générale—the outsourced customs, excise, and indirect tax operation of the period—any of the tax due. —Ed.

22 Louis Dominique Garthausen (1693 - 1721), known as Cartouche, who also went by the name of Louis Bourguignon and Louis Lamarre, was a highway robber who operated in the environs of Paris and who reputedly stole from the rich to give to the poor. He was eventually captured and broken at the wheel. —Ed.

Monks do with their rare books? He blamed it not for its principles, but because he thought it *a miserable composition: der elende Scottische ritter grade* are the terms in which he expresses his contempt. When he corrected this degree, the thefts were not the parts which he expunged; they were too serviceable to the order. Weishaupt, however, consented to let this degree (such as it was) serve as a preparation for the mysteries of his *Epoptes*; that is to say, for his priests of Illuminism; and when considered in that light it may be truly said, that the *Knights brigands* were but pitiful and miserable indeed. I will, however, give the reader an opportunity of judging for himself.

CHAPTER IX.

Seventh Part of the Code of the Illuminées.—Class of the Mysteries.—Of the Lesser Mysteries; the Epopt or Priest of Illuminism.

owever accurately the Sect may have ascertained the progress of its adepts in the preparatory degrees, still Weishaupt seems to fear that some may be startled when they come to be acquainted with the ultimate views of Illuminism. He wishes therefore to lead them to his darkest plots by gradual shades. Hence the division of lesser and greater mysteries, and the subdivision into degrees. The first degree into which the adepts are initiated in this class is that of *Epopt*; but these new dignitaries are only known by that title to the inferior class; the higher degrees call them *Priests*.[1]

Let not the reader take alarm at the denomination of *lesser mysteries*, as if they were of no consequence; for he will gradually, as he ascends, discover their dark designs and dealings. But before the adept is allowed to proceed, he must collect every thing that his mind, his memory, or all his former lessons can afford, of anti-religious and anti-social principles, to enable him to give written answers to the following questions:

Questions, or preliminary examination.

I. Do you think the present state of nations corresponds with the object for which man was placed upon earth? For example, do governments, civil associations, or religion, attain the ends for which they were designed? Do the sciences to which men apply furnish them with real lights; are they conducive (as they ought to be) to real happiness? Are they not, on the contrary, the offspring of numberless wants, and of the unnatural state in which men live? Are they not the crude inventions of crazy brains, or of geniuses laboriously subtle?

II. What civil associations and what sciences do you think tend or do not tend to the grand object? Did there not formerly exist an order of things more simple? What sort of an idea can you form of that ancient state of the world?

III. Now that we have passed through all those nullities (*or through all those useless and vain forms of our civil constitutions*), do you

---

1   Philo to Spartacus.—Instructions for this degree.

think that it would be possible to return back to the original and noble simplicity of our forefathers? Supposing we had returned to it, would not our past misfortunes render that state more durable? Would not all mankind be in a similar state with an individual who, having enjoyed the sweets of innocence during his childhood, and fallen a prey to error and his passions during his youth, at length, instructed by the risks he has run, and by experience, endeavours to return to that innocence and purity which rendered his childhood so happy?

IV. What means were best to be employed for restoring mankind to that happy state? Should it be by public measures, by violent revolutions, or by any means that should ensure success?

V. Does not the Christian Religion in all its purity afford some indications, does it not hint at some state or happiness similar to this? Does it not even prepare it?

VI. Is this holy and simple religion really what different Sects profess it to be at this present day, or is it more perfect?

VII. Can this more perfect Christianity be known or taught? Could the world (such as it now is) support a stronger degree of light? Do you not think that, before the numberless obstacles could be removed, it would be proper to preach to mankind a religion more perfect, a philosophy more elevated, and the art of each one's governing himself according to his greatest advantage?

VIII. Would not our moral and political views lead men to oppose this blessing? From our political and moral views then, or from an ill-judged interest, or even from deep-rooted prejudices, these obstacles originate. If men, therefore, oppose the renovation of human happiness, is it not because, slaves to ancient forms, they reject and reprobate every thing which is not to be found in those forms, though it should be the most natural, the grandest, and most noble of all possible things? Does not personal interest, alas! at present predominate over the general interest of mankind?

IX. Must we not then silently and gradually remedy those disorders before we can flatter ourselves with the re-establishment of the golden age? Meanwhile, is it not adviseable *to disseminate the truth in Secret Societies?*

X. Can we trace any such secret doctrine in the ancient schools of the sages, or in the allegorical lessons given by Jesus Christ, the Saviour and liberator of mankind, to his most intimate disciples? Have you not observed a sort of gradual education in that art which you see has been transmitted to our Order, from the highest antiquity?[2]

Initiation of the Epopts.

Should the answers of the Candidate to all these questions show that the progress he has made in his gradual education is not what the Order had reason to expect, he will solicit in vain the advancement he hoped for. Should his answers be equiv-

---

2   Instruction for this degree.

ocal, he will receive orders to prepare new ones, or to be more explicit.[3] But if he show the proper dispositions, and the Sect foresee no probability of his being startled at the lessons of the Hierophant on those grand objects which are to be disclosed to him, the Superiors give their assent, and a synod of the illuminized priesthood is held. The day of the initiation is fixed. At the hour agreed upon, the introducing adept waits upon his new proselyte and takes him into a carriage. The windows being closed, the Candidate blind-folded, and the coach-man continually winding and varying his course, are precautions more than sufficient to hinder the proselyte from ever being able to trace the spot to which he is conducted. Led by the hand, and still blind-folded, he slowly ascends to the porch of the temple of the mysteries. His guide then divests him of the Masonic insignia, puts a drawn sword into his hand, takes off the bandage from his eyes, and leaves him, strictly forbidding him to proceed a step until he hears the voice which is to call him. He is then left to his reflections.

With respect to the pomp of the mysteries, when the Brethren celebrate them in all their splendour, the walls of the temple are hung in red, and lighted up with an immense number of candles or lamps. A voice is at length heard, saying, "Come, enter, unhappy fugitive! The fathers wait for you; enter and shut the door after you." The proselyte obeys

3   *Ibid.* Further instructions on the admission to the degree of Priest.

the voice which calls him. At the bottom of the temple he beholds a throne under a rich canopy with a table before it, on which he a crown, a sceptre, a sword, some pieces of gold money, and precious jewels, all interlaid with chains. At the foot of this table, on a scarlet cushion, is thrown a white robe, a girdle, and the simple ornaments of the sacerdotal costume. The proselyte, standing at the bottom of the temple and in front of the throne, is addressed by the Hierophant as follows:

Behold and fix thine eyes on the splendour of the throne. If all this childish mummery, these crowns, these scepters, and all these monuments of human degradation, have any charms in your eyes, speak; and it may be in our power to gratify your wishes. Unhappy man! if such are your objects, if you wish to rise to power that you may assist in the oppression of your Brethren, go, and at your peril make the trial. Are you in quest of power, of force, of false honours, and of such superfluities, we will labour for you; we will procure such transient advantages for you, we will place you as near the throne as you can desire, and will leave you to the consequences of your folly; but observe, our sanctuary shall be for ever shut against you.

On the contrary, do you wish to be initiated into wisdom, would you teach the art of rendering men better, more free and more happy, then be welcome, be thrice welcome. Here you behold the attributes of Royalty, and there, on the cushion, you see the modest vestment of inno-

cence; make thy choice, and let it be the choice
which thy heart shall dictate.

If, contrary to all expectations, the Candidate
should make choice of the Regalia, he hears a
thundering voice exclaim, "Monster, retire! cease
to pollute this holy place! Begone, fly, before it is
too late." At these words he is led out of the temple
by the Brother who introduced him.—But should
he chuse the white robe, how different will be the
language! "Health and salutation to thy great and
noble soul! Such was the choice we expected from
you. But stop; it is not permitted to you to invest
yourself with that robe, until you have learned to
what you are in future destined by us."[4]

The Candidate is then ordered to be seated. The
Code of the Mysteries is opened, and the Brethren
in silence attend to the oracles of the Hierophant.

Now, reader, you who have been through so
long a course of trials, questions, rituals, and insidious degrees; who have been led through all the
preparatory labyrinth of illuminized education, if
still you be in the dark as to the object of such
precautions and artifices, follow me into this den
which the Sect dares to call the holy place; seat
thyself by the adept, and listen to their Oracles.—
This is the master-piece of the founder. Hear with
patience, though your indignation should be excited by his monstrous fertility in Sophism, in im-

---

4   *Ibid.* Further instructions on the admission to the degree of
    Priest.

piety, in blasphemy against your gospel and your God, treachery against your Magistrates, your country, and its laws, against your titles and your rights, against those of your ancestors and your progeny—Let Kings and Subjects, the rich and poor, the merchant and the labourer, let every class of citizens attend; let them hearken, and learn at length what hellish plots are contriving against them in the dark recesses of these diabolical dens. In vain shall the lethargic soul accuse us of credulity or groundless terrors. Those lessons which the Sect view as the master-piece of their code lie before me, such as they flowed from the pen of the Legislator, such as they were published by order of the Sovereign who seized the archives of the Sect, that all nations might learn the dreadful dangers with which they were menaced.[5] I have them again embellished by the compiler of the Sect, corrected and reviewed by the Council of the Areopagites, attested by the compiler as true and conformable to the copy signed and sealed with the signet of the Sect.[6]

Read then, and rock thyself to sleep in the cradle of voluntary ignorance if thou canst, content with having assured thyself that every conspiracy against the existence of civil society or of all government whatever, every conspiracy against the existence of property, can be but a chimera.

---

5   *Original Writings*, vol. II., part 2.

6   Last works of Philo and Spartacus, from page 10 to 70, and certificates of Philo at the beginning of this degree.

It is to the Candidate, and in presence of the Brethren already initiated to these mysteries, that the Illuminizing President addresses the following discourse:

Discourse of the Hierophant for the Degree of Priest or Epopt of the Illuminées.[7]

At length (he says) the time of your reward suc-ceeds to the trials of an assiduous preparation. At present you know yourself, and have learned to know others; you are what you ought to be, such as we wished to see you. It will now be your duty to conduct others.—What you already know, and what you are about to learn, will ex-pose to your view the extreme weakness of hu-man nature. In this advantage alone lies the true source of power which one man exercises over another. The dark clouds dissipate; the sun of light rises; the gates of the sanctuary unfold; a

---

7   I have compared the two editions of this discourse. The first gives it just as Weishaupt composed and pronounced it at his first initiations. The second has been corrected by his adept the Baron Knigge, known by the characteristic of Philo. All the difference that I could observe was, a slight refinement of the style in some parts, while prolix passages had been added in others. I remarked, that the Compiler Knigge had literal-ly copied all the impious, seditious, and frantic lessons of the original—I have given the preference to the original. In place of adding, I shall rather retrench, and only mention the most striking passages, making such reflexions as circumstances may require. Weishaupt, according to the idiom of the German language, always addressed the Candidate in the third person plural: in this particular, we have followed Knigge's correction, as more suitable with our language.

portion of our mysteries is going to be revealed to you. Let the gates of the temple be shut against the prophane; I will only speak to the Illustrious, to the Holy, to the Elect. I speak to those who have ears to hear, who have tongues which they can command, and who have minds sufficiently enlightened to understand.

Surrounded by the Illustrious, you are about to enter into that class which bears an essential part in the government of our sublime Order. But do you know what it is to govern, can you conceive what this right can be in a secret society? To exercise such an empire, not over the vulgar or the grandees of the people, but over the most accomplished men, over men in all stations, of all nations, of all religions; to reign over them without any exterior constraint, to keep them united by durable bonds, to inspire them all with one spirit; to govern with all possible precision, activity, and silence, men spread over the whole surface of the globe, even to its utmost confines. This is a problem which no political wisdom has ever been able to solve. To reunite the distinctions of Equality, Despotism, and Liberty; to prevent the treasons and persecutions which would be the inevitable consequences; of nothing, to create great things; to stand firm against the swelling torrent of evils and abuse; to make happiness universally shine on human nature; would be a master-piece of morality and polity re-united. The civil constitutions of states offer but little aid to such an undertaking. Fear and violence are their grand engines; with us, each one is voluntarily to lend his assistance.... Were men what they ought to be, we might on their first admission into

our society explain the greatness of our plans
to them; but the lure of a secret is perhaps the
only means of retaining those who might turn
their backs upon us as soon as their curiosity
had been gratified: The ignorance or imperfect
education of many makes it requisite that they
should be first formed by our moral lessons.
The complaints, the murmurs of others against
the trials to which we are obliged to condemn
them, sufficiently show you what pains we must
bestow, with what patience and what constancy we must be endowed; how intensely the love
of the grand object must glow in our hearts, to
make us keep true to our posts in the midst of
such unthankful labour; and not abandon for
ever the hope of regenerating mankind.

It is to partake with us of these labours that
you have been called. To observe others day and
night; to form them, to succour them, to watch
over them; to stimulate the courage of the pusil-
lanimous, the activity and the zeal of the luke-
warm; to instruct the ignorant; to raise up those
who have fallen, to fortify those who stagger; to
repress the ardour of rashness, to prevent dis-
union; to veil the faults and weaknesses of others; to guard against the acute inquisitiveness
of wit; to prevent imprudence and treason; in
short, to maintain the subordination to and esteem of our Superiors, and friendship and union among the Brethren, are the duties, among
others still greater, that we impose upon you.

Have you any idea of secret societies; of the
rank they hold, or of the parts they perform in
the events of this world? Do you view them as

insignificant or transient meteors? O, Brother! God and Nature, when disposing of all things according to the proper times and places, had their admirable ends in view; *and they make use of these secret societies as the only and as the indispensable means of conducting us thither.*

Hearken, and may you be filled with admiration! This is the point whither all the moral tends; it is on this that depends the knowledge of the rights of secret societies, of all our doctrine, of all our ideas of good and bad, ofjust and unjust. You are here situated between the world past and the world to come. Cast your eyes boldly on what has passed, and in an instant ten thousand bolts shall fall, and thousands of gates shall burst open to futurity—You shall behold the inexhaustible riches of God and of Nature, the degradation and the dignity of man. You shall see the world and human nature in its youth, if not in its childhood, even there where you thought to find it in its decrepitude and verging toward its ruin and ignominy.

Should this long exordium, which I have nevertheless abridged, have fatigued the reader, let him rest and reflect for an instant. The enthusiastic strain which predominates in this first part pervades the whole. Weishaupt thought it necessary to his object to afford his proselytes no time for reflection. He begins by inflaming them; he promises great things; though this impious and artful mountebank knows that he is going to fob them off with the greatest follies, the grossest impieties and errors. I have called him an impious and artful mountebank; but that is falling far short of what the proofs attest. Weishaupt knows that he deceives, and wishes to delude his proselytes in the most atrocious manner. When he has misled, he scoffs at them, and with his confidants derides their imbecility. He has, however, his reasons for beguiling them, and knows for what uses he intends them when he has infused into them his erroneous and vicious principles. The greater the consideration they may enjoy in the world, the more heartily he laughs at their delusion. He thus writes to his intimate friends:

> You cannot conceive how much my degree of Priest is admired by our people. But what is the most extraordinary is, that several great protestant and reformed divines, who are of our Order, really believe that that part of the discourse which alludes to religion contains the true spirit and real sense of Christianity; *poor mortals! what could I not make you believe?*—Candidly I own to you, that I never thought of becoming the founder of a religion.[8]

In this manner does the impostor delude his followers, and then scoffs at them in private. These great divines were probably of that class among the protestants which we should, among us, call apostates, a Sieyès or an Autun, for example; for it

---

8   *Orig. Writ.*, vol. II., let 18, from Weishaupt to Zwack.

is impossible that any man endowed with common sense or candour could avoid seeing that the whole tendency of this long discourse is the total overthrow of all religion and of all government.

A second observation well worthy the notice of our readers is, the extreme importance which the Sect gives to *secret societies*, and what mighty expectations it grounds on their mysterious existence. Let nations and chiefs of nations examine themselves, reflect whether they have ever calculated the means and importance of these secret societies so well as those who founded them; and say, whether fear and diffidence on the one side should not keep pace with the expectations and confidence of the other. But let us return to the Lodge wherein Weishaupt initiates his adepts.

Continuing his enthusiastic strain, the Hierophant informs the proselyte, that Nature, having a great plan to develope, begins by the lesser and most imperfect parts; that she then regularly proceeds to the middle terms, to bring things to a state of perfection; which state may serve as a point whence she may again depart, to raise them to a higher order of perfection.

> Nature (says he) makes us begin at infancy, from infancy she raises us to manhood. She at first left us in the savage state, but soon brought us to civilization, perhaps that we might be more sensible, more enraptured and tenacious of what we are, from viewing the contrast of what we were. But to what changes, and those

of an order infinitely more important, does our
future destiny lead us!

Were the candidate master of his own reason,
he must conclude from these principles, that human nature had acquired perfection when passing
from the savage state to that of civil society; that
if he is still to acquire perfection it can never be
by returning to his primitive state. But sophisters
have their tortuosities, and the adepts are involved
in a folly and blindness, with which the Almighty
God permits them to be stricken, since they prefer
error to truth, and impiety to Christianity.

As has the individual man (continues the Hierophant) so human nature in the aggregate has
its childhood, its youth, its manhood, and its
old age. At each of these periods mankind learn
and are subject to fresh wants—hence arise
their political and moral revolutions—It is at
the age of manhood that human nature appears
in all its dignity. It is then that, taught by long
experience, man conceives at length how great
a misfortune it is for him to invade the rights of
others, to avail himself of some few advantages,
purely exterior, to raise himself, to the prejudice of others. It is then that he sees and feels
the happiness and dignity of man.

The first age of mankind is that of savage and
uncouth nature. A family is the whole society;
hunger and thirst easily quenched, a shelter
from the inclemency of the seasons, a woman,
and, after fatigue, rest, are then the only wants.

At that period men enjoyed the two most in-estimable blessings EQUALITY *and* LIBERTY; *they enjoyed them to their utmost extent; they would have forever enjoyed them, had they chosen to follow the track which Nature had traced for them*—or had it not entered the plans of God and Nature first to show man *for what happiness he was destined*; happiness the more precious, as he had begun by tasting it; happiness so early lost, but instantaneously regretted and fruitlessly sought after, until he should have learned how *to make proper use oj his strength*, and how to conduct himself in his intercourse with the rest of mankind. In his primitive state he was destitute of the conveniencies of life, but he was not on that account unhappy; not knowing them, he did not feel the want of them. Health was his ordinary state, and physical pain was his only source of uneasiness—*Oh happy mortals! who were not sufficiently enlightened to disturb the repose of your mind*, or to feel those great agents of our miseries *the love of power and of distinctions*, the propensity to sensuality, the thirst after the representative signs of all wealth, those *truly original* sins with all their progeny, envy, avarice, intemperance, sickness, and all the tortures of imagination!

Thus we see this primitive and savage state, this first essay of Nature, already transformed (in the mouth of the Hierophant) into the happiest state that man ever knew: *Equality and Liberty* are the sovereign principles of happiness in that state. Should the reader be as much blinded as the proselyte, and not see whither all this is tending, let him proceed, and hear how man was deprived of this happiness by the institution of civil societies.

An infortunate germ soon vivifies in the breast of man, and his primitive peace and felicity disappear.

As families multiplied, the means of subsistence began to fail; *the nomade* (or roaming) *life ceased, and PROPERTY started into existence*; men chose habitations; agriculture made them intermix. Language became universal; living together, one man began to measure his strength with another, and the weaker were distinguished from the stronger. This undoubtedly created the idea of mutual defence, of one individual governing divers families reunited, and of thus defending their persons and their fields against the invasion of an enemy; *but hence* LIBERTY *was mined in its foundation, and* EQUALITY *disappeared.*

Oppressed with wants unknown until that period, man perceived that his own powers were no longer sufficient. To supply this defect, the weakest imprudently submitted to the strongest or to the wisest; not however to be ill-treated, but that he might be protected, conducted, and enlightened.—All submission, therefore, even of the most unpolished mortal, has an existence only in as much *as he wants* the person to whom he subjects himself, and on the express condition that that person can succour him. *His power ceases when my weakness no longer*

exists, or when another acquires superiority.
Kings are fathers; the paternal power is at an
end when the child has acquired his strength.
The father would offend his children if he pre-
tended to prolong his rights beyond that term.
Every man having attained to years of discre-
tion may govern himself; when a whole nation
therefore is arrived at that period, there can
exist no further plea for keeping it in wardship.

In putting such language into the mouth of the
Hierophant, the founder of Illuminism had too
well studied the strength and illusion of words;
he had been too cautious in the choice and preparation of his adepts ever to fear that any of them
would answer,

> You who thus give oracles, what do you under-
> stand by nations having attained their major-
> ity? Without doubt such as, having emerged
> from ignorance and barbarism, have acquired
> the lights necesssary for their happiness; and
> to what can they be indebted for these lights
> and this happiness, if not to their civil associ-
> ation? It will be then, if ever, that they will find
> it both reasonable and necessary to remain un-
> der the *guardianship* of their laws and of their
> government, lest they should fall back into the
> barbarism and ignorance of the roaming clans,
> or be precipitated into the horrors of anarchy,
> from revolution to revolution, under the suc-
> cessive tyrany of the brigand, of the executioner
> of the sophisticated despot, or under that of a
> sophister Sieyès and his colegislative Marsel-
> lois, of a Robespierre and his guillotines, of the

Triumvirs and their proscriptions. The populace alone in the *minority* of ignorance, the sophisters alone in the *majority* of wickedness and corruption, shall applaud thy mysteries.

Certain of not meeting with such reflexions from the adepts, the Hierophant continues to inculcate his principles by attributing every thing to strength, and destroying all principles of morality or of reason, though he will affect the tone of both; and ends by forming his judgment on man in society, as he would judge tigers and wild beasts in the forests.—These are his new doctrines.

Never did strength submit to weakness.—Nature has destined the weak to serve, because they have wants; the strong man to govern, because he can be useful. Let the one lose his force, and the other acquire it, they will then change situations, and he that obeyed will command. He that stands in need of another, also depends upon him, and he has renounced to him his rights. Hence few wants is the first step towards liberty. *It is for this reason that the savages are the most enlightened of men, and perhaps they alone are free.*[9] When wants are durable, servitude is also lasting. Safety is a durable want. Had men refrained from all injustice, they would have remained free; it was injustice which made them bend beneath the yoke. To acquire safety, they deposited the whole force in the hands of one man; and thus

9   *Darum sind wilde, und im hochsten grad aufgeklarte, vieleicht, die einzige ffeye menschen.*

created a new evil, that of fear. The work of their
own hands frightened them; and to live in safety they robbed themselves of that very safety.
This is the cause of our governments.—*Where
then shall we find a protecting force? In union*; but how rare, alas! is that union, except in
our new and secret associations, better guided
by wisdom, and leagued in straiter bonds! and
hence it is that nature itself inclines us toward
these associations.

Subtle as is the artifice in this description of human nature, and in that affectation of beholding on
the one side nothing but tyrants and despots, and
on the other only oppressed and trembling slaves
in the state of society; whatever share Nature may
have had in the institution of social order, or in reclaiming mankind from forests and wildernesses
to live under laws and a common chief; the Hierophant nevertheless exultingly exclaims,

Such is the faithful and philosophic picture of
despotism and of liberty, of our wishes and of our
fears. Despotism was engrafted on liberty, and
from despotism shall liberty once more spring.
The re-union of men in society is at once the cradle and the grave of despotism; it is aso the grave
and cradle of liberty. *We were once possessed of
liberty, and we lost it but to find it again and
never lose it more; to learn by the very privation of it the art of better enjoying it in future.*

Reader, observe these words; if they do not evidently point out the object of the Sect, if you do

not perceive the wish of bringing mankind back to those times of the *nomade herds* of *savages,* and of men destitute of *property,* laws, or government, read and convince yourself by what follows:

> *Nature drew men from the savage state and re-united them in civil societies; from these societies we proceed to further wishes, and to a wiser choice (aus den staaten tretten wir in neue klüger gewählte). New associations present themselves to these wishes, and by their means we return to the state whence we came, not again to run the former course, but better to enjoy our new destiny let us explain this mystery.*

> *Men then had passed from their peaceable state to the yoke of servitude; Eden, that terrestrial paradise, was lost to them. Subjects of sin and slavery, they were reduced to servitude and obliged to gain their bread by the sweat of their brow.*—In the number of these men some promised to protect, and thus became their chiefs—at first they reigned over herds or clans—these were soon conquered, or united together in order to form a numerous people; hence arose nations and their chiefs—kings of nations. At the formation of states and nations, the world ceased to be a great family, to be a single empire; the great bond of nature was rent asunder.

The impudence of such assertions must astonish the reader; he will ask himself can there possibly exist beings thus belying evidence itself, and pretending to show the universe forming but one and the same family, and the grand bond of nature in those roaming and scattered herds, where the child can scarcely walk when he is separated from his father? How is it possible to represent mankind as divorcing from the great family, at the very period when they unite under the same chiefs and the same laws, for their mutual protection and safety? But, reader, suspend thy indignation. Let us call up in evidence against the Sect those brigands and sophisticted murderers which it decorated with the high-sounding title of *Patriots*, and which it stimulated to bloodshed and methodized murder by the fanaticizing sounds of *people, nation, country*. At the very time that they rend the air with such accents, with names so dear as they pretend, hear the maledictions which their mysteries heap upon every *people*, every *nation*, every *country*.

At that period, when men re-united and formed nations,

> they ceased to acknowledge a common name— *Nationalism, or the love for a particular nation,* took place of the general love. With the division of the globe, and of its states, benevolence was restrained within certain limits, beyond which it could no longer trespass.—Then it became a merit to extend the bounds of states at the expence of the neighbouring ones. Then it became lawful to abuse, offend, and despise foreigners, to attain that end—*and this virtue was styled patriotism*; and he was styled *a patriot* who, just toward his countrymen, and unjust to

others, was blind to the merits of strangers, and believed the very vices of his own country to be perfections.—In such a case, why not restrain that love within a narrower compass, to citizens living in the same town, or to the members of one family; or why even should not each person have concentrated his affections in himself. *We really beheld Patriotism generating Localism, the confined spirit of families, and at length Egoism. Hence the origin of states and governments, and of civil society, has really proved to be the seeds of discord, and Patriotism has found its punishment in itself . . . . Diminish, reject that love of the country, and mankind will once more learn to know and love each other as men.* Partiality being cast aside, that union of hearts will once more appear and expand itself—on the contrary, extend the bonds of *Patriotism*, and you will teach man that it is impossible to blame the closer contraction of love, to a single family, to a single person, in a word, to the *strictest Egoism.*

But let us abridge these blasphemies. The Hierophant, under pretence of his universal love, may vent his spleen against the distinctions of Greeks or Romans, of French or English, of Italian or Spanish, of *Pagan or Jew*, of *Christians* or *Mahometans*, which denote nations and their religions: he may repeat, if he pleases, that amidst these different denominations that *of man is overlooked*; what will be the result of such declamation?—With our illuminizing doctor, in common with every class of the disorganizing Sophisters, is not this pretended universal love to be a cloak for the most odious hypocrisy? He only pretends to universal philanthropy, that he may dispense with loving his neighbour. He detests the love of one's country, only because he detests the laws of nations; he cannot even brook the love of one's family (he has given us a fine specimen in the person of his sister), and he will substitute that universal love because he is no more attached to them than he is to the Chinese, the Tartar, or the Hottentot, which he neither has seen nor ever will see, and that all human nature may be equally indifferent to him. He extends the bond that it may lose its elasticity and discontinue its action.—He calls himself citizen of the universe, that he may cease to be a citizen in his own country, a friend in society, or a fond father and dutiful child in his own family. His love, he tells us, extends from pole to pole, that he may love nothing that is near him. Such is the philanthropy of our Cosmopolites!

The proselyte stands astonished in stupid admiration at these expressions of universal love.—The Hierophant proceeds to the *Codes of Nations*. Still in extasy at these doctrines, he learns that they are in direct opposition *to the laws of nature*; nor will he even perceive that his new code is in direct opposition to the very first laws of nature, as it eradicates the love of one's own family and that of one's country. Nor will he ask, why the fulfilling of his duty toward his fellow-countrymen should hinder him from treating the barbarian or the savage with proper affection? Then follow new sophisms, to persuade the adept that the original fault of man was, the dereliction of the Equality and Liberty of the savage state by the institution of civil laws.

Here, more than ever, are calumny and hatred blended with enthusiasm by the Hierophant, who, reviewing the different ages of the world since the existence of civil institutions, pictures nations as groaning under oppression, despotism, and slavery, or glutted with the blood of wars and revolutions, which always terminate in tyranny. At one time it is the representation of Kings surrounding themselves with herds or legions called soldiers, in order to gratify their ambition by conquests on strangers, or to reign by terror over their enslaved subjects; at other times, it is the people themselves brandishing their arms, not to attack tyranny in its source, but merely to change their tyrants. If they think of giving themselves representatives, it is these very representatives, *who, forgetting that they only hold their missions and powers from the people, form Aristocracies and Oligarchies*, which all end by flowing into the general reservoir of Monarchy and Despotism. He never loses sight of his sophism of human nature degraded and vilified under the yoke of tyranny. These declamations, enthusiastically pronounced, at length make the proselyte exclaim, in unison with his master,

Are such then the consequences of the institution of states and of civil society? O folly! oh people!

175

that you did not foresee the fate that awaited
you; that you should yourselves have seconded
your despots in degrading human nature to ser-
vitude, and even to the condition of the brute!

Could a true Philosopher have been present, his heart must have burst with generous indignation; he would have abruptly challenged the Hierophant to declare whence he had learned to metamorphose the annals of society into those of brigands and monsters? Is the history of man then reduced to the records of plagues, famines, storms, tempests, or of convulsed elements? Have no serene days shone on man? Shall the sun be represented as a malevolent object, because it is sometimes obscured by fogs or clouds? Are we to fly from our habitations because many have been destroyed by fire? Shall we curse life and health because we are subject to pains and infirmities? Why else this fable painting of the disasters which have in the course of ages befallen civil society? Why are we to be silent on the misfortunes from which it has preserved us, or on the advantages which it has heaped on man, in reclaiming him from the forests?

But the voice of reason cannot penetrate into the den of conspiracy. The oracles of Weishaupt shall there be confidently repeated by the Hierophant. He draws nigher and nigher to the grand object, to the means of making those misfortunes disappear, which originate, as he pretends, in the institution of laws and governments. "Oh nature!" he continues,

> how great and incontestible are thy rights? It is from the womb of disaster and mutual destruction that the means of safety spring! Oppression disappears because it meets with abettors, and reason regains its rights because people wish to stifle it. He, at least, who wishes to mislead others, should seek to govern them by the advantages of instruction and science. Kings themselves at length perceive, that there is little glory in reigning over ignorant herds— Legislators begin to acquire wisdom, and they favour *property* and industry:—perverse motives propagate the sciences, and Kings protect them as agents of oppression. Other men profit of them to investigate the origin of their rights. They at length seize on that unknown mean of forwarding a revolution in the human mind, and of thus triumphing for ever over oppression. But the triumph would be of short duration, and man would fall back into his degraded state, had not Providence in those distant ages husbanded the means which it has transmitted down to us, of secretly meditating and at length operating the salvation of human kind.
>
> *These means are, the secret schools of Philosophy. Those schools have been in all ages the archives of nature and* OF THE RIGHTS OF MAN. *These schools shall one day retrieve the fall of human nature,* AND PRINCES AND NATIONS SHALL DISAPPEAR FROM THE FACE OF THE EARTH, *and that without any violence.* Human nature shall form one great family, and the earth shall become the habitation of the man

of reason.—Morality shall alone produce this great Revolution. *The day shall come when each father shall, like Abraham and the Patriarchs, become the Priest and absolute Sovereign of his family.* REASON SHALL BE THE ONLY BOOK OF LAWS, *the sole Code of man.* THIS IS ONE OF OUR GRAND MYSTERIES. *Attend to the demonstration of it, and learn how it has been transmitted down to us.*

I have already said, that had my object been only to prove the reality of a Conspiracy formed by Illuminism against the existence of every society, every civil Code, and every nation; these lessons of the Hierophant would render every other proof superfluous. But that the reader may know the full extent of the dangers which threaten us, it is necesssary that he should be shown how those plots of frenzy become really transformed into plots of profound wickedness; that he should be acquainted with the means employed enthusiastically to inflame the minds of whole legions of adepts. Let us then attend to the Hierophant. If patience be necessary to follow him, greater still has it been necessary to enable me to transcribe such doctrines.

What strange blindness can have induced men to imagine that human nature was always to be governed as it has hitherto been.

Where shall we find a man acquainted with all the resources of nature? Who dare prescribe limits, and say *thus far shalt thou proceed, and no farther*, to that nature, whose law is unity in the variegated infinite? Whence shall issue the command, that it shall always run the same course, and for ever renew it again—Where is the being who has condemned men, the best, the wisest, and the most enlightened of men, to perpetual slavery? *Why should human nature be bereft of its most perfect attribute, that of governing itself? Why are those persons to be always led who are capable of conducting themselves? Is it then impossible for mankind or at least the greater part, to come to their majority?* If one be enabled to do it why should not another; show to one person what you have taught another; teach him the grand art of mastering his passions and regulating his desires; teach him, that from his earliest youth he stands in need of others; that he must abstain from giving offence if he wishes not to be offended; that he must be beneficent if he wishes to receive favours. Let him be patient, indulgent, wise, and benevolent. Let these virtues be made easy to him by principles, experience, and examples; and you will soon see whether he needs another to conduct him? If it be true, that the greater part of mankind are too weak or too ignorant to conceive these simple truths, and to be convinced by them; Oh then our happiness will be at an end, and let us cease to labour at rendering mankind better, or at seeking to enlighten them.

Oh prejudice! oh contradiction of the human mind! shall the empire of reason, the capacity of governing ourselves, be but a chimerical dream for the greater number of men, while

> on the other hand prejudice leads us to believe
> that such is the inherent right of the children
> of Kings, of reigning families, and of every man
> whom wisdom or particular circumstances ren-
> der independent!

What horrid artifice is contained in these sentences! The poor proselyte really imagines that he
sees the most striking contradictions in the very
foundations of our civil societies. He really thinks
that we believe them to rest on the hereditary privilege of Kings and of their children, to be born with
all the necessary wisdom to conduct themselves,
while nature has refused such gifts to other mortals; though Weishaupt, who scoffs in private at
the credulity and folly of his adepts, knows as well
as we do, that such has never been the idea even
of the most ignorant populace. He knows that we
believe Kings to be born children like other men,
with the same weaknesses, the same passions, and
like incapacity; he knows as well as we do, that the
gift of conducting ourselves and others is to be acquired by education, and by the helps and lights
with which a man may be encompassed; and we
know as well as he does, that the child of the most
obscure parentage would often make a better king
than many Sovereigns; as he might also be an excellent magistrate, or a great general, had he received
a proportionate education. But does there hence
follow any contradiction in civil society, because,
uncertain as to the persons who would be the most
proper for governing, but certain of the intrigues

and broils which would accompany the election of Kings, it has obviated those inconveniencies by hereditary crowns and empires? And after all, what is the meaning of that sophisticated pretence founded on the power of being able to conduct oneself? Question the most prudent and the wisest of men, and he will readily say, though I do not stand in need of laws, magistrates, or Kings, to restrain me from being unjust toward others, or from oppressing and plundering, I yet want their assistance to secure me from being oppressed or plundered. The less I am inclined to injure others, the more I need the protection of the law from all injury. You are pleased to call my submission to the laws slavery; I, on the contrary, look to it as my safety, and as the guarantee of that liberty which enables me to do good and to live happy and at peace in society. I have never heard of laws which forbad me to live like an honest man. It is the wicked man only who recognises liberty but in the impunity of his crimes; I scorn such liberty, and bless the hand that deprives me of it. You call him a tyrant and a despot, I call him my King and my benefactor. The better I know how to conduct myself with respect to others, the more thankful I am to him who hinders others from behaving ill to me.

The reader must pardon me these reflexions; I know they are superfluous to those who think; but may not this work fall into the hands of persons as credulous as the unhappy proselyte. In exposing the envenomed weapons of the Sect, let it not be said that I withhold the antidote. Should any be still blind enough not to perceive the tendency of all these sophisms of Illuminism, let them hearken to the Sect ardently declaring their hopes; the Hierophant continues:

> Are we then fallen from our dignity so low as not even to feel our chains, or to hug them, and not cherish the flattering hope of being able to break them, or to recover our liberty, not by rebellion or violence (for the time is not yet come), but by force of reason. Because a thing cannot be accomplished to-morrow, should we despair of ever being able to effect it? *Abandon such short-sighted men to their own reasonings and their own conclusions; they may conclude again and again; but nature will continue to act. Inexorable to all their interested remonstrances, she proceeds, and nothing can impede her majestic course. Some events may take place contrary to our wishes; but they will all rectify of themselves; inequalities will be levelled, and a lasting calm shall succeed the tempest.* The only conclusion to be drawn from all these objections is, that we are too much accustomed to the present state of things, or perhaps self-interest has too great sway over us, *to let us own that it is not impossible to attain universal independence—Let then the laughers laugh and the scoffers scoff.* He that observes and compares what Nature has done with what she does at present, will soon see, that in spite of all our intrigues she tends invariably toward her object. Her proceedings are imperceptible to him who reflects but little; they are visible

only to the sage whose mind's eye penetrates
even to the womb of time.—From the summit of
the mount he discovers in the horizon that distant country, the very existence of which is not
surmised by the servile multitude of the plain.

The principal means which Weishaupt offers to
his adepts for the conquest of this land of promise,
this soil of independence, are, to diminish the wants
of the people, and to enlighten their minds. Heark-
en to his lessons, you who, heretofore protected by
your laws, peaceably exercised an honourable and
lucrative profession, and you who, once rivals of
the flourishing commerce of Great Britain on the
immensity of the ocean, are now but the sorrowful
and dejected coasters of the Texel, imprudent disciples of a disorganizing Sect.—Learn, that it is in
the secret hatred sworn against you by the Sect in
its mysteries that you are to seek the destruction of
Lyons, the pillage of Bourdeaux, the ruin of Nantes
and Marseilles, the fate, in short, of so many other towns flourishing in commerce, even the fate
of Amsterdam itself; and then let your aching eye
glance on your trees of Equality and Liberty. At
the very time when you thought that you were seconding the views of the Sect against the Nobles,
Priests, and Monarchs, only to reinstate the people in their rights of Equality and Liberty, the Sect
was aiming its blows at you as the grand artificers
of Despotism. At that very period your profession
was already proscribed by the mysteries, as that
which of all others most surely tended to retain

the people in slavery; the Illuminizing Jacobin was teaching his adepts, that

> he who wishes to subject nations to his yoke, need but to create wants which he alone can satisfy.—Erect the *mercantile tribe* (*die kaufmanschaft*) into an hierarchical body; that is to say, confer on it some rank or some authority in the government, and you will have created the most formidable, the most *despotic* of all powers. You will see it giving laws to the universe, and on it alone will rest the independence of one part of the world and the slavery of the other. For that man dictates the law who has it in his power to create or foresee, to stifle, weaken, or satisfy want. And who are better enabled to do this than merchants?

Thus we see that those men who were such ardent supporters of Jacobinism in our commercial towns, with a view to partake of the government, are precisely those whose profession the profound Jacobin chiefly detests in every form of government. May the elucidation of this mystery inspire the industrious inhabitants of hospitable Britain with new zeal for their laws! The discovery of such a snare is of too great importance to their safety, to allow me to conceal it from them.

In the next place the Hierophant proceeds from the art of diminishing wants in order to operate the independence of nations, to the duty of diffusing what he calls light. "He on the contrary" (those are his words)

who wishes to render mankind free, teaches
them how to refrain from the acquisition of
things which they cannot afford: he enlight-
ens them, he infuses into them boldness and
inflexible manners. He that teaches them so-
briety, temperance, and œconomy, is more
dangerous to the throne than the man who
openly preaches regicide.—If you cannot diffuse at the same instant this degree of light
among all men, at least begin by enlightening yourself, and by rendering yourself better. *Serve, assist, and mutually support each
other; augment our numbers; render yourselves at least independent, and leave to time
and posterity the care of doing the rest.* When
your numbers shall be augmented to a certain
degree, when you shall have acquired strength
by your union, *hesitate no longer, but begin
to render yourself powerful and formidable to
the wicked* (that is to say to all who will resist
their plans); the very circumstance of your being sufficiently numerous to talk of force, and
that you really do talk of it, that circumstance
alone makes the prophane *and wicked* trem-
ble—That they may not be overpowered by
numbers, many will become good (like you) of
themselves, and will join your party.—*You will
soon acquire sufficient force to bind the hands
of your opponents, to subjugate them and to
stifle wickedness in the embryo.*

That is to say, as it may be understood in future,
you will soon be able to stifle every principle of
law, of government, of civil or political society,
whose very institution in the eyes of an Illuminée

is the germ of all the vices and misfortunes of human nature.

> The mode of diffusing universal light, is not to proclaim it at once to the whole world, *but to begin with yourself; then turn toward your next neighbour; you two can enlighten a third and fourth; let these in the same manner extend and multiply the number of the children of light, until numbers and force shall throw power into our hands.*[10]

I observe in the ritual of this degree, that should the Hierophant be fatigued by the length of this discourse, he may take breath, and let one of the adepts continue the instruction of the proselyte.[11] Our readers also may avail themselves of this permission, and they have copious matter for reflection in what they have hitherto read. They may perhaps be inclined to ask, to what degree the people must dinimish their wants not to stand in need of laws? They will perceive that bread itself must be denied them; for as long as fields are cultivated, laws will be necessary to protect the crops and to restrain men from reaping that which they have

---

10 See Discourse on the lesser Mysteries of Illuminism.

11 This Discourse actually requires at least two hours to read it. That part from which I have made extracts extends in vol. II. *of the Original Writings*, from page 44 to 93, and in the *last works of Philo and Spartacus*, (which are in much smaller print) from page 10 to 48. I mean to abridge the remaining part still more; but shall be scrupulously exact in the translation of all remarkable passages.

not sown; and if on the first view the Sophism appears wicked, the reader will soon perceive that it is but folly in the garb of Sophistry.

The better to form their judgments on the lessons of the Hierophant, they will have to compare that Revolution, which is to be the effect of instruction alone, and which is insensibly to take place without the least shock or rebellion, with that period when the adepts shall have acquired numbers, force, and power, enabling them to bind the hands of their opponents, and to subjugate all who may still show any affection for their laws, or for that civil order in society which the Sect wishes to suppress.

Continuation of the Discourse on the Lesser Mysteries.

In that part of the discourse which remains to be laid before the reader, the Hierophant, insisting on the necessity of enlightening the people to operate the grand revolution, seems to fear that the Candidate has not clearly conceived the real plan of this revolution, which is in future to be the sole object of all his instructions. "Let your instructions and lights be univerally diffused; so shall you render mutual security universal; *and security and instruction will enable us to live without prince or government.* If that were not the case, why should we go in quest of either?"[1]

Here then the Candidate is clearly informed of the grand object towards which he is to direct all his future instructions. To teach the people to live without *princes or governments*, without laws or even civil society, is to be the general tendency of all his lessons. But of what nature must these lessons be to attain the desired object?—*They are to treat of morality, and of morality alone.*

> For (continues the Hierophant) if light be the work of morality, light and security will gain strength as morality expands itself. *Nor is true morality any other than the art of teaching men to shake off their wardship, to attain the age of manhood, and thus to need neither princes nor governments.*[2]

When we shall see the Sect enthusiastically pronouncing the word morality, let us recollect the definition which it has just given us of it. Without it, we could not have understood the real sense of the terms *honest men, virtue, good* or *wicked men.* We see that, according to this definition, the honest man is he who labours at the overthrow of civil society, its laws, and its chiefs: for these are the only crimes or virtues mentioned in the whole

---

1   *Und allgemeine aufklarung und sicherheit machen fürsten und staaten entbehrlich. Oder wo zu braucht man sie sodann.*

2   *Die moral ist also die kunst welche menschen lehrt volljahrig zu werden, der vormundschaft los zu werden, in ihr mannliches alter zu tretten, und die fürsten zu entbehren.*

CHAPTER X

Code. Pre-supposing that the Candidate may object that it would be impossible to bring mankind to adopt such doctrines, the Hierophant anticipates the objection, and exclaims,

> He is little acquainted with the powers of reason and the attractions of virtue; he is a very novice in the regions of light, who shall harbour such mean ideas as to his own essence, or the nature of mankind . . . . If either he or I can attain this point, why should not another attain it also? What! when men can be led to despise the horrors of death, when they may be inflamed with the enthusiasm of religious and political follies, shall they be deaf to that very doctrine which can alone lead them to happiness? *No, no; man is not so wicked as an arbitrary morality would make him appear.* He is wicked, because Religion, the State, and bad example, perverts him. It would be of avantage to those who wish to make him better, were there fewer persons whose interest it is to render him wicked in order that they may support their power by his wickedness.

> Let us form a more liberal opinion of human nature. We will labour indefatigably, nor shall difficulties affright us. May our principles become the foundation of all morals! *Let reason at length be the religion of men, and the problem is solved.*[3]

---

3   *Und endlich macht die vernunft zur religion der menschen, so ist die aufgabe aufgelosst.*

This pressing exhortation will enable the reader to solve the problem of the altars, *the worship, and the festivals of Reason*, in the French Revolution; nor will they be any longer at a loss to know from what loathsome den their shameless Goddess rose.

The Candidate also obtains the solution of all that may have appeared to him problematic in the course of his former trials.

Since such is the force of morality and of morality alone (says the Hierophant), since it alone can operate the grand revolution which is to restore liberty to mankind, and abolish the empire of imposture, superstition, and despotism; you must now perceive why on their first entrance into our Order we oblige our pupils to apply closely to the study of morality, to the knowledge of themselves and of others. You must see plainly, that if we permit each Novice to introduce his friend, *it is in order to form a legion that may more justly be called holy and invincible than that of the Thebans*; since the battles of the friend fighting by the side of his friend are those which are to reinstate human nature in its rights, its liberty, and its primitive independence.

The morality which is to perform this miracle is not a morality of vain subtleties. It is not that morality which, degrading man, renders him careless of the goods of this world, forbids him the enjoyment of the innocent pleasures of life, and inspires him with the hatred of his neighbour. It must not be a morality favouring the interests only of its teachers, which prescribes persecution and intoleration, which militates against reason, which forbids the prudent use of the passions; whose virtues are no other than inaction, idleness, and the heaping of riches on the slothful.—*Above all, it must not be that morality which, adding to the miseries of the miserable, throws them into a state of pusillanimity and despair, by the threats of hell and the fear of devils.*

It must, on the contrary, be that morality so much disregarded and defaced at the present day by selfishness, and replete with heterogeneous principles. It must be a divine doctrine, such as Jesus taught to his disciples, and of which he gave the real interpretation in his secret conferences.

This sudden transition naturally leads Weishaupt to the developement of a mystery of iniquity for which we have long since seen him preparing his *Major Illuminées*, and particularly the *Scotch Knights* of illuminization. The better to understand this mystery, let us recall to mind how the *Insinuators* or the teachers began by solemnly assuring their different Candidates, Novices, or Minerval Academicians, that in all the lodges of Illuminism there never arises a question in the least degree prejudicial to religion or the state. All these promises have been gradually lost sight of, and the proselyte has had time to accustom his ears to declamations against the priesthood and royalty. It has already been insinuated, that the Christianity of our times is very different from that taught by Jesus Christ; the time was not arrived for numbering Christ himself among the impostors; his name, his virtues, might still be venerated by certain adepts. Some there were, perhaps, who would be shocked at bare-faced Atheism; and it is on their account that Weishaupt has thus treated of Christ. In the preceding degree he had contented himself with hinting, that the doctrines of this divine teacher had been perverted; nor had he declared what species of political revolution was (as he pretended) pointed out in the Gospel. But here the execrable sophister apostrophizes the God of the Christians in language similar to that in which we have since seen the too famous Fauchet declaiming in the revolutionary pulpit. It is here that Weishaupt declares Jesus Christ to be the Father of the Jacobins, or rather (to speak the revolutionary language) the great Doctor of the *Sans-culottes*. But, to enable us the better to judge of the cunning and premeditated villainy of this detestable artifice, let us first attend to the correspondence of the adept who, under Weishaupt, is charged with the compiling of the Code. Knigge, like the monstrous prototype of Illuminism, subdivides the adepts into those who scoff at and detest revelation, and those who stand in need of a revealed religion to fix their ideas. It is to explain this that Knigge writes the following letter to Zwack:

> To unite these two classes of men, to make them concur and co-operate toward our ob-

ject, it was necessary to represent Christianity
in such a light as to recall the superstitious to
reason, and to teach our more enlightened sages not to reject it on account of its abuse. This
should have been the secret of Masonry, and
have led us to our object. Meanwhile despotism strengthens daily, though liberty universally keeps pace with it. It was necessary then
to unite the extremes. We therefore assert here,
that Christ did not establish a new religion, but
that his intention was simply to reinstate natural religion in its rights; that by giving a general
bond of union to the world, by diffusing the light
and wisdom of his morality, and by dissipating
prejudices, *his intention was, to teach us the
means of governing ourselves, and to re-estab-
lish, without the violent means of revolutions,
the reign of Equality and Liberty among men.*
This was easily done by quoting certain texts
from Scripture, and by giving explanations of
them, *true or false is of little consequence*, provided each one finds a sense in these doctrines
of Christ consonant with his reason. We add,
that this religion, so simple in itself, was afterwards defaced; but that, by means of inviolable
secrecy, it has been transmitted in purity to us
through Freemasonry.

Spartacus (Weishaupt) had collected many
materials for this, and I added my discoveries
in the instructions for these two degrees. Our
people, therefore, being convinced that we
alone are possessed of the real secrets of Christianity, *we have but to add a few words against
the Clergy and Princes.* In the last mysteries we
have to unfold to our adepts *this pious fraud,*

and then by writings demonstrate *the origin of all* religious impositions, and their mutual connexion with each other.[4]

If the reader be not too much disgusted with *this pious fraud*, but can still attend to the declamations of the Hierophant, let us once more enter that den of demons wherein presides the triple genius of impiety, hypocrisy, and anarchy.

The Hierophant is about to say,

> that their grand and ever-celebrated master, Jesus of Nazareth, appeared in an age when corruption was universal; in the midst of a people who from time immemorial had been subjected to, and severely felt the yoke of slavery;[5] and who eagerly expected their deliverer announced by the Prophets. Jesus appeared and taught the doctrine of reason; to give greater efficacy to these doctrines, he formed them into a religion, and adopted the received traditions of

---

4 *Orig. Writ.,* vol. II., letter from Philo to Cato, page 104, and following.

5 Here is another example of the manner in which history is falsified—The Jews were enslaved from time immemorial! Does this nation then make its whole history consist in the years of its captivity? Had it forgot its liberty and its triumphs under Joshua, David, Solomon, and its other Kings? Was it just emerged from its captivity when it fell under the dominion of the Romans, a dominion under which it remained at the time of Christ's birth? The adept has heard talk of the captivity of the Jews, of those periods when Almighty God, as a punishment for their crimes, delivered them over to their enemies; and he inconsiderately concludes, that their whole history is but one continued scene of bondage.

the Jews. He prudently grafted his new school on their religion and their customs, which he made the vehicle of the essence and secrets of his new doctrines. He did not select sages for his new disciples, but ignorant men chosen from the lowest class of the people, to show that his doctrine was made for all, and suitable to every one's understanding; to show too, that the knowledge of the grand truths of reason was not a privilege peculiar to the great. He does not teach the Jews alone, but all mankind, the means of acquiring their liberty, by the observation of his precepts. He supported his doctrines by an innocent life, and sealed them with his blood.

His precepts for the salvation of the world are, simply, the love of God and the love of our neighbour; he asks no more. . . . Nobody ever reduced and consolidated the bonds of human society within their real limits as he did—No one was ever more intelligible to his hearers, or more prudently covered the sublime signification of his doctrine. *No one, indeed, ever laid a surer foundation for liberty than our grand master, Jesus of Nazareth.* It is true, that on all occasions (*in ganzen*) he carefully concealed the sublime meaning and natural consequences of his doctrines; *for he had a secret doctrine, as is evident* from more than one passage of the Gospel.

It was during the time that he was writing this hypocritical history of the Messiah, that Weishaupt was turning the credulous proselyte into ridicule;

as to the other adepts, he well knew that they anticipated such explanations, or at least would be delighted with them. Hence that impudence with which he falsifies the Scriptures. To prove the existence of this secret school, the doctrines of which are reserved for the initiated alone, he cites these words of Christ: "To you is given to know the mystery of the kingdom of God; but to them that are without, all things are done in parables."[6] But he carefuly avoids mentioning the order which Christ gives to his disciples, "That which I tell you in the dark, speak ye in the light; and that which you hear in the ear, preach ye upon the house-tops."[7] Weishaupt then proceeds to these words: "And their princes have power over them—but it is not so among you; but whoever will be greater shall be your minister."[8] This precept, as well as all those on Christian humility, he transforms into principles of disorganizing equality inimical to all constituted authorities.—With equal ease he avoids all those lessons so often repeated both by Christ and his Apostles, on the obligation of rendering to Cæsar what is Cæsar's, of paying tribute, and of recognizing the authority of God himself in that of the law and of the magistrates. If Christ has preached the love of our neighbour, or fraternal love, his words are immediately perverted by *Weishaupt* into a love of *his* Equality. If Christ exhorts his disciples

6   St. Mark, ch. iv., v. 11.

7   St. Matthew. ch., x., v. 27.

8   St. Mark, ch. x., v. 42, 43.

to contemn riches, the impostor pretends it is *to prepare the world for that community of riches* which destroys all property. In fine, the conclusions drawn from these impious and deriding explanations, and from many others of a similar nature, are contained in the following words:

> If therefore the *object* of the secret of Jesus, which has been preserved by the institution of the mysteries, and clearly demonstrated both by the conduct and the discourses of this divine master, *was to reinstate mankind in their original Liberty and Equality,* and to prepare the means; how many things immediately appear clear and natural, which hitherto seemed to be contradictory and unintelligible! *This explains in what sense Christ was the saviour and the liberator of the world. Now the doctrine of original sin, of the fall of man, and of his regeneration, can be understood. The state of pure nature, of fallen or corrupt nature, and the state of grace, will no longer be a problem. Mankind, in quitting their state of original liberty, fell from the state of nature and lost their dignity. In their civil society, under their governments, they no longer live in the state of pure nature, but in that of fallen and corrupt nature. If the moderating of their passions and the diminution of their wants, reinstate them in their primitive dignity, that will really constitute their redemption and their state of grace. It is to this point that morality, and the most perfect of all morality, that of Jesus, leads mankind. When at length this doctrine shall be generalized throughout*

the world, the reign of the good and of the elect shall be established.[9]

This language is surely not enigmatical. The proselyte, once master of the mysteries it contains, needs only to be informed, how the great revolution, which they foretell, became the object of secret societies, and what advantages accrue to these societies from the secresy in which they exist.

The Hierophant then, for the instruction of the proselyte, goes back to the origin of Masonry; he declares it to be the original school and depository of the true doctrine. He takes a view of its hieroglyphics, and shapes them to his system. The *rough stone* of Masonry becomes the symbol of the primitive state of man, savage but *free.—The stone split or broken is the state of fallen nature, of mankind in civil society, no longer united in one family, but divided according to their states, governments, or religions. The polished stone represents mankind reinstated in its primitive dignity, in its independence.* Yet Masonry has not only lost these explanations; but the illuminizing orator goes so far as to say, *"The Freemasons, like Priests and chiefs of nations, have banished reason from*

---

9   *Orig. Writ.,* part II., p. 106,7.—*The Last Works of Spartacus,* p. 58.—The author has transcribed the whole of what is printed in Italics in German, lest his translation of this extraordinary passsage should be suspected of being exaggerated. As he perfectly understands the German language, and is a man of undoubted veracity, I have omitted it, but in so doing think it my duty to mention it.—Tr.

the earth. They have inundated the world with ty-rants, impostors, spectres, corpses, and men like to wild beasts."

Should any reader be surprised at seeing the Hierophant give this account of Masonry, let him reflect on the hatred which Weishaupt had sworn against every school where the name of any deity was preserved. The *Jehovah* or the *Grand Architect* of Masonry, the *two-fold god* of the Rosycrusian magicians, still render the occult lodges a school of some sort of Theosophy. But how reserved soever the Hierophant may be with regard to Atheism, the proselyte must, nevertheless, foresee, that should he be admitted to one degree higher, neither the *Grand Architect* nor the *two-fold God* will meet a better fate than the God of the Christians. And therefore it is that Weishaupt declaims against those *spirits, apparitions,* and all the *superstitions* of Freemasonry; hence the theosophic Masons are involved in the general malediction pronounced against the priesthood and the throne.

It can be easily conceived, that Weishaupt must represent true Masonry, or the pretended real Christianity, as solely extant in Illuminism. But the Hierophant enjoins the proselyte *not to think that this is the only advantage which the Order and the whole universe draw from this mysterious association.*

Here let magistrates, the chiefs of nations, every man who still retains any regard for the support of laws and empires, and of civil society, let them, I say, read and meditate on these other advantages. The lesson is of the utmost importance—Whoever you are, all honest citizens, whether *Masons, Rosycrusians, Mopses, Hewers of Wood, Knights*; all you who thirst after the mysteries of the lodges, cease to accuse me of conjuring up chimerical dangers. I am not the man who speaks: it is he who of all others has been the *best acquainted* with your association, and has known what advantages could be drawn from them by able and patient conspirators.—Read; and tell us which is the most impressive on your mind, the pleasures you may find in your lodges, or the dangers of your country. Read; and if the name of citizen be still dear to you, reflect whether yours should remain inscribed on the registers of a secret society. You were ignorant of the dangers; the most monstrous of conspirators will lay them open to you, and he will call them advantages. He literally says,

> Though these mysterious Associations should not attain our object, they prepare the way for us; they give a new interest to the cause; they present it under points of view hitherto unobserved; they stimulate the inventive powers and the expectations of mankind; *they render men more indifferent as to the interests of governments*; they bring men of divers nations and religions within the same bond of union; *they deprive the church and the state of their ablest and most laborious members*; they bring men together who would never otherwise

have known or met each other. *By this meth-od alone they undermine the foundation of states, though they had really no such project in view.* They *throw them together and make them clash one against the other.* They teach mankind the power and force of union; they point out to them the imperfection of their *po-litical constitutions*, and that without exposing them to the suspicions of their enemies, such as magistrates and public governments. They *mask our progress, and procure us the facility of incorporating in our plans and of admitting into our Order, after the proper trials, the most able men, whose patience, long abused, thirsts after the grand ultimatum.* By this means they weaken the enemy; and though they should never triumph over him, *they will at least di-minish the numbers and the zeal of his parti-zans*; they divide his troops *to cover the attack.* In proportion as these new associations or se-cret societies, formed in different states, shall acquire strength and prudence at the expence of the former ones (that is to say, of civil socie-ty), *the latter must weaken, and insensibly fail.*

Beside, our Society originates, and must nat-urally and essentially deduce its origin from those very governments whose vices have ren-dered our union necessary. We have no object but that better order of things for which we incessantly labour; *all the efforts, therefore, of Princes to stop our progress will be fruitless; the spark may long remain hidden in the ash-es, but the day must come in which shall burst forth the general flame.* For nature nauseates always to run the same course. The heavier the yoke of oppression weighs on man, the more sedulously will he labour to throw it off; and the liberty he seeks shall expand itself. *The seed is sown whence shall spring a new world; the roots extend themselves; they have acquired too much strength, they have been too industriously propagated, for the day of harvest to fail us.*—Perhaps it may be necessary to wait thousands and thousands of years; but sooner or later nature shall consummate its grand work, and she shall restore *that dignity to man for which he was destined from the beginning.*

Reader, you have heard them. These conspirators have said more than I should have dared to hint at on the nature and danger of these associations. It would be useless for me to rest longer on that point. I shall end by showing by what artifices the Hierophant endeavours to tranquilize the consciences of those adepts who may have been startled at these predictions. Notwithstanding all that he has said of those times when Illuminism shall find means of *binding hands* and *subjugating*; notwithstanding all that aversion against governments which he seeks to infuse into the adepts, he concludes in a hypocritical strain peculiar to his wickedness.

We are here at once the observers and the instruments of nature.—We do not wish to precipitate her steps. To enlighten men, to correct their morals, to inspire them with benevolence, such are our means. Secure of success, we ab-

stain from violent commotions. To have foreseen the happiness of posterity, and to have prepared it by irreproachable means, suffices for
our felicity. The tranquility of our consciences
is not troubled by the reproach of aiming at the
ruin or overthrow of states and thrones. Such
an accusation could with no more propriety be
preferred against us, than it might against the
statesmen who had foreseen and foretold the
impending and inevitable ruin of the state.—As
assiduous observers of Nature, we admire her
majestic course; and, burning with the noble
pride of our origin, we felicitate ourselves on
being the chidlren of men and of God.

But carefully observe and remember, that we
do not impose our opinions; we do not oblige
you to adopt our doctrines. Let the truth you
can acknowledge be your only guide. Free man,
exercise here thy primitive right; seek, doubt,
examine; do you know of, or can you find elsewhere, any thing that is better?—Make us acquainted with your views, as we have exposed
ours to you. We do not blush at the limits of our
understandings; we know that we are but men;
we know that such are the dispositions of nature, such the lot of man, that he is not to expect
to attain perfection at his outset; he can attain it
but by degrees. It is by gaining experience from
our errors, by profiting of the lights acquired by
our forefathers, that we shall become at once
the children of wisdom, and the parents of a
still wiser progeny. If, therefore, you think that
you have found truth in the whole of our doctrine, adopt the whole. Should you perceive any
error to have stolen in with it, remember that

truth is not the less estimable on that account. If you have met with nothing that pleases you here, reject the whole without fear; and remember, that in many things, at least, we only need further research, or a new investigation. Do you observe any thing blameable or laudable, see and make choice of what you approve. Should you be more enlightened yourself, then your eye may have discovered truths which are still denied to us. The more art we employ in the instruction of our pupils to lead them to the paths of wisdom, the less you will be inclined to refuse us a portion of your applause.

Thus ends the discourse of the Hierophant.— The proselyte who has heard it without shuddering, may flatter himself with being worthy of this priesthood. But before he is sacrilegiously anointed, he is led back to the porch, where he is invested with a white tunic. He wears a broad silken scarlet belt; the sleeve is tied at the extremity and middle with bandages of the same colour, which make it bulge out.[10] I am particular in the description of this dress, because it was in a similar one that, during the French revolution, a comedian appeared personally attacking Almighty God, saying, "No! thou dost not exist. If thou hast power over the thunder bolts, grasp them; aim them at the man who dares set thee at defiance in the face of thy altars. But no, I blaspheme thee, and I still live. No, thou dost not exist." In the same costume, and to

10   *Last Works of Philo and Spartacus*, at the end of the Discourse.

prepare him for the same blasphemies, the Epopt is recalled into the temple of mysteries. He is met by one of the Brethren, who does not permit him to advance till he has told him, "that he is sent to enquire whether he (the proselyte) has perfectly understood the discourse which has been read to him—whether he has any doubts concerning the doctrines which are contained in it—whether his heart is penetrated with the sanctity of the principles of the Order—whether he is sensible of the call, feels the strength of mind, the fervent will, and all the disinterestedness requisite to labour at the grand undertaking—whether he is ready to make a sacrifice of his will, and to suffer himself to be led by the most excellent superiors of the Order."

I will spare the reader the disgusting impiety of the ceremonial which immediately follows.—The rites of the preceding degree were in derision of the Last Supper; these are an atrocious mimicry of the sacerdotal ordination. A curtain is drawn, and an altar appears with a crucifix upon it. On the altar also is a Bible; and the ritual of the Order lies on a reading desk; on the side a censer, and a phial full of oil. The Dean acts the part of a Bishop, and he is surrounded with acolytes. He prays over the proselyte, blesses him, cuts hair from the top of his head, clothes him in the vestments of the priesthood, and pronounces prayers after the fashion of the Sect. On presenting the cap he says, *"Cover thyself with this cap, it is more valuable than the crown of kings."* The very expressions of the Jacobin with his red cap. The communion consists in honey and milk, which the Dean gives to the proselyte, saying, "This is what Nature gives to man. Reflect how happy he would still have been, if the desire of superfluities had not, by depriving him of a taste for such simple food, multiplied his wants, and poisoned the balm of life."

All the preceding part of this degree sufficiently explains the real meaning of these words. The ceremonies are terminated with delivering to the Epopt that part of the code which relates to his new degree. I shall relate all that is necessary for the reader to be informed of, when, after having treated of the degree of Regent, and of the Grand Mysteries, I shall come to investigate the government of the Order.

CHAPTER XI.

Eighth Part of the Code of Illuminées.—The Regent, or the Prince Illuminée.

hen one of our Epopts has sufficiently distinguished himself to
bear a part in the political government of our Order; that is to say,
when he unites prudence with *the
liberty of thinking and of acting*; when he knows
how to temper boldness with precaution, resolution with complaisance; subtlety with good
nature; loyalty with simplicity; singularity with
method; transcendency of wit with gravity and
dignity of manners; when he has learned oppor-
tunely to speak or to be silent, how to obey or
to command; when he shall have gained the esteem and affection of his fellow-citizens, though
feared by them at the same time; when his heart
shall be entirely devoted to the interests of our

Qualities
required.

209

Order, and the common welfare of the universe shall be uppermost in his mind;—then, and only then, let the Superior of the province propose him to the National Inspector as worthy of being admitted to the degree of *Regent*.

Such are the qualities required by the Sect for the admission of its adepts to the degree which in the Code is sometimes termed *Regent*, at others the *Prince Illuminée*. Such are the very words to be found in the preamble of the rules of this degree.

Three things of the utmost consequence (says the Code) are to be observed. In the first place, the greatest reserve is necesssary with respect to this degree. Secondly, those who are admitted into it must be as much as possible *free men and independent of all Princes*: they must indeed have clearly manifested their *hatred for the general constitution* or the actual state of mankind; have shown how ardently they wish for a change in the government of the world; and how much the hints thrown out in the degree of Priest has inflamed their wishes for a better order of things.

Precautions and preliminary questions.

If all these requisites are to be found in the Candidate, then let the National Inspector once more examine, in his records, every thing relative to the conduct and character of the new adept, let him inspect the divers questions which have been put to him, and discover where he has shown his strong or his weak side. According to the result of this examination, let the Inspector propose some new questions on those articles on which the Candidate may have shown the greatest reserve. For example, some of the following:[1]

> I. Would you think a society objectionable, which should (till nature shall have ripened its grand revolutions) place itself in a situation, that would deprive Monarchs of the power of doing harm, though they should wish it; a society whose invisible means should prevent all governments from abusing their power? Would it be impossible, through the influence of such a society, to form a new state in each state, *status in statu;*"

that is to say, would it be impossible to subject the rulers of every state to this Illuminizing Society, and to convert them into mere tools of the Order even in the government of their own dominions?

> II. Were it to be objected, that such a society would abuse its power, would not the following considerations do away such an objection?—Do not our present rulers daily abuse their power? And are not the people silent, notwithstanding such an abuse? Is this power as secure from abuse in the hands of Princes, as it would be in those of our adepts whom we train up with so much care? If then any government could be harmless, would it not be our's, which would be entirely founded on morality, foresight, wisdom, liberty, and virtue?

---

1   Instructions for conferring the degree of Regent, nos. 1, 2, 3. *Last Works of Philo and Spartacus.*

THE ANTISOCIAL CONSPIRACY

III. Though this universal government, founded on morality, should prove chimerical, would it not be *worth while to make an essay of it?*

IV. Would not the most sceptical man find a sufficient guarantee against any abuse of power on the part of our Order, in the liberty of abandoning it at pleasure; in the happiness of having Superiors of tried merit, who, unknown to each other, could not possibly support each other in their treasonable combinations against the general welfare; Superiors, in short, who would be deterred from doing harm by the fear of the existing chiefs of empires?

V. Should there exist any other secret means of guarding against the abuse of that authority entrusted by the order to our Superiors, what might they be?

VI. Supposing despotism were to ensue, would it be dangerous in the hands of men who, from the very first step we made in the Order, teach us nothing but science, liberty, and virtue? Would not that despotism lose its sting, in the consideration that those chiefs who may have conceived dangerous plans will have begun by disposing a machine in direct opposition to their views.[2]

To understand the tendency of these questions, let us reflect on the meaning given by the Sect to *liberty* and *general welfare*. Above all, let us not forget the lesson already given to the adepts on

_____

2   Instructions for conferring the degree of Regent, nos. 1, 2, 3. *Last Works of Philo and Spartacus.*

morality; the art of teaching men to shake off the yoke of their minority, to set aside Princes and Rulers, and to learn to govern themselves. This lesson once well understood, the most contracted understanding must perceive, in spite of the insidious tenour of these questions, that their sole tendency is to ask, whether

> a Sect would be very dangerous who, under pretence of hindering the chiefs of nations, Kings, Ministers, and Magistrates, from hurting the people, should begin by mastering the opinions of all those who surrounded Kings, Ministers, or Magistrates; or should seek by invisible means to captivate all the councils, and the agents of public authority, in order to reinstate mankind in the rights of their pretended majority; and to teach the subject to throw off the authority of his Prince, and learn to govern himself; or, in other words, to destroy every King, Minsiter, Law, Magistrate, and public authority whatever?

The Candidate, too well-trained to the spirit of Illuminism not to see the real tendency of these questions, but also too much perverted by it to be startled at them, knows what answers he is to give to obtain the new degree. Should he still harbour doubts, the ceremonies of his installation would divest him of them. These are not theosophical or insignificant ceremonies;—every step demonstrates the disorganizing genius, and the hatred for all authority, which irritates the spleen of their impious author; and it is therefore that Weishaupt, when writing to

Zwack, represents them as *infinitely more important* than those of the preceding degree.[3]

The Inauguration.

When the admission of the new adept is resolved on, he is informed,

> that as in future he is to be entrusted with papers belonging to the Order, of far greater importance than any that he has yet had in his possession, it is necessary that the Order should have further securities. He is therefore to make his will, and insert a particular clause with respect to any private papers which he may leave in case of sudden death. He is to get a formal and juridical receipt of that part of his will from his family, or from the public Magistrate, and he is to take their promises in writing that they will fulfil his intentions.[4]

This precaution taken, and the day for the initiation fixed, the adept is admitted into an antichamber hung with black. Its furniture consists in a skeleton elevated on two steps, at the feet of which are laid a crown and a sword—There he is asked for the written dispositions he has made concerning the papers with which he may be entrusted, and the juridical promise he has received that his intentions shall be fulfilled. His hands are then loaded with chains, as if he were a slave; and he is thus left to his meditations.[5] The Provincial

---

3   *Original Writings*, vol. II., letter 24, from Weishaupt to Cato.

4   Instructions for conferring this degree. no. 5.

5   Ritual of this degree, no. 1.

who performs the functions of Initiator is alone in the first saloon, seated on a throne. The Introducer, having left the Candidate to his reflections, enters this room, and in a voice loud enough to be heard by the new adept, the following Dialogue takes place between them.

Provincial. Who brought this slave to us?"

Introducer. He came of his own accord; he knocked at the door.

Prov . What does he want?

Introd. He is in search of Liberty, and asks to be freed from his chains.

Prov. Why does he not apply to those who have chained him?

Introd. They refuse to break his bonds; they acquire too great an advantage from his slavery.

Prov. Who then is it that has reduced him to this state of slavery?

Introd. Society, governments, the sciences, and false religion. "*Die geselschaft, der staat, die gelehrsamkeit, die falsche religion.*"

Prov. And he wishes to cast off this yoke to become a seditious man and a rebel?

Introd. No; he wishes to unite with us, to join in our fights against the constitution of governments, the corruption of morals, and the profanation of religion. He wishes through our means to become powerful, that he may attain the grand ultimatum.

Prov. And who will answer to us, that after having obtained that power he will not also abuse it, that he will not be a tyrant and the author of new misfortunes?

Introd. His heart and his reason are our guarantees—the Order has enlightened him. He has learned to conquer his passions and to know himself. Our Superiors have tried him.

Prov. That is saying a great deal—Is he also superior to prejudice. Does he prefer the general interest of the universe to that of more limited associations?

Introd. Such have been his promises.

Prov. How many others have made similar promises who did not keep them? Is he master of himself? Can he resist temptation? Are personal considerations of no avail with respect to him? Ask him, whether the skeleton he has before him is that of a king, a nobleman, or a beggar?

Introd. He cannot tell; nature has destroyed all that marked the depraved state of inequality; all that he sees is, that this skeleton was man like us; and the character of man is all that he attends to.

Prov. If such be his sentiments, let him be free at his own risk and peril. But he knows us not. Go and ask him why he implores our protection?[6]

This dialogue ended (and the reader will not be at a loss to perceive the drift of it), the Introducer returns to the Candidate, and says,

Brother, the knowledge you have acquired can no longer leave you in doubt as to the grandeur, the importance, the disinterestedness and lawfulness of our great object. It must therefore be indifferent to you whether you are

---

6   Ritual of this degree, no. 1.

acquainted with our Superiors or not; nevertheless, I have some information to impart to you on that subject.

This information is nothing more than a summary of a pretended history of Masonry, going back to the deluge; and of what the Sect calls the fall of man, the loss of his dignity, and of the true doctrine. The story then continues to Noah and the few who escaped the deluge in the ark; these, he says, were a few Sages or Freemasons, who have maintained the true principles in their secret schools. It is for that reason, says the Instructor, that Masonry has preserved the denominations of *Noachists* and *Patriarchs*—Then comes a recapitulation of what had been said in the degree of *Epopt* on the pretended views of Christ, on the decline of Masonry, and on the honour reserved to Illuminism to preserve and revive these true and ancient mysteries—

> When questioned (says the Instructor) as to whom we are indebted to for the actual constitution of our Order, and the present form of the inferior degrees, the following is the answer we give:
> Our founders, without doubt, had extensive knowledge, since they have transmitted so much to us.—Actuated by a laudable zeal for the general welfare, they formed a code of laws for our Order; but, partly through prudence, and partly to guard against their own passions, they left the direction of the edifice they had raised

to other hands, and retired. Their names will for ever remain in oblivion—The chiefs who govern the Order at present are not our founders; but posterity will doubly bless those unknown benefactors who have despised the vain glory of immortalizing their names. Every document which could have thrown light on our origin has been committed to the flames.

You will now be under the direction of other men; men who, gradually educated by the Order, have at length been placed at the helm. You will soon make one of their number—Tell me only, whether you still harbour any doubt as to the object of the Order.

The Candidate, who has long since been past all possibility of doubt, advances with his Introducer toward another saloon; but, on opening the door, several of the adepts run and oppose their entrance.—A new dialogue takes place in the style of the first—Who goes there? Who are you?—Is it a slave who fled from his masters— No slave shall enter here—He has fled that he might cease to be a slave; he craves an asylum and protection—But should his master follow?—He is safe, the doors are shut.—But should he be a traitor?—He is not one, he has been educated under the eyes of the Illuminées. They have imprinted the divine seal on his forehead.—The door opens, and those who opposed the Candidate's entrance escort him to the third saloon. Here new obstacles occur, and another dialogue takes place between an adept in the inside and the Introducer. In the mean time the Provincial has left his former station, and has seated himself upon a throne in this third room. [It is worthy of remark that these enemies of thrones are themselves always seated on a throne.] The Provincial gives orders that the Candidate may be admitted, and desires to see whether he really bears the print of the seal of liberty. The Brethren accompany the new adept to the foot of the throne,

Prov. Wretch! You are a slave: and yet dare enter an assembly of free men! Do you know the fate that awaits you? You have passed through two doors to enter this; but you shall not go hence unpunished, if you prophane this sanctuary.

Introd . That will not happen; I will be his guarantee. You have taught him to thirst after liberty; and now keep your promise.

Prov. Well, Brother, we have subjected you to various trials. The elevation of your sentiments has made us conceive you to be both proper and worthy of being admitted into our Order. You have thrown yourself with confidence and without reserve into our arms: and it is time to impart to you that liberty which we have painted to you in such bewitching colours. *We have been your guide during all the time that you stood in need of one. You are now strong enough to conduct yourself; be then in future your own guide, be it at your own peril and risk. Be free; that is to say, be a man, and a man who knows how to govern himself; a man who knows his duty, and his imprescriptible rights; a man who serves the universe alone; whose actions*

> are solely directed to the general benefit of the
> world and of human nataure. Every thing else
> is injustice—Be free and independent; in future
> be so of yourself—Here, take back the engage-
> ments you have hitherto contracted with us. To
> you we return them all.

As he pronounces these words, the Provinical
returns him all the writings which concern him,
such as his oaths, his promises, the minutes of his
admission to the preceding degrees, the history of
his life which he had transmitted to the Superiors,
and all the notes taken by the Scrutators concerning him.

This perhaps is one of the most delicate traits of
policy of the Sect. The chiefs have had full leisure
to pry into the most secret recesses of his heart,
and the Scrutators have no further discoveries to
make. The Candidate may take back his oaths and
his secrets, but recollections (perhaps copies) still
remain, and the Initiator may well continue:

> In future you will owe us nothing but that which
> your heart shall dictate. We do not tyrannize
> over men, we only enlighten them. Have you
> found contentment, rest, satisfaction, happi-
> ness, among us? You will not then abandon us.
> Can we have mistaken you, or can you have mis-
> taken us! It would be a misfortune for you; but
> you are free. Remember only that men free and
> *independent* do not offend each other; on the
> contrary, they assist and mutually protect each
> other. Remember, that to offend another man,

is to give him the right of defending himself. Do you wish to make a noble use of the power we give to you? rely on our word: you shall find zeal and protection among us. Could a disinterested zeal for your brethren glow in your heart, then labour at the grand object, labour for unfortunate human nature, and thy last hour shall be blest. We ask nothing else from you, we ask nothing for ourselves. Question your own heart, and let it say whether our conduct to you has not been noble and disinterested. After so many favours, could you be ungrateful, your heart should avenge us, and chastise you. But no; many trials have proved you to be man of constancy and resolution. Be such your character, and in future govern with us oppressed man, and labour at rendering him virtuous and free.

Oh, Brother! what a fight, what hopes! when one day happiness, affection, and peace shall be the inhabitants of the earth! when misery, error, and oppression, shall disappear with superfluous wants! when, each one at his station labouring only for the general good, every father of a family shall be sovereign in his tranquit cot! when *he that wishes to invade these sacred rights shall ot find an asylum on the face of the earth!* when idleness shall be no longer suffered! *when the clod of useless sciences shall be cast aside*, and none shall be taught but those which contribute to make man better, and to reinstate him in his primitive freedom, his future destiny! when we may flatter ourselves with having forwarded that happy period, and complacently view the fruits of our labours! when, in fine, each man viewing his brother in his fellow-creature, shall extend a succouring hand—with us and ours you shall find happiness and peace, should you continue faithful and attached to us. You will also remark, that the sign of this degree consists in extending your arms to a brother with your hands open, to show that they are not sullied by injustice and oppression, and the gripe is to seize the brother by the two elbows, as it were to hinder him from falling. The *word* is *redemption*.

The foregoing passsages so clearly demonstrate the meaning of this word *redemption*, that the reader must be surprised at learning that there still remain further mysteries to be revealed.—The candidate is not yet admitted into the highest class. He is only the Prince Illuminée, and has to gain admission to the two degrees of *Philosopher*, and of the *Man King*. He is invested in his new principality by receiving a buckler, boots, a cloak, and a hat. The words pronounced at the investiture are worthy of the reader's attention.

On presenting the bucket, the Initiator says, "Arm thyself with fidelity, truth, and constancy; *be a true Christian*, and the shafts of calumny and misfortune shall not pierce thee." *Be a Christian! (und sey ein Christ)!!* What a strange Christian; what a wicked wretch then must be the Initiator who dares carry his dissimulation to such lengths, and prophane that sacred name in mysteries so evidently combined for the eradication of every trace of Christianity! But the adepts smiles, or his stupidity must be beyond expression if he does not see through so miserable a cant.

On presenting the boots: "Be active in the service of the good, and fear no road which may lead to the propagation or discovery of happiness." This will recall to our minds the principle, *whatever may be the means*, fear not to employ them when they lead to what the Sect calls happiness.

On giving the cloak: "*Be a prince over thy people*; that is to say, be sincere and wise, the benefactor of thy brethren, and teach them science." The reader will not be at a loss to understand what science.

The formula of *the hat* is, "Beware of ever exchanging this hat of liberty (*diesen frey heitshut*) for a crown."

Thus decorated, the Prince Illuminée receives the fraternal embrace.—He then hears read the instructions for his new degree; but as they entirely relate (like those of the preceding degree) to the government of the brethren, they will be treated of in the last part of the code. It is now time to proceed to the Grand Mysteries.

CHAPTER XII.

Ninth Part of the Code of the Illuminées.—Class of the Grand Mysteries; the Mage or the Philosopher, and the Man King.

y the great importance which the Sect places in the last mysteries of Illuminism, and the many precautions it has taken to conceal them from the public view, I am compelled to begin this chapter with candidly declaring, that every attempt to discover the original text of this part of the Code has been fruitless. Such an avowal, however, should not disconcert the reader. Though the real text may be wanting, we have abundant matter to supply its place. We have Weishaupt's familiar correspondence; we are in possession of the letters of many of the adepts who enthusiastically admired them; and the avowals are still extant of

The text not to be obtained.

225

other adepts, who indignantly beheld such abom-inations. Our judgement will be guided by laws laid down by Weishaupt himself; and the famous apology of this monstrous legislator will teach us how to appreciate them. Such materials are more than sufficient to supply the deficiency of the liter-al text. It is true, that the crafty cant and affected enthusiasm of the Hierophant will be wanting; but the substance of his declamation, the extent and monstrosity of his ultimate plots will lose nothing of their evidence. Let us begin then by attending to their author, and from him receive our first im-pressions.

Weis-haupts opinion on these mysteries.

Weishaupt, when writing to *Zwack*, his *in-comparable* man, and speaking of the degree of *Epopt*, wherein impiety and rebellion seem to have strained every nerve to disseminate their vene-mous principles against church and state, says,

> One might be tempted to think that this degree was the last and the most sublime: I have, nev-ertheless, THREE MORE *of infinitely greater im-portance, which I reserve for our Grand Mys-teries*. But these I keep at home, and only show them to the Areopagites, or to a few other breth-ren the most distinguished for their merit and their services.—Were you here, I would admit you to my degree, for you are worthy of it—But I never suffer it to go out of my hands. *It is of too serious an import*; it is the key of the ancient and modern, the religious and political history of the universe.

"That I may keep our provinces in due subordination, I will take care to have only three copies of this degree in all Germany; that is to say, one in each Inspection." He soon after writes again to the same adept: "I have composed four more degrees above that of Regent; and with respect to these four, even the lowest of them, our degree of Priest will be but child's play"—*Wo gegen den schlechesten der priester grad kinder spiel seyn soll.*[1]

Before we draw any conclusion toward forming our judgment, let me recall to the mind of the reader those letters wherein Weishaupt declares, that every degree shall be an apprenticeship for the next, *a sort of Noviciate for the higher degrees.* That these degrees were always to be *in crescendo;* in fine, that in the last class of the mysteries a perfect statement of the maxims and polity of Illuminism was to be given. *Und am endefolgt die totale einsicht in die politic und maximen des ordens.*[2] After such letters, the text of these mysteries is scarcely necessary. I know that these degrees were reduced to two for the last class of the mysteries; I know, from the agreement made by the founder and his intimate adepts, that the first was the *Mage,* or *Philospher,* the other, the *Man King.*[3] I will start from these data, and shall not hesitate to say, that this monster of impiety and of wickedness

---

1   *Orig. Writ.,* vol. II., let. 15, 16, 24, to Cato-Zwack.

2   *Ibid.,* vol. I., let. 4, to Cato.

3   *Ibid.,* vol. II., let 1, to Philo, and Second Part of Agreement of the Areopagites.

imposes on himself when he speaks of *degrees infinitely more important* for the higher mysteries, or when he pretends that those of *Epopt* and *Regent* are but *puerile* in comparison with those which he reserves for his intimate adepts. His execrable pride may flatter him with surpassing even the devils themselves, in his wicked inventions for sending forth the pestiferous blast; but their combined efforts could not suggest more hideous plots than those in which Weishaupt glories when calling them his *lesser mysteries.*—What! the vow of annihilating every idea of religion, even to the very name of a God; the plan for overthrowing every government, even to the obliteration of every vestige of laws, authority, or civil society; the wish of destroying our arts and sciences, our towns, and even villages, that they may realize their systems of Equality and Liberty; the desire of exterminating the greater part of human nature, to work the triumph of their vagabond clans, over the remaining part of mankind. These vows and wishes, these plots and plans, have already appeared in the lesser mysteries, and his adepts must have been as stupid as he wishes them to be impious and wicked, if they have not seen through the web that veils from their sight the baleful abyss. And, after all, it is not the *object* or the *substance* of their plots which is thus slightly veiled; the *terms* alone are concealed. There only remains to say, that all religion shall be destroyed for the adoption of Atheism; every constitution, whether Monarchical or Republican,

shall be overthrown in favour of absolute Independence; property shall be annihilated; science
and arts shall be suppressed; towns, houses, and
fixed habitations, reduced to ashes, for the re-establishment of the roaming and savage life, which
the hypocrite, in his cant, calls *the patriarchal life*.
Such are the terms; and the scroll of this hideous
pantomime needed only to be unrolled, to tell the
names of those who were to appear on the gloomy
stage of the last mysteries. The adept had long since
inhaled the deleterious air with which Weishaupt
had spared no pains to surround him; and could
he nauseate this, or turn away from these disastrous machinations, the gates of the mysterious
pit were shut against him. At such a sight nature
shudders—The reader will cry out, None but monsters could have conceived or abetted such plots.
Be it so; I will not contradict him; I only wish to
name these monsters.—Behold Weishaupt and his
profound adepts! The reader will find the proofs of
this exclamation in their own writings.

Weishaupt, who divided his mysteries into two
classes, also distributed his last secrets under two
heads. First, Religion; which was the object of the
Mages: The other comprehended what he called
his Polity; and he reserved it for the *Man King*. Let
us separately investigate each of these degrees,
commencing with that principle which he himself
lays down, and from which he never deviates, that
each degree shall be a preparatory concatenation
of principles and doctrines, the ultimate tendency

of which was to form the object of the last mysteries. Such a principle is more than sufficient to demonstrate that the secret to be imparted to his *Mages* can be no other than the most absolute Atheism, and the total subversion of every Religion. The adept, however, has already imbibed such horrid principles; and the secret consists in telling him, in plain terms, that it was toward that point the Sect had long since been leading him, and that in future all his thoughts, words, and actions, must tend to second the views of the Sect in their monstrous undertaking; that in the preceding degrees the name of *Religion* had only been preserved the better to destroy the thing; but that in future the very name would only be the expression of chimeras, of superstition, of fanaticism, supported by despotism and ambition, as a tool for enslaving mankind.

Secret of the Mage; Atheism.

This explication is no vain fancy of mine. See Weishaupt confidentially writing to his intimate and incomparable Cato- Zwack:

Proved by Weishaupt's letters,

> I firmly believe, that the secret doctrine of Christ had no other object in view than the re-establishment of Jewish Liberty, which is the explanation I give of it. I even believe, that Freemasonry is nothing but a Christianity of this sort; at least, my explanation of their Hieroglyphics perfectly coincides with such an explanation. In this sense, nobody could blush at being a Christian; *for I preserve the name, and substitute reason,—denn ich lasse den namen, und substituiere ihm die vernunjt.*

—He continues: "It is no trivial matter to have discovered a new Religion and a new Polity in these tenebrous Hieroglyphics;" and he goes on to say, "One might be induced to think that this was my highest degree; I have, nevertheless, three of infinitely more importance, for our grand mysteries."[4] Here then is Weishaupt's decision on the degree of *Epopt* or *Illuminized Priest.*—It is Christianity preserving the name of Religion, with the Gospel converted into a Code by means of which Christ taught the Jacobinical *Equality and Liberty.*[5] Here Weishaupt is transcendant in his wickedness and his impiety; it is under the sacred *name of Religion* that he teaches his disorganizing principles of *Equality and Liberty.* After having led his Epopts to the pinnacle of Impiety, to what farther lengths can he possibly lead his *Mage?*—He may erase the *names* of *Religion* and *God?* And this he will do in his higher mysteries; for who can expect to find them when he says, "You know that the *Unity of God* was one of the secrets revealed in the mysteries of Eleusis; *as for that, there is no fear of any such thing being found in mine.*"[6]

After this, can the name of God be expected ever to be found in the mysteries of the *Illuminized Mage* for any other purpose than to be blasphemed? We see this same Weishaupt reserving

---

4   *Original Writings*, vol.II., let. 15, to Cato.

5   See the Discourse on the Degree of Epopt.

6   *Original Writings*, vol. I., let 4, to Cato.

all the Atheistical productions for this degree; he writes again to his incomparable man:

> With our beginners let us act prudently with respect to books on Religion and Polity. *In my plan, I reserve them for the grand mysteries.* At first we must put only books of history or of metaphysics into their hands. Let Morality be our pursuit. *Robinet, Mirabeau* (that is to say, the System of Nature written by Diderot, though attributed to Mirabeau), *the Social System, Natural Polity, the Philosophy of Nature,* and such works, are reserved for my higher degrees.—At present they must not even be mentioned to our adepts, and particularly Helvétius' *On Man.*[7]

The reader here sees a list of the most Anti-religious and the most Atheistical works,[8] and that they are reserved for these last mysteries. As a preparation for them (*horribile dictu!*) the very idea of a God must be eradicated from the mind of the adept. Can we doubt this, when we see Weishaupt thus write: "Do put Brother *Numenius* in correspondence with me; I must try to cure him of his Theosophical ideas, and properly prepare him for our views.—*Ich will ihn suchen von der Theosophie zu curieren, und zu unseren absichten zu bestimmen.*"[9] The Theosopher, or the man still believing in a God, is not fit for these mysteries;

---

7   *Ibid.,* let 3, to Cato.

8   See the Helvian Letters on these Works.

9   *Ibid.,* vol. II., let. 15, to Cato.

Religion then must, of course, be irreconcileable with them. Were the consequences less evident, and should we reject these secret correspondences, or condemn the last oracles of the Hierophant to remain *within the hundred bolts* which keeps them hidden from the adepts; I say, even then, to ascertain what the tenets of the Sect are as to any worship or religion, we should not be necessitated to enter that den of mysteries. Though Weishaupt had not mentioned Religion in his intimate correspondence, the Atheistical Conspiracy of his mysteries would be evident, and why seek private documents when he has given us irrefragable proofs of guilt in that which he publishes as his apology?

Two years after his flight, Weishaupt most by his daringly asserts, that the Systems of his Illumi- apology, nism (as published by the civil powers) are but a mere sketch, a plan as yet too ill-digested for the public to form any judgment either on him or his adepts, from the *Original Writings* or his Confidential Correspondence. He publishes a new Code, and calls it *The corrected System of Illuminism, with its Degrees and Constitutions, by Adam Weishaupt, Counsellor to the Duke of Saxe Gotha.* Here at least we have a right to judge him and his mysteries, both in his apology and his corrected degrees. But the reader will now view him in a new light. He is not only the conspiring infidel, but the insolent Sophister, insulting the Public with all the haughtiness of the most daring Atheist, shrugging his shoulders in disdain at the rest of mankind, and with impertinent pity saying to us all, as he did of the adepts whom he had duped, *poor creatures! what could one not make you believe!*

I deign to cast my eyes on this apology, or the Illuminism corrected. He begins by telling us, that to have supposed him capable of composing so extensive a work in two years *was doing him the honour of supposing him gifted with most extraordinary talents*; and it is in such terms that the Sophister informs the public that he takes them for great fools. Let the contempt with which he treats his readers be retorted upon himself; let neither him nor his accomplices expect to descend to posterity with any other distinction than as the phenomena of vice and infamy. Are we to crouch in token of homage before the men who insolently scoff at their God and at the public weal? I know not whether Weishaupt needed extraordinary talents or not, though I grant him all the art and cunning of the Sophister; but most certainly he must have presumed much on the force of impudence when he flattered himself that the public would inevitably find that his corrected Code contained no principles but such as would elevate the mind and tend to form great men.[10] What I find is, that it is nothing more than a medley of all the arts of his original Code for the education or rath-

---

10 *So hoffe ich doch sollen alle darin übereinkommen, dass die in diesen graden aufgestellten grund-saze fahig seyen, grosse und erhabene menschen zu bilden—Introduction to his corrected System.*

er depravation of his Adepts. Did I wish to form a stupid atheist, this would be the work I should chuse to put into his hands. As early as the third degree, in place of a God reigning as freely as he does powerfully over this universe, I find the universe transformed into a vast machine, in which every thing is held together or put in motion by I know not what fatality, decorated sometimes by the appellation of God, at other of nature. Again: did I wish to decorate with the name of providence a destiny *which cannot annihilate a single atom without depriving the stars of their support and involving the whole universe in ruin*, this would be the work I should recommend: I would give it to the narrow-minded adept, who, in a world where every thing is said to be necessary, should still pretend to talk of virtue or vices, or who could comfort himself for all the harm which the wicked could do him, by learning that the wicked like the virtuous man only followed the course which nature had traced for him; and that they would both arrive at the same point as himself: In fine, I would put it into the hands of the imbecile, who would call *the art of making merry the art of being always happy (ars semper gaudendi)*; the art of persuading oneself that one's misfortunes are incurable, or that they are all necessary.[11] But what reader will brook the impudence of that conspiring infidel, who, dedicating his mysteries as an apology to the whole world and all mankind—*der welt und den*

---

11   See in the corrected System the Discourse on the third class.

menschlichen geschlecht—and pretending to prove that his original mysteries are not a conspiracy against Religion, puts a discourse in the mouth of his new Hierophants, whose very title characterizes the most determined one both against God and Religion; he calls it, *An Instruction for the adepts who are inclined to the fancy of believing in or of adoring a God!* I know it may be also translated, *An instruction for the Brethren inclining toward Theosopohical or Religious enthusiasm.*[12] But if both these translations be not synonimous in the language of the Sophisters, let the reader judge, from the exordium of the discourse, which is the most accurate.

> He who wishes to labour for the happiness of mankind, to add to the content and rest of the human species, to decrease their dissatisfaction (these are literally the words of our Antitheosophical Sophister), must scrutinize and weaken *those principles* which trouble their rest, contentment, and happiness. Of this species are all those systems which are hostile to the ennobling and perfecting of human nature; which unnecessarily multiply evil in the world, or represent it as greater than it really is: all those systems which depreciate the merit and the dignity of man, which diminish his confidence in his own natural powers, and thereby render him lazy, pusillanimous, mean, and cringing: all those also which beget enthusi-

---

12   *Unterricht für alle mitglieder, welche zu Theosophischen schwärmereyen geneight sind.*

*asm, which bring human reason into discredit,
and thus open a free course for imposture: All
the Theosophical and Mystical Systems; all
those which have a direct or indirect tendency to such Systems; in short, all the principles
derived from Theosophy, which, concealed in
our hearts, often finish by leading men back to
it, belong to this class.*

In the course of his instructions, the reader is
not to expect that Weishaupt will make any exception in favour of the revealed Religion, not even a
hint at such an exception is to be seen.—The Religion of Christ is represented as a medley of the
reveries of Pythagoras, of Plato, and of Judaism. It
is in vain for the Israelites to believe in the Unity
of God, in the coming of a Messiah; it is in vain to
assert that such was the faith of their forefathers,
of Abraham, Isaac, and Jacob, long before they entered Egypt or Babylon; it is in vain to prove, that
the adoration of the golden Calf, or of the god Apis,
was punished by the Almighty as a prevarication
of their Religion: Nothing will serve the Sophister;
he will declare in his *corrected code*, that the Religion of the Jews was but a modification of the
reveries of the Egyptians, of Zoroaster, or of the
Babylonians. To *correct* his adepts, he teaches
them to cast aside the Creation as a chimera unknown to antiquity, and to reduce all Religion to
two Systems—The one, that of matter co-etemal
with God, a part of God, proceeding from God, cast
forth and separated from God, in order to become

the world—The other, matter co-eternal with God, without being God, but worked by God, for the formation of the universe. On these foundations he builds a general history of all Religions, and makes all appear equally absurd. The reader might be tempted to think that these lessons had been composed before the hegira or rather proscription of the author of Illuminism. They may have been compiled for one of those discourses which he declares to be of more importance than that of the Hierophant in the degree of Epopt.—He precisely follows the course which Knigge represents as the grand object of the last mysteries. He makes, after his fashion, a general compilation of all the schools of Philosophism and of its Systems; and hence he deduces Christianity and all Religions. The result of the whole is, that all Religions are founded on imposture and chimera, all end in rendering man *cowardly*, *lazy*, *cringing*, and *superstitious*; all degrade him, and trouble his repose.[13] And it is thus that this Sophister, under pretence of his justification, daringly acts that part in public which before he had only ventured to act under the cover of his mysteries. He sallies forth from his baleful abyss but to proclaim to the world what heretofore he had only hinted to his adepts in private,—that the time was at length come for the overthrow of every Altar, and the annihilation of every Religion.

by Knigge's testimony, Are any further proofs necessary to demonstrate the object of the grand mysteries? The testimony

13   See the last Discourse of Illuminism corrected.

of Knigge cannot be objected to, nor can Knigge pretend or wish to mislead Zwack when confidentially corresponding with him. Both had signed the agreement of the Areopagites respecting the compilation of the degrees of Illuminism.[14] Let us then attend to these two adepts—Philo-Knigge has been exhibiting all that he has done, according to Weishaupt's instructions, in the degree of *Epopt*, to demonstrate that Christ had no other view than the establishment of natural Religion, or, in the language of Illuminism, the rights of Equality and Liberty. Knigge then continues:

> After having thus shown to our people that we are the real Christians, we have only *a word to add* against Priests and Princes. I have made use of such precaution in the degrees of Epopt and of Regent, that I should not be afraid of conferring them on Kings or Popes, provided they had undergone the proper previous trials. In our last mysteries we have to acknowledge this *pious fraud*; to prove, upon the testimony of authors, the origin of all the religious impostures, and to expose the whole with their connections and dependencies.[15]

---

14 See this agreement in the *Original Writings*, vol. II., part II., signed the 20 *Adarmeth* 1551, or Anno Domini 20 December, 1781.

15 Da nun die leute sehen dass wir die einzigen achten wahren Christen sind, so darfen wir da gegen ein word mehr gegen pfaffen and fursten reden; doch habe ich diess so gethan, dass ich papste und konige nach vorhergegangener prüfung, in diese grade aufnehmen wollte. Indem hoheren mysterien sollte man dann A diese *piam fraudem* entdecken, und B aus

Such, reader, is *that word to add*, which was
to be spoken only in the last mysteries of Illuminism! That *word* against Priests and the Ministers
of every worship! That *word* on the *pious fraud*,
or rather labyrinth of impiety, in which the Sect
had involved the Candidate on his first entrance
into the Order, only to extricate him when he was
judged worthy of their last mysteries! The adept
must certainly be of weak intellects, and his credulity must border on stupidity, if he has not in the
degree of Epopt, and long before, observed whither they were leading him. But should he really be
still in the dark, or could he view with indignation
the artifices which had been used with him; if all
reflection have not abandoned him; what will not
the very term of *pious fraud* discover to him? Will
it not recall to his mind,

> that on the first invitations of the Sect, to entice
> him into their Order, they began by telling him,
> that nothing contrary to Religion would ever
> enter the projects of the Order? Does he not re-
> member, that this declaration was repeated on
> his admission into the noviciate, and reiterated
> when he was received into the minerval acad-
> emy? Has he forgotten how strongly the sect
> enforced the study of morality and of virtue in
> the first degrees, and how carefully it isolated
> both from religion? When pouring forth its en-
> comium on religion, did not the Sect insinuate,

---

alien schrifften den ursprung aller religiozen lügen, und deren
zusammenhang entwickeln—*Original Writings, vol. II., let. I.,
from Philo to Cato.*

that true Religion widely differed from those mysteries and worship which had degenerated in the hands of the priesthood? Does he remember with what art and affected respect it spoke of Christ and his Gospel in the degrees of *Major Illuminée*, of *Scotch Knight*, and of *Epopt*; how the Gospel was insensibly metamorphosed into illuminized reason, its morality into that of Nature; and from a moral, reasonable, and natural religion, how a religion and a morality of the rights of man, *of Liberty and Equality*, were deduced? Does he reflect how all the different parts of this system and opinions of the Sect were insinuated to him, how naturally they occurred and appeared to have been fostered in his own breast? Could not the Sect say to him, 'tis true, we put you on the way, but you were much more earnest in solving our questions than we in answering yours. When, for example, we asked whether the religions which nations had adopted fulfilled the objects for which they were intended; whether the pure and simple religion of Christ was really that which different Sects professed at this present day, we knew what to believe, but we wished to know how far you had inhaled our principles. We had a multitude of prejudices to conquer in you, before we could succeed in persuading you that the pretended Religion of Christ was but an invention of Priestcraft, imposture, and tyranny. If such be the case with the much-admired and loudly proclaimed Gospel, what are we to think of all other religions? Learn, then, that they are all founded on fiction, all originate in imposition, error, imposture, and chimera. Such is our secret. All the windings we made; the hypotheses we assumed; the promises set forth; the panegyric pronounced on Christ and his secret schools; the fable, of Masonry being for a long time in possession of his true doctrines, and our Order being at present sole depositary of his mysteries, can no longer be subjects of surprise. If, to overturn Christianity and every Religion, we pretended solely to possess true Christianity, the true Religion, remember that the *end sanctifies the means*, that the sage *must make use of all those means for good purposes, which the wicked do for evil*. The means we have employed to rid you, and which we continue in order to rid mankind of all Religion, are but a *pious fraud*, which we always meant to reveal to you when admitted to the degree of *Mage*, or of *illuminized Philosopher!!!*

by the avowal of an honest adept.

To these reflections *on the word to be added* in the last mysteries (sufficiently demonstrated by the ascension of the degrees, by Weishaupt's apology, by his intimate correspondence, and that of his most perfect adepts) let us subjoin the avowal of a man little calculated indeed for a Member of such an abominable tribe, but who has better than any person known how to tear the mask from their hideous countenances, and expose their wickedness. I am acquainted with his real name; I am aware that it would greatly add to the confidence of the public; but I also know that could Illuminism discover his asylum, it would follow him to drink his blood, though it were to the southern pole. He is then entitled to secrecy; till now it has been observed, nor will I be the first to infringe his right. The Germans have paid him homage, and, ignorant of his name, they have surnamed him *Biederman*, or Man of Honour; at least, it is under that denomination that his works are generally cited. All that I can say in addition to what the public is already in possession of respecting this gentleman is that nothing could have induced him to continue so disgusting a course, but a zeal for the public welfare, and a just opinion, that the only means of preventing the effects of the conspiracy of the Sect was to make their machinations public.—Having passed through all the degrees, he was at length admitted to the last mysteries. He published those of *Epopt or Priest, and of Regent*, under the title of *Last Works of Philo and Spartacus*. He subjoined the instructions belonging to those degrees, with a *Critical History of all the Degrees of Illuminism*. Had I no other guarantee of the veracity of his assertions, than their glaring coincidence with the original writings, which is beyond all doubt with the attentive investigator, I should not hesitate in declaring him to be the man that has given the truest account, and was best acquainted with the Sect. The certificate at the head of the degree of *Epopt and Regent*, for a more perfect knowledge of which the public is indebted to him, I look upon as undoubtedly genuine. I know a person who has seen and read this certificate in the original, in *Philo-* Knigge's own hand-writing, and who has seen the seal of the Order attached to this certificate. I thus particularize because the public is entitled, in discussions of this importance, to know how far I have extended my researches, and how far the grounds I work upon deserve to be credited.—The passage I am about to quote is looked upon as fundamental by all German authors; it is from Biederman, and occurs near the end of his *Critical History*:

"With respect to the two degrees of *Mage* and of *Man King*, there is no reception, that is to say, there are no ceremonies of initiation. Even the Elect are not permitted to transcribe these degrees, they only hear them read; and that is the reason why I do not publish them with this work."

"The first is that of *Mage*, also called Philosopher. It contains the fundamental principles of Spinosism. Here every thing is material; God and the world are but one and the same thing; all religions are *inconsistent*, chimerical, and the invention of ambitious men."[16]

---

16 *Der erste, welcher Magus auch Philosophus heist, enthalt spinosistiche grund-satze, nach welchen alles materiell, Gotz und die welt einerley, alle religion unstatthaft, und eine erfindung hersüchtiger menschen ist.*

I might have quoted the testimony of another adept, who writes as follows to the authors of the Eudemonia: (vol. III. no. 2, Art. 4.) "I can also declare that I have been present at the grand mysteries; particularly, that in 1785 I was entrusted with the instructions of the degree of Mage or Philosopher, and that the short description given in the ENDLICHES SCHICKSAL (or the last object of Freemasonry) is perfectly exact and well grounded." The author of the *Endliches Schicksal* has

"Divers principles," continues the author, "thrown out in the preceding degrees might in some measure point out the object the Sect had in view." Certainly nothing could be better ground-

only, like myself, copied the text from *Biederman*. I have no knowledge of this new adept. I see he has signed his letter, desiring the authors of the Eudemonia not to make use of his name without an absolute necessity. "Besides," he adds, "I am a Roman Catholic; and in the country in which I live might find disagreeable consequences from not having asked to be absolved from my oath, *before I published what I had promised to keep secret.*" Sir, I am a Catholic as well as yourself, and should wish to know where you have learned, that the oath you had taken to the Illuminées was superior to that you had taken to the state. How then could you reconcile with your conscience the keeping back from the magistrate or the prince such proofs as you had acquired of a conspiracy against the state? Yes, do penance, and ask absolution for having taken such an oath, and for not having been true to the oath of allegiance which you had sworn to the state, and from which you could not be absolved by any power on earth.—What singular ideas are sometimes formed of probity! To persuade oneself that one is bound by an oath to a band of conspirators, while the oath of allegiance is overlooked!—Sir, you had said, that it was necessary to take proper precautions for your security, that *wretches pretending to the power of life and death* might not assassinate you, nothing could be more natural; take your precautions while informing the public magistrate, but do not come and give us as an excuse your fidelity to an oath, which in itself is nothing less than a peijury to the state.

Notwithstanding, however, the reproach jusdy merited by this adept, his testimony is not to be neglected, since he has sent his name to the editors of the Eudemonia, a journal printed at Franckfort on the Mein, and highly deserving of encouragement for the vigour with which the editors combat the Illuminées. Their writings have frequently corroborated materials that I had received from Austria and Bavaria, which give me great confidence in the researches I have made.

ed than such a surmise—Nature, so often united with God, represented active like God, following with the same immensity of power, the same wisdom as God, the course which it had traced; a hundred such expressions in the mouth of the Hierophant evidently indicated, that the God of Weishaupt was that of Spinosa or Lucretius, no other than matter and the universe; in fine, the God of Atheism. Let the Sieur d'Alembert assert, that nothing can be more opposite to Atheism than Spinosism;[17] or let Spinosa say, that, so far from being an Atheist, he converts every thing into God; will such an excuse raise pity or indignation in the reader? To deny that there is any other God than the world, is evidently denying the only being that can justly be called God. It is laughing at men, to wish to make them believe, that the person is preserved because they do not dare destroy the name, at the very time that the name of God is only used as an agent for the annihiliation of every idea of a Deity.

I think I have sufficiently demonstrated, that the first object of these grand mysteries of Illuminism, prepared with so much art and cunning, is no other than to plunge the adepts into a monstrous Atheism, to persuade all nations that religion is but an invention of ambitious impostors, and that to deliver nations from this despotism of imposture, and recover the famous rights of man, Equality and Liberty, they must begin by annihi-

---

17   Panegyric of Montesquieu.

lating every religion, every worship, every altar, and cease to believe in a God.

Let us continue the declaration of Biederman, and the object of the last part of the mysteries (or the degree of the Man King) will be equally clear.

The Man King, by the same adept.

"The second degree of the grand mysteries," he says,

> called the *Man King*, teaches that every inhab-
> itant of the country or town, every father of a
> family, is sovereign, as men formerly were in the
> times of the patriarchal life, to which mankind
> is once more to be carried back; that, in conse-
> quence, all authority and all magistracy must be
> destroyed.—I have read these two degrees, and
> have passed through all those of the Order.[18]

How well authenticated soever this testimony may be, still one is loth to think that there could have existed men at once so absurd and so wick-ed as to take such exquisite pains to educate their adepts merely to address them in the end to the following purpose:

> All that we have done for you hitherto was only
> to prepare you to co-operate with us in the an-
> nihilation of all Magistracy, all Governments,

---

18 *Der zweyte, Rex gennant, lehrt dass jeder Bauer, Burger und*
hausvater ein souverain sey, wie in dem patriarchalischen
leben, auf welches die leute wieder zurück-gebracht werden
müsten, gewesen sey; und dass folglich alle obrigkeit weg-
fallen müsse—Diese beyden graden habe auch ich, der ich in
dem orden alles durchgegangen bin, selbst gelesen. Ibid.

all Laws, and all Civil Society; of every Republic and even Democracy, as well as of every Aristocracy or Monarchy—It all tended to infuse into you and make you insensibly imbibe that which we plainly tell you at present—All men are equal and free, this is their imprescriptible right; but it is not only under the dominion of Kings that you are deprived of the exercise of these rights. They are annulled wherever man recognises any other law than his own will. We have frequently spoken of Despotism and of Tyranny; but they are not confined to an Aristocracy or a Monarchy: Despotism and Tyranny as essentially reside in the Democratic sovereignty of the people, or in the legislative people, as in the legislative King. What right has that people to subject me and the minority to the decrees of its majority? Are such the rights of nature? Did the sovereign or legislative people exist any more than Kings or Aristocratic Legislators at that period when man enjoyed his natural Equality and Liberty?— Here then are our Mysteries— All that we have said to you of Tyrants and Despots, was only designed insensibly to lead you to what we had to impart concerning the despotism and tyranny of the people themselves. Democratic governments are not more consonant with nature than any others. If you ask. How it will be possible for men assembled in towns to live in future without laws, magistrates, or constituted authorities,—the answer is clear, Desert your towns and villages, and fire your houses. Did men build houses, villages, or towns in the days of the Patriarchs? They were all equal and free; the earth belonged to them all, each had an equal right, and lived where he chose. Their

country was the world, and they were not confined to England or Spain, to France or Germany; their country was the whole earth, and not
a Monarchy or petty Republic in some comer of
it. Be equal and free, and you will be cosmopolites or citizens of the world. Could you but appreciate Equality and Liberty as you ought, you
would view with indifference Rome, Vienna,
Paris, London, or Constantinople in flames, or
any of those towns, boroughs, or villages which
you call your coun- try.—Friend and Brother,
such is the grand secret which we reserved for
our Mysteries!!!

It is painful indeed to believe, that stupidity,
pride, and wickedness, should have thus combined
to prepare adepts, who, attending Weishaupts Mysteries, could mistake them for the Oracles of tme
wisdom and transcendant Philosophy. How many
Jacobins and those pretended patriots of Democracy blush, when they learn the real object of the
Sect which directs their actions; when they learn
that they have only been the tools of a Sect whose
ultimate object is to overturn even their Democratic Constitutions!—But in attributing such language
to the Hierophant of the last Mysteries, what more
have I said than the Illuminizing Legislator has already declared? What other can be the meaning By the
of his *Patriarchal* or of his *Nomade* or *roaming* foregoing
life, of those vagabond clans, or of man still in the degrees.
savage state?[19] What Democracy even could con-

---

19   *Original Writings*, vol. II., let. 10, to Cato.

sist with the Patriarchal life or the vagabond clan? Where is the necessity for attending the last Mysteries, to learn from the Sect itself the extent of their conspiracies? We have seen Weishaupt cursing that day as one of the most disastrous for mankind, when, uniting themselves in civil society, they instituted Laws and Governments, and first formed *nations and people*. We have seen him depreciate *nations* and the *national spirit* as the grand source of Egoism; call down vengeance on the laws and the rights of nations as incompatible with the *laws and rights of nature*. What else can the Sect mean by saying, that *nations shall disappear from the face of the earth*, but the annihilation of all civil or national society? Why those blasphemies against *the love of one's country*, if not to persuade the adepts to acknowlege none?—Have we not heard the Hierophant teaching that true morality consisted *in the art of casting Princes and Governors aside and of governing oneself*, that the real original sin in mankind was their uniting under the laws of civil society; that their *redemption* could be accomplished only by the abolition of this civil state? And when his frantic hatred against all government exalts his imagination, does he not enthusiastically exclaim, *Let the laughers laugh, the scoffers scoff; still the day will come, when Princes and Nations shall disappear from the face of the earth; a time when each man shall recognize no other law but that of his reason?* Nor does he hesitate to say, *that this shall be the grand work of* SECRET SOCIETIES.

They are to reinstate man in his rights of Equality and Liberty, in an independence of every law but that of his reason. Such he formally declares to be one of the grand mysteries of his Illuminism;[20] and can the reader quietly sit down and think that all these declarations of the author of Illuminism, who must be superior to his Mysteries, have not the absolute ruin of every law, government, and civil society, in view? Has he not seen the Sect anticipating those objections which evidence might have suggested against systems still more wicked than stupid; forewarning the adepts, that independence once more restored among men, it was not to meet the same fate it formerly had, and was never to be lost again;—teaching that mankind, having acquired wisdom by its disasters, will resemble a man corrected of his errors by long experience, and who carefully avoids those faults which were the cause of his past misfortunes? Has not the reader heard him proclaim to his elect, that this independence once recovered, the empire of the laws and all civil society would cease; and will he still continue to disbelieve the existence of the most deliberate and most dangerous Conspiracy that ever was formed agaisnt society!

Should any of my readers be weak enough to be seduced by the imaginary sweets of a patriarchal life, so artfully promised by Weishaupt, let them receive the explanation of that life from these pretended Apostles of Nature.

20 See the Degree of Epopt.

At my outset I did not only declare, that the destruction of civil society was the object of their views; I did not confine myself to saying, that should Jacobinism triumph every Religion and every Government would be overthrown; but I added, *that to whatever rank in society you may belong, your riches and your fields, your houses and your cottages, even your very wives and children would be torn from you.*[21] I also rejected *fanaticism and enthusiasm* in my own and my reader's name. I have said it, and adopting the simplest construction, do not proofs of the most extensive plots croud upon us from the very lessons of the Sect? Can common sense, nay can the strongest prejudice, refuse to admit such powerful evidence?

Plots of the Sect against PROPERTY.

Let him who may wish to preserve his field, his house, or the smallest part of his property, under this patriarchal life, go back to the *lesser Mysteries*; there let him hear the Hierophant teaching the adept, that it would have been happy for man,

> Had he know how to preserve himself in the primitive state in which nature had placed him!—But soon the unhappy germ developed itself in his heart, and rest and happiness disappeared. As families multiplied, the necessary means of subsistence began to fail. *The Nomade or roaming life ceased; Property began; Men chose fixed habitations; Agriculture brought them together.*

21   Chap. I.

What were in the eyes of the Sect the dreadful consequences of this deviation from the Nomade or
Patriarchal life?—Why the Hierophant hastens to
tell us. *Liberty was ruined in its foundations, and
Equality disappeared.* This *Patriarchal* or *Nomade* life is then no other than that which preceded *property*, the building of *fixed habitations*, of
houses, cottages, *or the cultivation of your fields.* It
was this beginning of property therefore, the building of habitations, the cultivation of lands, which
struck the first mortal blow at Equality and Liberty.
Should any one wish to return to the *Patriarchal* or
Nomade life with such wretches as these apostles
of Equality and Liberty, let him begin by renouncing his property; let him abandon his house and
his field; let him, in unison with the Sect, declare,
that the first blasphemy which was uttered against
Equality and Liberty was by the man who first said
my field, *my* house, *my* property.

It must be voluntary blindness, indeed, in the
man who will not see the hatred conceived and the
Conspiracies entered into by the Sect against titles
or pretensions to, nay against the very existence of
property. It will acknowledge none, nor can it in
any shape be compatible with their explanations of
Equality and Liberty, or with that primitive state
of nature which no more entitles you or me to the
possession of this gold or silver, or that field, than
it does a third person.

Here it is not simply the question of establishing
the *Agrarian Laws*, where lands, riches, and other

properties are to be equally distributed among all; it is not simply to abolish the distinction of *rich* and *poor*; no, every property is to be destroyed, that of the poor like that of the rich. The first man who was weary of the *Nomade*, roaming, vagabond, and savage life, built a cot and not a palace. The first who furrowed the earth was in quest of bread and not of gold; but he nevertheless, according to the principles of the Sect, was the man who struck the first deadly blow at Equality and Liberty. Poor or rich man then, according to the doctrine of the Sect, the field you have recovered from the waste, and that you have cultivated, belongs to me equally as to you, or else to nobody; I, though idle, and inactive, am entitled to the fruit of your labours; I have a right to share those fruits which you have raised on the land which I left uncultured. Does not *Equality* disappear, whether it be a poor or rich man who shall pretend to be entitled to or say this field is mine, I have that property? If the poor man has a title to his property, has not the rich man also one? Treasures and palaces are no more property than the cot or cottage. Here an Illuminée spies want, there abundance; Equality and Liberty are every where banished; Despotism or Slavery is universal. Nevertheless, Equality and Liberty in his eyes are the rights of Nature, and he beholds them mortally wounded on the first appearance of property, when man became stationary. Poor or rich, you all imbrued your hands in this foul assassination of Equality and Liberty when you pretended to property; from that instant you are both involved in the curse pronounced in the mysteries; you are both objects of the Conspiracies of the Sect from the first instant that you dared assert your right to your habitations whether cots or palaces, to your properties whether fields or domains. But these cannot be the whole of the secrets; they are only those of the lesser mysteries. Weishaupt has revealed them to his Epopts; he reserves the grander secrets for his *Mage* and *Man-King*; then let any man rich or poor harbour, if he can, a hope of seeing the Sect respect his property. Or rather, let him behold the Sect at present pillaging the rich in favour of the poor. The last mysteries or ultimate conspiracy will take place; and then the poor man will learn, that if Illuminism begins by pillaging the rich, it is only to teach him that he is no better entitled to his property than the rich man was, and that the time is near when he will also be pillaged and fall a victim to the curse which has been pronounced against every proprietor.

The progress of this Sophism is worthy of remark. If we judge by its present growth, what a gigantic form will it assume for posterity! The Genevese Sophister of Equality and Liberty, anticipating the modern *Spartacus*, had already dogmatically asserted, "That the man who, having enclosed a piece of ground, first took upon himself to say *this is mine*, and found beings *simple enough to believe him*, was the true founder of civil society." He then continues:—

THE ANTISOCIAL CONSPIRACY

> What crimes, what wars, what murders, what
> miseries, what horrors would that man have
> spared mankind, who, tearing down the fences
> or filling up the ditches of this new enclosure,
> had called out to his equals, beware of hearken-
> ing to this impostor, you are ruined if ever you
> forget that *the fruits belong to all, though the
> land belongs to none.*[22]

How many crimes and spoliations would Rousseau have spared the French Revolution, if, con-
temning so disastrous a paradox, he had said with
more judgement and veracity, "The first man who
enclosed a piece of land and took upon himself to
say, *this belongs to nobody,* I will cultivate it, and
from sterile it shall become fertile; I will follow the
course which nature shall point out to me, to raise
sustenance for me, my wife and children, and this
land will become my property. The God of nature,
who as yet has given it to nobody, offers and will
give it to him who shall first cultivate it in reward
for his labour.—The first man who held such language, seconding the views of nature, and meeting
with beings *wise* enough to imitate him, was *the
true benefactor of mankind.* He taught his children and his equals, that they were not made to
dispute the wild fruits of the earth one with another, nor with the savage beasts of the forest; no, he
taught them, that there existed social and domestic virtues far preferable to the roaming and often
ferocious life of the *Nomades.* His posterity was

22 Discourse on the Inequality of Stations, vol. II.

blessed, his generations were multiplied. If it was not in his power to avert all the evils, he at least destroyed the first of them, that sterility which stinted the very growth of life and drove the scanty population of the earth into the forests like wild beasts, and too often assimilated them to the lion or the tyger, to whom they frequently fell a prey."

Had the Sophister of Geneva held this language, he would not have exposed himself to the ignominy of being the precursor of Weishaupt.—But human imbecility has lavished its praises on this paradox, and have decorated it with the name of Philosophy! The Bavarian Sophister adopts the doctrine of Rousseau, and the delirium of pride has only refined on the phrenzy of wickedness. That which in the mouth of the master had been but a paradox in support of the wildest independence, becomes in the scholar (without divesting itself of its folly) the blackest of conspiracies.

It is now too late to say, that those were the wild chimeras of the Sophisters; at present we are compelled to say, such are the plots contriving against all and each one's property, plots which have been awfully illustrated by the spoliation of the Church, of the Nobility, of the Merchants, and of all rich proprietors—Let them be called chimeras if you are so determined; but remember, that they are the chimeras of Weishaupt, of the genius of conspiring brigands, of a genius the most fertile in sophisms and artifice for the execution of those plans supposed to be chimerical. What Jean

Jaques teaches his Sophisters, the modern Sparta-cus infuses into his Illuminized legions, *The fruits belong to all, the land to none.* He farther states in his dark recesses, When property *began, Equality and Liberty disappeared*; and it is in the name of this Equality and of this Liberty that he conspires, that he invites his conspirators to restore mankind to the Patriarchal or wandering life.

Against paternal authority. Let not the reader be imposed upon by the term *patriarchal* life. The Illuminizing Hierophant speaks of Abraham and of the Patriarchs, of the father *priest and king*, sole *sovereign* over his family. He is not to expect to see the father sur-rounded by his children, exercising the sweetest of all dominions, and each child, docile to the dic-tates of nature, revering the orders and anticipat-ing the will of a beloved father. No; this empire is as imaginary as his priesthood. We have seen in the degree of *Mage*, that the iluminized Patriarch can no more pretend to the acknowledgement of a God than can an Atheist. We must then begin by withdrawing from the Patriarchal life that inter-esting sight of the father offering up to heaven the prayers of his children, sacrificing in their name, and exercising in the midst of them the functions of the priest of the living God. In the next degree of the mysteries all his dominion over his chil-dren is to disappear, as his priesthood has already done. Nor was I afraid to assert in the beginning of this work. *If Jacobinism triumphs—your very children shall be torn from you.* I now repeat it;

all this pretended sovereignty of the father is but a conspiracy against the paternal authority. The proofs are extant in the codes of the Sect.

Here again is Weishaupt deprived of the glory of the invention. Rousseau and the Encyclopedists had long since told us, that *the authority of the father ceased with the wants of the son*; this was one of their principles of rebellion. The man who invented his Illuminism only to convert it into the common sewer of every antichristian and antisocial error, could not leave your children in the dark as to these lessons of independence, though under the sanctuary of the paternal roof; nor with respect to the pretended right of governing themselves, and of acknowledging no other law than that of their reason, as soon as they were strong enough to disobey, or no longer needed your assistance. Tell the illuminizing Hierophant, that your children belong to you; it will be useless, for he has already answered, *"The paternal authority ceases with the wants of the children; the father would wrong his children, should he pretend to any authority over them after that period."* This is but a principle laid down in the lesser mysteries. Follow up the consequences, or rather leave it to the revolution to develope such a principle. The reader will soon see to what this authority of the father is reduced. Scarcely can the child lisp the words Equality and Liberty, or that of Reason, when the commands of his parents become the most horrid despotism, oppression, and tyranny.—Nor is the

Patriarchal sovereign to expect any more affection than obedience from his subjects or his children. In imparting the doctrines of Equality and Liberty, the Hierophant had taught them to blaspheme the *love of one's family even still more than the national love, or the love of one's country*, as being the more direct and innnediate principle of the most disastrous *Egoism*. Let the father then enquire by what bonds his children still remain united to him, or how they are subjected to him, when, without fear, they may openly resist his Patriarchal power as soon as their feeble arms have acquired sufficient strength to gather the fruits which were to serve them as food. No, this hellish Sect acknowledges no ties. All those of nature, as well as those of government or religion, were to be dissolved in Weishaupt's last mysteries. The child, like the savage tyger of the forest, was to abandon his parents when strong enough to go alone in quest of his prey. And this is what the Sect calls restoring man to his primitive state of nature, to the Patriarchal life, to those days when filial piety compensated for all the necessary laws of civil society. Yes, it is by the most abandoned depravation of all morals, by the extinction of the purest and justest sentiments of nature, that these conspirators consummate their last mysteries. In the name of Equality and Liberty, they abjure the love and authority of their country; in that name they curse the authority and love of their own family.

As I proceed in revealing these plots, I know not

whether the reader does not frequently ask himself, What then can these men want? Have they not fortunes to preserve in our state of society? Have they not children in their families? Can they be conspiring against themselves? or, are they ignorant that their conspiracies will fall back upon themselves?— Those who can propose such questions are little acquainted with the enthusiasm of error when inflated by the spirit of independence and pride, of impiety and jealousy. They have not, like us, heard the cant of the heroes, demi-heroes, and *sans-culottes* of the revolution—They will be equal and free; they will it above all things.—It must cost them many sacrifices, but they are ready to make them—They will lose their fortunes in the pursuit, but you will not preserve yours—He that served will become the equal, nor will he recognize either God or man above him.—Have we not seen the prince of the fallen angels exclaiming in his pride,

> — Here at least
> We shall be free;—
> Here we may reign secure, and in my choice
> To reign is worth ambition, tho' in hell:
> Better to reign in hell, than *serve* in heaven.

It is not to one of Weishupt's adepts that the ties of nature are to be objects. He must be as heedless of the duty he owes to his parents as of the affection due to his children, or the baleful consequences of the mysteries cannot affect him. Can the reader have forgotten the precept laid down for the *Insinuators or Recruiters?—The principles; look always to the principles, never to the consequences.* Or, in other words, strenuously support and insist upon these great principles of Equality and Liberty; never be frightened or stopped by their consequences, however disastrous they may appear. These wretches, blinded by their pride, do not know, then, that one single consequence proved to be false, contrary to nature, or hurtful to mankind, is a sufficient demonstration that both nature and truth hold the principle in detestation as the prime mover of these disasters. These madmen, with all the confidence of an atheistical Condorcet, when once become the adepts of Weishaupt, will exclaim even in the very tribune of the National Assembly, *Perish the universe, but may the principle remain!* They will not see, that this principle of Equality and Liberty, devastating human nature, cannot be an Equality and Liberty congenial to mankind. These unhappy men fall victims, perishing under the axe of these disorganizing principles, and spend their last breath in crying, *Liberty and Equality* for ever. No; they are all ignorant of the power of error stimulated by pride, who could think of counteracting the plots of the Sect by the cries of nature, or even by the self-interest of the illuminized adept.—They have not sufficiently comprehended the artifice with which the Hierophant insinuates, vivifies, and inflames the enthusiastic zeal of his adepts.

The reader may rest assured, that villany never slumbers; it watches incessantly the opportunity for the completion of its views. It will persuade the imbecile adept, that all his wants are to disappear on the establishment of the reign of Equality and Liberty; that he will be as free from wants as the savage; that Nature shall provide for them; and this heedless adept thirsts after such an Equality. If the adept ruffian be taught that *the fruits belong to all, though the land to none,* he will easily find means of obtaining his share.

But am I really thinking of reconciling the adepts with their plots? What is it to them whether you see any agreement between them or not? Villany, we all know, is replete with contradictions; but is it the less wicked on that account, or are its crimes less real? In vain would the reader object and say, What can these men want with their monstrous Equality, with their plots against our civil laws, our title to even the very name of property? Must we then, to please them, abandon our habitations; must we renounce all arts and sciences, and end with burning our cities, towns, and villages, to follow them in herds like the savage and Nomade clans?—Are half the inhabitants of the globe to be slaughtered, the better to scatter these roaming herds? What can be the object of those arts and sciences, and particularly of those Minerval academies of Illuminism? Can it be for the propagation of science, or the involving mankind again in the disasters of barbarism, that all this parade of science is made? Can these Illuminées resemble the Goths, Eluns, or Vandals? And is Europe once more threatened with an inundation of barbarians like those which formerly sallied from the North?—In answering such questions, the reader may expect that I would put certain restrictions on the views of the Sect. Nothing like a restriction or qualification. No; you must renounce all the arts, all the sciences; you must begin by firing your habitations, not only your cities, towns, and villages, in short all your fixed habitations, unless you stop the disorganizing career of the Sect. Yes, wherever its legions shall be at liberty to act and accomplish the grand object of the Sect, there you may expect to see those scenes of plunder, rapine, and devastation, which heretofore traced the awful progress of the Huns, Goths, or Vandals; and this inference is fairly drawn from the very Code of the Sect.

Has not the reader heard the Hierophant insinuating the designs of the Sect upon the arts and sciences? Has he not taught the adept to answer, when asked what misfortunes reduced human nature to slavery, that *it was civil society, the state, governments, and sciences?* Has he not heard him exclaim, When shall the day come when, *the clod of useless sciences banished form the earth,* man shall recognize no other but the savage or nomade state, and which the Sect styles patriarchal, primitive, natural? Has he not declared, that the happiness and glory of the Sect would be at its zenith when, beholding those happy days, it could say, *This is our work? (Wenn die beschleünigung dieser periode, unser werk ist?)*[23] Are we to be duped by the name of *Minerval Academies*, with which the Sect decorates its schools? Can we observe there any other study than that of applying the sciences to the subversion of science, as well as to the total annihilation of all religion or society, when we remark the anxiety with which the Sect puts the following questions to the adept on his coming out of these academies, wishing to know what progress he has made in its principles before he is admitted to the illuminized priesthood:

"Do the *general* and *common* sciences to which men apply infuse real light? Do they lead to true happiness? Are they not rather the offspring of variegated wants, or of the anti-natural state in which men exist? Are they not the invention of crazy brains laboriously subtle?"[24] The reader has heard these questions, he has heard the Sect blaspheme science, and will he still believe that Illuminism recognizes any other sciences but those of the man-savage equal and free, roaming in the forests? Have not the revolutionary devastations, the multitude of monuments fallen beneath the hatchet of the Jacobin brigand, already demon-

---

23 See above, the Prince Illuminée.

24 *Befordem die gemeine wissenschaften warhafte aufklärung, wahre menschliche glückseligkeit; oder sind sie viel mehr kinder der noth, der verfielfältigten bedürfnisse, des wiedematürlichen zustandes errindungen spitzfindiger eider köpfe?*

strated the frantic hatred of the modern Vandals? But the mysteries elucidate this enigma in a clearer manner.

Reader, give vent to your indignation. Ask again. What can this Weishaupt be? What are these adepts of Illuminism? Treat them as barbarians, as Huns, as Ostrogoths; but see him smiling at your contempt, and teaching his adepts to honour themselves by imitating, and glory in the hope of hereafter surpassing, the disastrous devastations of those barbarians.—Do you know in what light the illuminizing legislator views these northern clans sallying from their forests and desolating the most flourishing countries of Europe, firing its towns, beating down its empires, and strewing the earth with ruins? He complacently beholds the precious remains of the patriarchal race, the true offspring of Nature; it is with their hatchets that he means to regenerate mankind, and shape them out to the views of the Sect. I did not note the lessons of the Hierophant on this subject, when lecturing the future Epopt.—Hear the account which Weishaupt gives of these clans, when he pretends to historify human nature, at that epoch marked in the annals of Europe as a scourge, and called the inundation of the barbarians. Here is his description:

At that period when all Europe had fallen prey to corruption,

> Nature, which had preserved the true race of men in its original vigour and purity, came to

the assistance of mankind. From distant, but poor and sterile countries, she calls those *savage nations* and sends them into the regions of luxury and voluptuousness to infuse new life into the enervated species of the south; and with new laws and morals to restore that vigour to human nature which flourished until an ill-extinguished germ of corruption infected even that portion of mankind which originally arrived in so pure a state,

or those barbarians the pretended regenerators of Europe sent by Nature.

Such are the encomiums lavished by the Sect on the Goths and Vandals. You thought it would be offending this illuminized tribe to compare them to barbarians; whereas they glory in the comparison. History has described these northern clans as carrying every where fire and sword, as ravaging countries, firing towns, destroying the monuments of the arts, depopulating empires; their course is to be traced by ruins and wastes, and in their train appear ignorance and the iron age. But in the eyes of the adept this is not the exceptionable part of their conduct; on the contrary, it was by such means that they were to regenerate mankind, and second the grand object of nature. These barbarians leave the regeneration in an imperfect state; in time they adopt our usages and manners; they are civilized; the plains rise once more in fertile crops; society is re-established; science returns; the arts flourish under the protection of the laws; towns are re-peopled; the *savage and primitive* race, confounded among the citizens, is subjected to the same laws, and governments acquire their pristine lustre.

Here, in the eyes of the adept, is the grand crime of these barbarians; the Hierophant, deploring their fall, exclaims,

> Oh had there remained any sages among them, happy enough to have preserved themselves from the contagion, how would they sigh after, and ardently wish to return to the former abodes of their ancestors, there again to enjoy their former pleasures on the banks of a rivulet, under the shade of a tree laden with fruit, by the side of the object of their affections! It was then that they conceived the high value of Liberty, and the greatness of the fault they had committed in placing too much power in the hands one one man—It was then that the want of Liberty made them sensible of their fall, and seek means of softening the rigour of Slavery;—but even then their effors were only aimed against the tyrant, and not against tyranny.

It is thus that the insidious and declaiming Sophister, but able Conspirator, leads the adept through the labyrinth of his lesser mysteries, not barely to imitate these barbarians, but to surpass their devouring rage, by constancy, perseverance, and the perpetuation of their devastations. Thus are to be explained all those questions on the danger of reconquering *Equality and Liberty* only to lose them again. Hence those exhortations to unite and support each other; to increase their numbers; and to begin by becoming powerful and terrible—You have already done it, for the multitude sides with you—The wicked, who fear you, seek protection beneath your banners—Henceforward your strength will be sufficient to bind the remainder of mankind, subjugate them, and stifle vice in its origin.[25]

Such will be the explanation of the revolutionary rage and madness which has levelled beneath its blows such a multitude of majestic and invaluable monuments of the arts and sciences—The cry of indignation rising from every class suspends for a moment the sanguinary crimes of the Jacobin Vandal, and he even pretends to weep.—Wait, and the last mysteries shall be accomplished; wait, and you shall see the awful bodings of the Hierophant fulfilled, and with fire and sword shall he annihilate your laws, your sciences and arts, and erase your towns and habitations.

Here in particular is to be found the origin of that revolutionary ferocity, that thirst of blood, those insatiable proscriptions, those incessant executions, and finally those banishments more artfully cruel than the relentless guillotine. Yes, the time draws near when they shall *bind the hands, subjugate, and crush* in their origin, what the Sect calls the *wicked*, or, in other words, all who are

---

25 *Nun seyd ihr stark genug den noch übrigen rest die hande zu binden, sie zu unterwerfen, und die bosheit eher in ihrem keime zu ersticken.*

proof against their vile efforts; the time for *subjugating* and *destroying* every citizen zealous in the cause of Religion, or wishing to support the laws, civil society, or property. Like Huns and Vandals, the Sect has begun its career; but it will carefully avoid terminating it like them; the devastations of its followers shall be perpetuated, and they will be Vandals to the last, until Religion, property, and the laws shall be irrecoverably lost. Such atrocious plots are only the consequences of the lesser mysteries; but trust the author of the Sect, the modern Spartacus, for the farther developement of them. Has he not told you, that his last mysteries were but the consequences, a clearer and more absolute exposition of the foregoing secrets of the Order? He informed you, that nations, together with their laws and social institutions, shall vanish, and that they shall disappear before the all-powerful arm of his adepts, or his modern Vandals. What new secret then remains to be discovered, unless it be that no time shall blunt the sword or slack the unrelenting fury of his proselytes; that they shall persevere until the end of time in their Vandalism, lest Religion, society, science, arts, the love of their country, and respect for property, should shoot forth again, and overshadow the venemous growth of his Illuminized Equality and Liberty?

But Spartacus is not to be contented with these last secrets of the Conspiracy; his pride cannot endure that others shoud usurp the glory of the invention. Hitherto we have seen him play upon the credulity of his adepts, inflame their zeal, and acquire their respect by the pretended antiquity of his Order; and successively attribute the honour of instituting his mysteries to the children of the Patriarchs, the Sages, even to the god of Christianity, and to the founders of the Masonic Lodges. But now the time is come when the adept, initiated in the higher mysteries, is supposed to be sufficiently enthusiastic in his admiration of the Order for the chiefs no longer to fear *to disclose the real history of Illuminism.*[26] Here they inform him, that this secret society, which so artfully led him from mystery to mystery, which has with such persevering industry rooted from his heart every principle of Religion, all false ideas of love of the country or affection for his family, all pretensions to property, to the exclusive right to riches, or to the fruits of the earth; this society, which took such pains to demonstrate the tyranny and despotism of all that he calls the laws of empires; this society, which has declared him free, and teaches him that he has no sovereign but himself, no rights to respect in others, but those of perfect Equality, of absolute Liberty, and of the most entire independence; this society is not the offspring of an ignorant and superstitious antiquity, it is that of modern philosophy; in a word, it is of our own invention. The *true father of Illuminism is no other than* SPARTACUS WEISHAUPT.

---

26   *Original Writings,* vol.II., letter from Knigge to Zwack.

We must also perceive by many of Weishaupt's letters, that this latter part of the secret, which attributed to him the whole honour of the invention, always remained a mystery to the greater part of his *Mages* and *Men-Kings*. Those alone who, under the title of Areopagites, formed the grand council of the Order, were to be made acquainted with the real chief and founder, except in certain cases where an adept was judged worthy of so distinguished a mark of confidence.[27] Whatever merit the adept might boast, Weishaupt knew no higher recompence than to tell them in the end, "This general overthrow of the Altar, of the Throne, and of all Society, is a conception of my own; to me and to me alone is due the whole glory."

I have revealed the disastrous secrets of Illuminism; I have laid open the gradation and progressive degrees, the long chain of artifice, by which the Sect prepares its adepts for the last mysteries, to behold them stript of their veil without shuddering, and to embrace them with enthusiastic ardour.—We must either commit the Code of the Sect to the flames, and deny the truth of its annals; even refuse the evidence of the familiar correspondence of *Spartacus* Weishaupt the founder, and of *Philo*-Knigge the principal compiler; we must dispute all the agreements of its most arduous co-operators, or else must we wait, as the only possible demonstration, the entire and fatal execution of these disastrous plots, before we positively pro-

---

27　*Original Writings*, vol. I, let. 25, to Cato. Vol. III.

nounce, that the sole object of their infernal plans and of their frantic wishes is no other than the total overthrow of every Altar, of every Throne or Magistracy; the annihilation of all authority and of all civil or religious society; the destruction of property whether in the hands of the rich or of the poor; and the very arts and sciences which can only be cultivated in civil society are to be banished from the face of the earth. *Liberty and Equality*, together with the most absolute independence, are to be the substitutes for all rights and all property: Our morals and social intercourse are to make place for the savage, vagabond, roaming life, which the Sect alternately decorates with the name of *Nomade* and of *Patriarchal*. The means to be employed in operating this change will be found in the artifice, deceit, illusion and wickedness which the Sophisters are masters of, until the force of numbers shall have declared for the Sect; but when at length, powerful in numbers, the Sect shall have acquired strength, it shall not only *bind hands*, *subjugate*, murder, ravage, and renew all the horrors and atrocities of the barbarians of the North, but also surpass those Vandals in the arts of destruction, and without pity or distinction butcher all that part of mankind that shall dare to oppose the progress of the Sect, presume to heave a sigh over the ruins of religion, society, or property, or attempt to raise them from their ashes.—If I have not proved that such are the wishes, the secret machinations of the Sect and of its flagitious principles, let me be informed what is to be understood by proof, or what is to be the operation of evidence on the human mind.—Were it possible that any of my readers still consoled themselves with the idea that the frantic extravagance of these plots surpassed their wickedness, let them remember that I have still something more to say.—I have still to investigate the laws and interior government of the Sect, laws adopted for the destruction of every other law or government, and that it might hereafter prove, that however monstrous the object of the plots of the Sect may be, it was far from being chimerical.

Tenth and Last Part of the Code of the Illuminées.—Government of the Order—General Idea of that Government, and of the Share which the Inferior Classes of Illuminism Bear in It.

I t is not enough for the founder of a Sect of Conspirators to have fixed the precise object of his plots, the trials and degrees through which his adepts are to rise insensibly to the acquisition of his profoundest mysteries. His accomplices must form but one body animated by one spirit; its members must be moved by the same laws, under the inspection and government of the same chiefs, and all must tend toward the same object. Such a genius as Weishaupt's could not be suspected of having overlooked in his Code so important a means of success. From what I have already said, the reader will have observed what connection

Of the separate and collective government of the Lodges.

and subordination subsisted in the gradation of his mysteries; how all the adepts of a given town formed, notwithstanding the inequality of their degrees, but one and the same academy of Conspirators, while each one laboured separately at the overthrow of religion and the laws in the state in which he lived. In this academy the *Candidate* and the Novice are under the direction of the *Insinuator*, who introduces them into the *Minerval Lodges*; these Lodges are governed by the *Minor Illuminées*, who in their turn are inspected by the *Major Illuminées*. Next to these preparatory degrees follow the intermediary or Masonic degree, called the *Scotch Knight*; and his power extends on the one side over the *Major Illuminées*, and on the other over the Illuminized Masons; or, in general, over all that part of the Order stiled in the Code the *lower part of the edifice*. After these we meet the *Epopts* and *Regents* or *Princes* of the lesser mysteries, and lastly, in the higher mysteries, the *Mage* and *Man-King*.

The aggregate of all these degrees forms a complete academy of Conspirators, and impendent ruin threatens the country where such a one exists. The Magistrate and the Citizen may expect to see their property and their religion annihilated. The Sect recognizes no country but the universe, or rather acknowledges none; the very term *country* is a blasphemy against the rights of man, against Equality and Liberty. What each member in his particular academy performs by himself, is performed throughout all of them by the Sect in general, and the combined efforts of the whole are regularly directed toward the concerted plan of devastation. The Miners have received their instructions, that each may bore his subterraneous galleries, and lodge the chamber of his mines in such a manner that partial explosions may forward the views of the Sect, without endamaging the grand chamber, which shall involve the whole world in the premeditated explosion of universal destruction. To produce this effet, general laws and mutual communications, common chiefs and directors are requisite. Each Conspirator, wherever his field of action may lie, must be certain that he acts in concert with his Brethren, that he will not be crossed in his plans, but on the contrary meet every where with support and corresponding agents.

Weishaupt was aware, that the farther the sphere of disorganization was to extend the more perfect should be the organization of his power. The more eager he was to call down universal anarchy, and make it take place of all laws, the more did he wish to establish subordination, and concentrate the forces of the Order, the better to direct its motions. To accomplish this, the oath of implicit obedience to Superiors was not enough.—It was not sufficient for the adept to have blindly submitted his life and fortune to the despotic power of unknown chiefs, should they ever suspect him of treachery or rebellion. The Superiors themselves were to be bound by laws and principles common to all, that they might proceed in all points by a regular and uniform impulse.

Weis-haupt meditates on the laws of his Government.

It cost Weishaupt much meditation before he could perfect his plan of government as he wished. Five years after the establishment of the Sect, he writes *"This machine of ours must be so perfectly simple that a child could direct it;"* and still later he writes, "allow me time to digest my speculations, that I may properly marshal our forces."[1]

So preoccupied was Weishaupt with his speculations on the government of the Sect, that all his letters written to his principal adepts are replete with his maxims and political councils. One must have heard or read them one's self to credit the deep-laid villany of his means and his infernal policy. Here is an example:

In the same letter which I have justed quoted of the 15 Asphandar 1151 he gives two rules to be inserted among the instructions of the Areopagites—The one, to be on the reserve with Candidates *from among the class of the rich*, because that sort of men, *proud, ignorant, averse to labour, and impatient of subordination*, only seek admission to our mysteries in order to make them an object of ridicule and mockery; the other, not to take the smallest pains to prove, that Illuminism is in the sole possession of the true Masonry, *because the best possible demonstration is to give none*. Let Weishaupt himself explain a third law, which is to make a part of his political collection.

---

1   Letters to Cato, 15th March 1781, and 16th February 1782.

That we may be uncontrolled in our dis-
course, let our pupils remark, that the Superi-
ors enjoy a great latitude in that respect; that
we sometimes speak in one way, sometimes in
another; that we often question with great as-
surance only to sound the opinions of our pupils, and to give them an opportunity of showing it by their answers. This subterfuge repairs
many errors. Let us always say, that the end will
discover which of our observations conveys our
true sentiments.—Thus we may speak sometimes in one way, at others in a quite different
one, that we may never be embarrassed, and
that our real sentiments may always be impenetrable to our inferiors. Let this be also inserted in the instructions, *etiam hoc inseratur in-*
structioni. It would still have a better effect, if
you gave in charge to our *Major Illuminées* to
vary their conversation with their inferiors, for
the above reasons, *ex rationibus supra dictis*.

These insertions of Latin are from Weishaupt, who
frequently makes use of that language in his letters.
It is immediately after having given these principles of government to the Areopagites, the chief
superiors of his Illuminism, that Weishaupt adds,

I entreat that the maxims which are so often to
be found in my letters may not be lost. Collect
them for the use of our Areopagites, as they are
not always present in my mind. With time they
might form an excellent *political* degree. Philo
has long since been employed about it. Communicate also your private instructions to each
other, which may in time grow into an uniform

Code. Read them attentively, that they may become familiar to you. Though I know them well and practise them (*und auch damach handle*) they would take me too much time to digest them systematically. These maxims once engraved in your mind, you will enter better into my plans, and you will proceed more comformably to my mode of operation.[2]

Let the reader also profit of these instructions. They must bear evidence in my behalf while revealing all the monstrous artifices of the remaining part of the Illuminized Code. From these long meditated combinations, sprang forth that chain of laws which was to direct each Illuminée in all his procedings.

General subordination and gradation of the superiors.

We first remark in this government, as a means of subordination, a general division of command, as well as of locality. Each department has a particular Lodge for its adepts; each Minerval Lodge has a Superior from among the preparatory class, under the inspection of the intermediary class. In the second place, we find the division into districts which contain several Lodges, all which as well as the Prefect are under the direction of the superior of the district whom the Order calls *Dean*. He is also subjected to the *Provincial*, who has the inspection and command over all the lodges and deanries of the province. Next in rank comes the *National Superior*, who has full powers over all within his nation, Provincials, Deans, Lodges, &c.

---

2   Letter to Cato, 15th March, 1781.

&c. Then comes the supreme council of the Order, or the *Areopagites*, presided by the real General of Illuminism.

The same hierarchy is preserved in their communications. The simple Illuminée corresponds with his immediate superior, the latter with his Dean, and thus gradually ascending to the National Superiors. These latter are in direct correspondence with the Areopagites; and they alone are acquainted with their residence. In this council there is always a member whose particular office is to receive and answer their letters, and to transmit orders, which gradually descend to the person or persons who are the objects of them. The Areopagites alone are entrusted with the name and residence of the General, excepting in cases which I have already noticed, where particular confidence or remarkable services have gained for an adept the signal honour of knowing and approaching the modern Spartacus.

Correspondence of the superiors and inferiors.

It is easy to perceive, from the very regulations of the first degrees, how voluminous this correspondence must be. Each brother, in the first place, as the *natural scrutator* of his co-adepts and of the prophane, is bound to transmit at least one letter each month, with a statement of all the observations he has made, whether favourable or detrimental to the Order. He is also to give an account of the progress which himself and his brethren have made; of the orders he has received, and of their execution; and he is each month to inform

Its object.

his higher superiors whether he is pleased with the conduct of his immediate superior. Each brother Insinuator is to report the progress of his Candidates, and the prospect he has of adding to their number. Next, to swell the volume, come all the portraits of the adepts, the extracts of tablets or daily observations made on the friends or enemies of the Order: also the minutes of initiations, the characters and lives of the initiated, the returns made by the Lodges, those by the superiors, and an infinity of other articles which the Illuminée is bound to make known to his chiefs.—All this occurs without noticing the numberless orders and instructions which are perpetually transmitting to the inferiors.

Its gradation.

Beside the secret language already explained, and of which the grand object was to render this correspondence unintelligible to the prophane, the Sect had secret means of transmitting their letters, lest they might be intercepted. The Order styles these letters relative to their illuminism *Quibus Licet*'s (or to those who have a right). The origin of this appellation is the direction of these letters which consists of the two words *Quibus Licet* or simply the initials Q. L. When, therefore, we find in the *Original Writings*, that such an adept has been fined in such a month for having neglected his Q. L., it must be understood that he let such a month pass without writing to his superiors.[3]

---

3   Vol. II., let. 2, from Spartacus to Cato.

When the letter contains secrets or complaints which the adept chooses to keep from the knowledge of his immediate superior, he adds to the direction *Soli* or *Primo* (*to him alone, to the first*); this letter will then be opened by the Provincial, the *National Superior*, or will reach the *Areopagites*, or *General*, according to the rank of the person from whom it comes.

Next to these general means of graduated correspondence, come the meetings proper to each degree, and their respective powers. We have already seen, that those of the Minerval academy are regularly held twice a month. The Minor Illuminées, who are the magistrates of this degree, and the Major Illuminée, or the Scotch Knight, who presides in them, have no direct share in the government, farther than to inspect the studies and watch over the conduct of the young Minervals, and report to the lodges of the Major Illuminées. It is in that degree that the authority begins to extend beyond the limits of the assembly. It is to the Major Illuminées that all the tablets or instructions relative to the brethren of Minerva are sent. Here these statements are digested, and receive additions and notes, before they are forwarded to the assembly of the next superior degree. Here are judged and determined the promotions of the Novices, Minervals, and Minor Illuminées; and also all differences and contests which may arise in the inferior degrees, unless the importance of the debate be such as to require the interference of a higher tri-

Powers of each degree respecting this correspondence.

bunal. They are the guardians of the first tablets and reversal letters of the brethren.—As to what knowlege a Major Illuminée may have acquired either relative to other secret societies, or to employments or dignities which might be obtained for adepts, he is bound to report it to his lodge, which will note it, and inform the assembly of the Directing Illuminées or Scotch Knights.[4]

When treating of the intermediary degree of Scotch Knight, I gave an account of their particular functions, and especially their charge of superintending the Masonic Lodges. The part they act in the general government of the Order chiefly consists in hearing all the *Quibus Licets* of the preparatory classes read in their chapters, even those of the Novices which had already been opened by the officers of the Minerval school: the latter having only the power of deciding provisionally on these letters.

The authority which the Scotch Knights exercise over this correspondence seems to give still more propriety to their denomination of intermediary degree. Their *Quibus Licets* are directly sent to the Provincial Lodge, which is composed entirely of adepts initiated in the mysteries of the Order. But the Knights read all letters coming from the preparatory class which have not the distinction of *Primo* or *Soli*. They classify and make extracts from all the *Quibus Licets* of lesser importance coming from the inferior degrees, and send the general ex-

---

4   Degree of Major Illuminée, Instruction 4th.

tract to the Provincial. To these extracts they subjoin a circumstantial account of every thing that
is going forward in the lodges of the preparatory
class, to which they transmit all the orders coming from the adepts initiated in the mysteries, even
from those of the highest degrees with the very
names of which they are unacquainted, and thus
constitute a link between the two extremities.[5]

Both the intermediary and preparatory classes,
however, form but the lower part of the edifice.
The Prefects of the Chapters of the Scotch Knights
are rather tools than superiors; they receive their
impulse from the higher mysteries. It is there that
the grand polity of the Order is to be sought for in
the instructions laid down for the Epopt and the
Regent, and these are the instructions which, beginning with those of the Epopt, demand our utmost attention.

---

5   See this degree, Instruction the 2d, No. 2.

CHAPTER XIV.

Of the Government and Political Instructions for the Epopts.

nlighten *nations*; that is to say, efface from the minds of the people what *we* call religious and political prejudices; make yourself master of the public opinion; and, this empire once established, all the constitutions which govern the world will disappear.—Such are the grand means, such the hopes, on which Weishaupt has been observed in his mysteries to have grounded his hopes of success. We have seen even the sciences involved in the vortex of his conspiracies. They were to be swept into the common mass of ruin with religion, laws, Princes, nations, our towns and stationary habitations.—Vandalism and the era of barbarism were

Object of these Instructions.

to be revived, and science was to be reduced to that of the *nomade* and *savage* clans *equal and free.* This gigantic mass of destruction could be the operation but of a general corruption and perversion of the public opinion, which is itself dependent on science, or at least upon the reputation of wisdom and knowledge which he possesses who pretends to instruct us. To prepare the attack, therefore, it was necessary to make the sciences serve under the banners of the Sect in the cause of their own annihilation, and through their means captivate the public opinion in favour of the Sect. Its errors once triumphant, and every thing dear and sacred to man *vandalized* and overthrown; sciences would of themselves shrink back and vanish from before the man savage and free. Such were the fruits of Weishaupt's meditations, such the spirit which dictated the laws given to his Epopts. This degree was to extend the conquests of the Sect over public opinion by science, or, in other words, to dispense its anti-religious and anti-social doctrines under the bewitching name of science. He entirely devoted his degree of Epopts to the sciences, and may be said to have forestalled them all, that he might usurp and dictate to the public opinion; or, rather, tainted them all, to make them subservient to his views; well assured that they would not survive the contagion. In his Minerval degree, it was the minds of the young adepts that he wished to pervert; but in his degree of Epopt, his means and views expand, and, under the same mask, he aims at nothing less than the perversion of the whole universe. He formed it into a secret academy, whose hidden ramifications, widely spreading throughout the globe, were, by means of the disastrous laws he had combined, at one blow to annihilate all society and the empire of science.

The plan may appear inconceivable, and above the reach of the most disorganizing genius; but let the reader remember how clearly it has been proved in the mysteries, that Weishaupt and his followers were firmly resolved to bring back the human race to the days of the Huns and Vandals, and, by means of this Vandalism, to all the ignorance of the *nomade* and *savage clans*; and to reduce the standard of science to that of the Equality and Liberty of *Sans-culotism*. Let the reader now condescend to follow me in the exposition of the lessons which the Sect has appropriated to the instruction of its Epopts, and the organization of their academy.

The illuminized Priests, or Epopts, are presided over by a Dean chosen by themselves. They are to be known to the inferior degrees only under the appellation of Epopt—their meetings are called *Synods*. All the Epopts within the circle of the same district compose a Synod; but each district shall contain no more than nine Epopts, exclusive of the Dean and Prefect of the Chapter. The higher superiors may attend these Synods.

The academy of the Epopts.

Of the nine Epopts, seven preside over the sciences distributed under as many heads in the following order:

I. *Physics.*—Under this head are comprehended Dioptrics, Catoptrics, Hydraulics and Hydrostatics; Electricity, Magnetism, Attraction, &c.

II. *Medicine*—comprising Anatomy, Chirurgery, Chymistry,&c.

III. *Mathematics.*—Algebra; Architecture, civil and military; Navigation, Mechanics, Astronomy, &c.

IV. *Natural History.*—Agriculture, Gardening, Economics, the Knowledge of Insects and Animals including Man, Mineralogy, Metallurgy, Geology, and the science of the earthly phenomena.

V. *Politics*—which embraces the study of Man, a branch in which the Major Illuminées furnish the materials; Geography, History, Biography, Antiquity, Diplomatics; the political history of Orders, their design, their progress, and their mutual dissentions.

This last article seems to have the divers Orders of Masonry in view. A *nota bene* is added in the original, with a particular injunction *to attend to this article*, which the dissentions of the Illuminées and Freemasons had probably rendered of great importance to the Sect.

VI. *The Arts.*—Mechanics, Painting, Sculpture, Engraving, Music, Dancing, Eloquence, Poetry, Rhetoric, all the branches of Literature; the Trades.

VII. *The Occult Sciences.*—The study of the
Oriental tongues, and others little known, the secret methods of writing, the art of decyphering;
the art of raising the seals of the letters of others,
and that of preserving their own from similar
practices; *Petcsh aften zu erbrechen, und fur das
erbrechen zu bewahren.* The study of ancient
and modern hieroglyphics; and, once more, of
secret societies. Masonic systems, &c. &c.

Should the reader feel his indignation roused by
the art of raising the seals and violating the secresy
of letters, and at seeing an adept named in each
district to preside over this strange science, let him
not forget that I am but the translator and tran-
scriber of the code of the Sect.[1]

The two remaining Epopts, who in the synod
are named to preside over any particular science,
are made secretaries to the Dean, and serve him as
coadjutors. These functions once distributed, the
Epopts are to renounce all other business political
or domestic, and every care but that of perfecting
themselves in the branch of science which they
are to superintend, and of secretly forwarding the
brethren of the inferior degrees in the sciences to
which they had devoted themselves.

The grand object of this institution is to inspire
the pupils with the greatest confidence in the Order, from an idea that it will furnish them with all
the means and lights necessary for the prosecution
of the study they have adopted. The Insinuators

---

1   Instructions for this degree, nos. 1, 2, 3, 4, 11.

have held out the promise to them, and the Order has engaged to fulfil it. This idea of a scientific society, and of which they have the honour of being members, is to encourage in them a docility and veneration for their chiefs naturally due to men whose precepts appear to be emanations of light and of the most transcendent wisdom. The artifice in some sort answers to the promise.

Every Novice, on being admitted into the Minerval schools, was to begin by declaring to what art or science he meant to devote himself, unless indeed his pocket was to be assessed for the tax which his genius could not pay. This declaration is transmitted from the inferior lodges to the Provincial, who forwards it to the Dean; by whom notice of it is given to the Epopt who presides over that particular branch of science; and he inscribes his name on the list of those pupils whose labours fall under his inspection. In future, and by the same conveyance, all the essays, discourses, treatises, &c. which the Sect requires of the young Minerval are transmitted to the same Epopt. The first advantage accruing to the Order from this law is the pointing out to the inspecting Epopt those whom the code calls the *best heads of the Order*.

Should any doubts arise in the minds of the pupils, any difficulties to vanquish, or any questions to propose; they have been taught that the Order is the fountain of science, that they have but to apply to their superiors, and light will instantaneously shine upon them. They are ignorant as to who these superiors may be; but that will not hinder their doubts and questions from reaching the presiding Epopt: and he has divers means of solving them, and of never being taken unawares.

In the first place the Epopt must have prepared himself for certain questions, which he either has or ought to have foreseen. Many of them will have been already solved by his predecessors, by his brother Epopts of other districts or even nations. The Order is exceedingly careful in collecting all these answers, and putting them into such hands as may employ them according to the views of the Sect. Each Epopt is particularly enjoined to study those which relate to his branch; he is even to make an alphabetical entry of them on his tablets, that he may always have them at hand whenever he wishes to turn to them. If, notwithstanding all these precautions, the Epopt should find himself unprepared or unable to solve the difficulty proposed, he will apply to the Dean, who will send the required solution or have recourse to the Provincial. But, lest the Superiors should find their occupations too often interrupted by such applications, it is expressly enjoined to the Epopt not to have recourse to them but in cases of absolute necessity, and not to make the acquisitions of their Superiors an encouragement to their own negligence.—It may so happen, that the Provincial is not able to give the required solution; he will then propose it to all the Epopts of his province. If that does not succeed, application is made to the

National Inspector, and from him it is referred to the Areopagites and General. On such occasions all the learned men of the Order are consulted. Before this last appeal, it is ordained in the statutes, that the Epopt may propose the questions to the prophane; but in so doing he is on no account to discover that the *Sect* has recourse to, or stood in need of their information, nor what use it makes of it. This is particularly enjoined to the presiding Epopt in the following terms:—"As often as your own knowledge and that of your pupils shall not suffice, you may ask the advice of learned strangers, *and turn their knowledge to the advantage of our Order, but without letting them perceive it:*" (*ohne dass sie es bemerken*). This precaution is the more to be insisted on, as one of the grand objects of the Epopts must be, "to attain such perfection in science, that Illuminism shall never be beholden to the prophane; but that the latter, on the contrary, shall perpetually stand in need of the lights of the Order."[2]

That the Epopt may not recur too frequently to the superiors, or to the prophane, an artifice has been invented by which he may profit of all the acquisitions of the pupils of his district, while he makes them believe that the whole flows from the unknown superiors. This artifice consists in proposing such questions as he is not perfectly master of, to the different lodges, and then studying and combining the various answers that he receives. All

2   Instructions for ths degree, no. 2, 5, 6, 9.

the Epopts of the province do as much in their several districts. Each one selects those parts which he has judged worthy of notice in the productions of the lodges; these he inspects, and lays them before the provincial and annual assembly. There other Epopts are employed in compiling from these selections, and in preparing the required solutions of the proposed questions, or in commenting on such passages as may elucidate others that may hereafter arise. The same plan is followed in all the provinces, and the reports of the provinces will form a new collection to be digested under the inspection of the National Chief, or even of the Areopagites. This will be a new treasure for the secret library of the Epopts, and furnish them with new means of maintaining in the minds of their pupils the high idea they have conceived of the knowledge of their Superiors.[3] It will also furnish materials for the formation of a systematic Code or complete course of study for the use of the Sect.[4]

Here we cannot but remark how much arts and sciences would be benefited and promoted by the labours of a society which, actuated by quite other views, and despising that affectation of secrecy, should employ the same means and be animated with a similar zeal in the discussion of useful truths. But the united efforts of the Epopts are concentrated in their pursuit of science, only to debase it, by directing all its powers toward the overthrow

3   Nos. 5 and 12.
4   No. 15.

of Religion and Governments, the triumph of their disorganizing systems, and always under the stale pretext of subjecting mankind to Nature alone.[5]

Should the reader be curious to know to what uses the Epopt turns all the science which he is supposed to acquire daily, let him observe the questions which this presiding Illuminée either solves himself, or proposes for the solution of the adepts. Let his judgement on the questions and on their tendency, be guided by the expressions of the Code:

"The Epopt," says the Code,

> must keep a list of a very great number of important questions proper for investigation, and which he may eventually propose to the young adepts.—In the branch of practical Philosophy, for example, he will propose for investigation the question, how far the principle is true, *that all means are allowable, when employed for a laudable end?* How far this maxim is to be limited to keep the proper medium between Jesuitical abuse, and the scrupulosity of prejudice?—Questions of this nature shall be sent to the Dean, who shall transmit them to the Minerval schools for the investigation of the young adepts, and their dissertations will swarm with a multitude of ideas, *new, bold, and useful,* which will greatly enrich our *Magazine.*[6]

---

5   *Das der Order die bisherigen systeme entbehren, und eigene, auf die natur allein gegründete systeme seinen anhanger vorlegen konne.*

6   *Ibid.,* no. 7.

We despise this infamous aspersion on the Jesuits. Let those pass sentence on them who have learned to judge them by their conduct and by their real doctrines, and not by calumnious assertions, or satires which, in spite of all the powers of genius and irony, have been justly condemned by various tribunals as replete with falsehood and misrepresentation.[7] Let those who have been educated by the Jesuits pronounce on these atrocious imputations of the Illuminées; I do not think myself bound to follow the example of the celebrated Hoffman, Professor at the University of Vienna, one of the most formidable adversaries of the Illuminizing Sect, by inserting a long justification of that persecuted Order.[8] But it is impossible not to observe, that the legislator of Illuminism has not the most distant idea of modifying or limiting this famous principle, *the end sanctifies the means*; his object is evidently to give rise to ideas, *new, bold, and useful* to the Sect; or, in other words, to dispose the young adepts hereafter to decide as he has already done, that *nothing is criminal*, not even robbery or theft, provided *it be useful* to the views and forward the grand object of Illuminism. He wishes by means of these questions to acquire an early insight into the minds of the adepts, and to distinguish those who will hereafter be the most

---

7   See Art. Pascal in the *Historical Dictionary* of Flexier Dureval [Flexier de Reval —Ed.], last Edition.

8   *Vide Hoch wichtige erinnerungen*—Von Leopold-Alois Hoffman, sect. V., page 279 to 307.

worthy of his higher mysteries, by the greater or smaller disposition they show to stifle the cries of conscience and remorse in the perpetration of the crimes necessary for the future success of his plots. This is the sum total of the science to be carefully inculcated by the Epopts in the branch of *practical* Philosophy.

With respect to Religion, it is not even admitted among the sciences to be studied by the Epopts; the Code has, however, furnished them with a means of traducing and blaspheming it.—That the Epopt may never be at a loss for questions of this nature to solve or propose, he will have them noted on a register in alphabetical order. "For example," says the Code, "at the Letter C in the register of secret sciences and hieroglyphics the word Cross is to be found, and under it is the following note—For the antiquity of this hieroglyphic, consult such a work, printed such a year, such a page, or else such a manuscript, signature M."[9] It is not necessary to be endowed with any extraordinary share of perspicacity to see that the whole object of these pretended *secret sciences*, or hieroglyphics, is merely to teach the young pupils to view the Cross in no other light than as an ancient hieroglyphic erected by ignorance and superstition into a symbol of the redemption of mankind. The illuminized explanation of this glorious symbol will, doubtless, long remain buried in the Occult Sciences of the Order. Meanwhile we may defy them to point out in the

9   *Ibid.,* no. 15.

history of mankind any nation whatever revering the cross as the symbol of salvation anterior to the grand epoch when the Son of Man died on the cross to consummate the triumph of Christianity.

The Epopts have also their historians and annalists, and their duties are laid down in the Code. The following rules may be remarked: Each province of Illuminism must have its historian, in imitation of the ancient annalists and chronologists. He is to keep a journal, in which, beside facts of public notoriety, he will particularly collect, and even give *the preference to, anecdotes of secret history.*—He will endeavour to redeem from oblivion all men of merit, however deep they may have sunk into obscurity— He will make them known to the Provincial, who will inform the Brethren of their situation—Each Provincial will have a Calendar of his own, in which (instead of saints) for each day of the year shall be inscribed the name of some man as an object of veneration or execration, according as he has merited or demerited of the Sect.

My name may perhaps be inscribed under the black letter; but I anticipate the glory and consolation of seeing it by the side of that of Zimmerman and of Hoffman, who, like myself, are entitled to the sable wreath twined by Illuminism for its most strenuous opponents. But how different is that to which the Code declares that all the Brethren *may aspire!*—Probaby, to be seated beside a Brother *Mirabeau* or a *Marat.*

The same laws ordain, that the Chronologist shall inform the Minerval Lodges of all memorable facts.—He will not fail to insert all mean and odious actions, nor to paint them in their proper colours. He will not pass unnoticed *those of men occupying the first dignities, or enjoying the highest consideration.*[10]

Next to the laws of the historian follow those for the Epopt who superintends that branch of science relating to politics, and particularly to the knowledge of mankind. The reader has already seen what stress the Order lays upon this science, and how much they make it depend on the spirit of observation—Let no Brother pretend to the dignity of Epopt, nor to the honour of presiding over any branch of science, until he has answered the three following questions—What is the spirit of observation?—How is this spirit to be acquired, and what constitutes a good observer?—What method is to be followed, in order to make just and exact observations?—When an Epopt has sufficiently distinguished himself by his answers on these heads, to be judged worthy of being chosen the chief of the observers or scrutators, he is entrusted with all those notes which the reader has seen the Sect so carefully collecting on the character, the passions, the talents, and history of the Brethren. When these notes contain the portrait or life of any adept more than commonly interesting, he will make him (without naming him) the object of various

---

10   *Ibid.*, no. 18.

questions to be proposed to the Minerval Schools. He will ask, for example, What are the ideas which a man, with such and such passions or dispositions, will adopt or reject?—How on such data can such and such inclinations be encouraged or weakened?—What adept could be employed with most advantage in such a business?—What must such a man's ideas be on Religion and Governments?—Can he be looked upon as being superior to all prejudices, and ready to sacrifice his own personal interest to that of Truth?—Should he be deficient in confidence and attachment, what means should be employed to invigorate them, and what sort of man would be the fittest for such an undertaking?—Finally, *what employment in the state, or in the Order, would he fill to the greatest advantage, or in which would he he the most useful?*

The Scrutator in chief digests these answers into a proper statement, which he sends to the Dean. The Provincial receives it from the Dean, and is thus enabled to form his judgement, whether that particular adept *be a moral, disinterested, beneficent man, and free from all prejudice; whether he can be useful to the Order, and in what way he can be best employed.*—From the result of such observations, the scrutinizing Epopt will carefully select rules and general maxims on the knowledge of mankind. He will make a compilation of them, and transmit them to the Superiors.[11]

---

11   *Ibid.*, no. 18.

"By means," says the Code, "of these and such like observations, the Order will be enabled to make discoveries of every kind, to form new systems, and to give on all subjects irrefragable proofs of its labours and its immense fund of science; and the public will give it credit for being in possession of all human knowledge."[12]

Lest any of the prophane should partake of this honour, or that any one of the members should not direct these sciences toward the object of Illuminism, precautions are taken in the Code to assure the exclusive advantage of these labours to the Sect.

> Particular parts of these sciences and discoveries may be printed by permission of the Superiors; but the law adds, not only these books shall not be communicated to any of the prophane, but as they will never be printed elsewhere than at the presses of the Sect, they will only be entrusted to the Brethren according to the rank they hold in the Order.[13]

> That our worthy co-operators may not be divested of the glory of their labours, every new principle laid down, machine invented, or discovery made, shall for ever bear the name of its inventor, that his memory may be revered by future ages.[14]

---

12   *Ibid.,* no. 20.

13   *Ibid.,* no. 17.

14   *Ibid.,* no. 23.

On the same grounds it is strictly enjoined, that no member shall ever communicate to the prophane any discovery that he may have made in the Order—No book treating of these discoveries shall be printed without the permission of the Superiors; and hence arises the general regulation, that no Brother shall publish any of his productions without leave of the Provincial. He also is to decide whether the work is of a nature to be printed by the secret presses of the Order, and what particular Brethren may be allowed the perusal of it—Should it be necessary to dismiss any of the Brethren from the Order, the local Superior is to receive notice that he may have the necessary time to withdraw from him not only the manuscripts, but even the printed works of the Order.[15]

The Illuminizing Legislator, in justification of all these precautions, alledges, in the first place, the undeniable right vested in the Order to all the labours of its Brethren; then the lure of secrecy, which stimulates curiosity and the thirst of science; finally, the advantage accruing to the sciences themselves, by being preserved among men who only impart them to others so prepared as to render them of the greatest possible utility—Beside, says he, every man has it in his power to make himself an Illuminée if he pleases, and to partake of their science; and who better able to render them useful to mankind, or to preserve them, than we are? After this justification, which the reader may ap-

15   *Ibid.*, no. 24.

preciate, he returns to his Epopts, and tells them, that it is incumbent on them to direct and turn all the sciences toward the views of Illuminism. "The wants of every country are to be maturely considered, as well as those of your district; let them be the objects of deliberation in your Synods; and ask instructions of your Superiors." Then the Legislator makes a sudden transition, and expands his views far beyond his Lodges. The reader will scarcely suspect whither they tend. Let him read, and learn the grand object of the Epopts, what conquests they are to make for the Order, and whither they are to extend the systems of Illuminism. "You will," abruptly exclaims the legislator, "incessantly form new plans, and try every means, in your respective provinces, to seize upon the public education, the ecclesiastical government, the chairs of literature, and the pulpit."[16]—This is one of the grand objects of the Sect; and we shall see the Code treating of it again in another part.

To enhance the merits of his plans, and to insinuate his adepts into the ecclesiastical seminaries, and even into the pulpit, under the shadow of his pretended science,

> the Epopt must find means of *acquiring* the reputation of a man of transcendent learning; wherever he appears, whether walking or stop-

---

16 *Müssen stets neue plane entworfen und eingeführt werden: Wie man die hande in erziehungswesen, geistliche regierung, lehr, und predigt-stühle in der provinz bekomme. Ibid.,* no. 28.

ping, sitting or standing, let *rays of light* en-
circle his head, which shall enlighten all who
approach him. Let every one think himself
happy in hearing the pure truth from his lips.
Let him on all occasions, combat prejudice; *but
with precaution*, and according to the rules laid
down, until dexterity and *with all the respect
due to the persons he is addressing*.[17]

Who could believe that these were lessons given
to a modern Vandal by his disorganizing legislator,
whose heart thirsts after the *happy* period when
that *encircling light* of his Epopts shall have *Vandalized* the whole universe, and nations shall have
disappeared from off the face of the earth?

But the Epopt has yet to aim at another conquest, that of the empire over the literary world.

In the literary world certain writings generally
take the lead for a time, according to the fashion, and inspire feeble minds with admiration.
At one time the enthusiastic productions of Religion, at another the sentimental novels of wit,
or perhaps philosophical reveries, pastorals,
romances on chivalry, epic poems, or odes, will
inundate the republic of letters. The Epopt will
turn all his skill toward bringing into fashion
the principles of our Order, the sole tendency of
which is the happiness of mankind.

Or, in other words, those baleful principles which,
under the pretence of rendering human nature

---

17   *Ibid.*, No. 2.

more happy and united in one family, aim at nothing less than destroying every Religion, every title to *property*, every town, every fixed residence, and every nation.

"Our principles must be made fashionable, that the young writers may diffuse them among the people, and serve the Order without intending it."[18]

"In order to raise the public spirit, he must with the greatest ardour preach up *the general interest of humanity, and inculcate the utmost indifference for all associations or secret unions which are only formed among the subjects of one particular nation.*"[19] Here the impious legislator blasphemously cites for an example Christ, and his pretended indifference for his family. Because Christ died for the redemption of *all* mankind, because his affection for the most holy of mothers never made him lose sight of that great work, is that a ground on which the illuminizing Epopt shall persuade his simple auditory, that to love all mankind is to dissolve the bonds of nations?

As a farther rule for acquiring this literary empire, "He will take care that the writings of the members of the Order shall be cried up, and that the trumpet of fame shall be sounded in their honour. He will also find means of hindering the reviewers from casting any suspicions on the writers of the Sect."[20]

---

18   *Damit junge schriftsteller dergleichen unter das volk ausbreiten, und uns, ohne dass sie es wissen, dienen.*

19   *Ibid.*, no. 3.

20   *Ibid.*, no. 4.

With respect to the *Literati*, and *writers who, without belonging to the Order, show principles coinciding with ours*, should they be what we call good, *"class them among those who are to be enrolled. Let the Dean have a list of those men, and from time to time he unit hand it about among the brethren."*[21]

Let us now take a cursory view of these laws, and of their gradual tendency to infect the whole literary world. In its Minerval academies the sect begins by forming its pupils; and the care with which its disorganizing principles are instilled into the young adept has already been displayed. Lest any of these principles should swerve from the grand object, the Epopts oversee all the schools of the same district; these latter have their provincial assemblies, where every thing is prepared, combined, and foreseen. At this assembly the Epopt attends, bringing with him *his notes* and observations on his particular district, and on those means which may there contribute to the advancement or disparagement of the Illuminizing principles and science. The minutes of these assemblies are sent to the National Inspector, who overlooks the whole, and sees that the original spirit is every where preserved; and the Areopagites hold the same line of conduct with respect to all nations that he does within his particular one. Hence then the Minerval academies, the Epopts, the Provincials, the National Inspectors, in a word, the disorganizing

21   *Ibid.*, no. 5.

whole, form but one and the same invisible academy, spreading its subterraneous ramifications, every where infusing the same principles, actuated by the same spirit, and subjected to the same laws: and these laws, this science, are but the machinations and the forebodings of universal impiety and disorganization.

But the union and universality of this conspiring academy is not sufficient for the Sect; it extends its views to the public schools and to the pulpit. The man of letters, the transcendent genius, all are to bend beneath its laws, and fashion is to aid its plots. From the child that spells, to the Doctor enveloped in mazy science, all are to be subjected to Illuminism; and science itself, so instrumental to the progress of the Sect, shall sink beneath the effort of bringing forth that Vandalism which is to annihilate the altar and the throne, all laws, individual property, and national society.

Let the reader compare the mysteries of the Sect with the code of its Epopts, and pronounce if such be not the real tendency of this Empire of Science. Horror impresses the mind, and indignation rises at such a sight.—But the monstrous legislator who has compiled them pretends that they are entitled to the admiration of the young adepts; and it is his Epopts who are to inspire them with this admiration. "You must," says he, "infuse so great a respect for the sublimity and sanctity of our Order, that a promise made by the adepts on the honour of Illuminism shall be more binding than the most sacred oath."[22] At length the Atheist has found an equivalent for the name of God. He seeks bonds to bind his followers, and he has broken those of conscience; he appeals to honour, and perverts it into a bond of villany.

> *He* (says Weishaupt) *who shall dare violate the oath he shall have sworn on the honour of my Society, shall be declared infamous. I care not what his rank may be, his infamy shall be proclaimed throughout the whole Order, and it shall be so without remission or hope of pardon.* My intention is, that the Members should be informed of this, that they should deliberately reflect on the sacredness of this oath in my Order, I mean that the consequences of it should be clearly and warmly represented to them.[23]

The Epopts charged with this mission are of a degree too much revered in the Order to compromise their dignity. They attend, at pleasure, the meetings of the inferior degrees, but they are never to occupy any office in them, excepting that of Prefect of the Scotch Knights. Their presence might overawe and intimidate the young adepts, and thus be detrimental to the observations they are ordered to make; for (so far from constraint), the Epopt is to endeavour to study them in their most unguarded moments. He is therefore never to intermix with them but as their equal. There is

---

22   *Ibid.*, no. 29.
23   *Original Writings*, vol. II., let. 8, to Cato.

a particular law forbidding him to disclose the degree or the class to which he belongs, or even his costume.[24] Thus, hiding his superiority, and seated on the same benches beside the young adepts, he exercises his functions of Scrutator more freely among them in thier mutual intercourse, and he judges better of the talents of each. His lessons, coming apparently from an equal, will sink deeper into their minds; and, without betraying his authority, he will the better observe their progress and their failings.—Should any of these pupils have shown a zeal and fidelity beyond all doubt, he may take them into his confidence; he will point them out to the Dean, who may call them about his person and make them his *Acolites*. The Dean may even throw a great part of the weight of his correspondence on them, and carry them to the Synod of the Epopts, until they shall have shown themselves worthy of being initiated to all the mysteries reserved for this class.[25]

Thus ends that part of the Code which is to be communicated to the Epopts. The following Chapters will delineate the laws and instructions which are to guide their conduct when admitted to the degree of *Regent* or *Prince* of *Illuminism*.

---

24 *Ibid.*, no. 31.

CHAPTER XV.

Instructions for the Regent or Prince Illuminée, on the Government of the Order.

T he prominent feature of all the instructions given by the Illuminizing Legislator to his Epopts is the consecration of their degree to the perversion of the public opinion, and to the attainment of the empire of sciences, that he may direct them all to the support of his disorganizing Equality and Liberty and to universal anarchy. This mission of perversion requires an assiduity to which not many men are equal; but adepts may be found, who, unable to distinguish themselves in such missions, may yet be endowed with a sufficient zeal and with the necessary talents for the superintendance and direction of the Brethren.

First part of these Instructions.

There are others again whose disastrous successes are to be recompensed by the higher employments in the Order; and it is from these two classes of Epopts that the Order selects its Regents. It is also for their instruction that the Legislator descends into all the gubematory minutiæ of his Illuminism.—His instructions are comprised under four different heads. I. General System of Government for the Order.—II. Instructions for the degree of Regent.—III. Instructions for the Prefects or Local Superiors.—IV. Instructions for the Provincial.[1]

I have, it is true, been obliged to anticipate many parts of this Code when unfolding the artifices of the lower degrees; but as a confirmation of what has already been exposed, in order to bring the different objects within one point of view, and to show the dangers of his disastrous combinations, let us attend to the Legislator when treating of the whole collectively. What particularly endeared this degree of Regent to Weishaupt was, that part of his instruction which takes a general view, and which lays open the progressive plan to be observed in the government of the Brethren. The reader perusing the instructions in the same order in which Weishaupt has written them, will more easily conceive the cause of his predilection.

---

1   *Last Works of Philo and Spartacus*, degree of Regent.

Chapter XV

Instruction A.
Plan of the General Government of the Order.

I. The most high and excellent Superiors of the illustrious Order of true *Freemasonry* do not immediately attend to the minutiæ of the edifice.—They must not, however, on that account be considered as contributing less to our happiness, by their counsels, their lessons, their plans, and the many and powerful resources with which they furnish us.

II. These excellent and most gracious Superiors have established a class of Masons to whom they have entrusted the whole plan of our Order. This class is that of the *Regents* . . . . .

III. In this plan our Regents hold the first dignities. Until admitted to this degree, no person can hold the office of *Prefect* or of *Local Superior*.

IV. Every country has its national Superior, who holds an immediate correspondence with our *Fathers*, at the head of whom is a General who holds the helm of the Order.

V. Under the *National* and his *Assistants* are the *Provincials*, who each govern their Circle or their Province.

VI. Every Provincial is surrounded by his Counsellors.

VII. Each Provincial also commands a certain number of Prefects, who may in like manner have their coadjutors in their districts. All these, as well as the *Dean*, belong to the class of Regents.

VIII. All these offices are for life, excepting in cases of deposition or ejectment.

IX. The Provincial is to be chosen by the *Regents* of his province and the *National Superi-*

313

ors, and approved by the *National.*—[I do not understand how the Code distinguishes between the several *National Superiors* and the National in chief; unless it be, that it denotes in this place as Superiors those who are called a little higher up *Assistants (Gehulfen)* of this chief.]

X. The whole success of Illuminism depending on the *Regents,* it is but just that their domestic wants should be provided for. They shall therefore be the first supplied from out of the funds of the Order.

XI. The Regents of each Province form a particular body immediately under the Provincial, whom they are to obey . . . . .

XII. The offices of Illuminism not being considered in the light of dignities, nor of *places of honour,* but as mere *employments* freely accepted, the Regents must be always ready to labour for the good of the Order, each according to his situation and to his talents. Age is never to be set forth as a title. It may often happen, that the youngest is chosen Provincial, and the eldest only a Local Superior or Counsellor, should the one live in the center, while the other only inhabits the extremity of the Province; or, should the former, on account of his natural activity or his station in life, be more fitted for the place of Superior than the latter, though far more eloquent. In many cases, for example, a Regent is not to think it beneath his dignity to offer himself to discharge any of the lesser offices in the *Minerval churches* (lodges) in whch he may be useful.

XIII. That the Provincial may not be overburdened with too extensive a correspondence, all the *Quibus Licets,* and all the letters of the Regents, shall pass through the hands of the

Prefect, unless the Provincial gives Orders to the contrary.

XIV. But the Prefect shall not open the letters of the *Regents*. Those he must transmit to the Provincial, who will forward them to their proper destination.

XV. The Provincial has the power of convoking the whole of his Regents, or merely those whom he may think proper, considering the exigencies of the Province. He who cannot attend according to his summons must give the proper notice at least four weeks prior to the meeting. Beside, he is always to be ready to give in an account of what he has done for the Order until that period, and show willingness to fulfil the intentions of his Provincial and of his high Superiors. The convocation of Regents must take place at least once a year.

XVI. The following instruction (B) will point out more particularly to the Regents those objects to which they must chiefly attend.

XVII. It has been already observed, that great attention is to be paid to the gradually procuring of funds for the Order. This may be accomplished by attending to the following rules:

Each province is to be entrusted with the expenditure of its own monies, and only remit small contributions to the Superiors for the expences of postage. Each Lodge also is to enjoy the full propriety of its funds (*eigenthümlich*)— when *for any great enterprize* the assembly of the Regents levy contributions on the funds of the different Lodges, they shall be considered but as loans, and shall be made good to the Lodges with full interest.

Has the Illuminizing Legislator then forgotten, that it was PROPERTY which gave the first *deadly blow to Equality and Liberty?* Certainly not; but more than one *great enterprize* will be necessary to prepare the LAST, which is to *annihilate all property* whatsoever; meanwhile the Order is glad to enjoy its own, and to make the inferior Lodges believe that they are not to be pillaged of any thing that belongs to them.

> The Provincial has no fund allotted to him, but he has an exact return of all those of his province.

> The general *receipts* will consist—1°. In the contributions paid on the receptions of Masons (*freymaurer-receptions-gelder*)—2°. In the over-plus of the monthly contributions—3°. In voluntary subscriptions—4°. In fines—5°. In legacies and donations—6°. In our commerce and traffic (*handel und gewerbe*).

> The *expences* are—1°. The expences of the meetings, postage, decorations, and some few joumies—2°. Pensions to the poor brethren who have no other means of subsistence—3°. Sums paid for the *promotion of the grand object of the Order*—4°. Sums paid for the encouraging of talents—5°. The expences of experiments and trials—6°. For widows and children—7°. For foundations.

Thus terminates the first part of the instructions for the Regent. After the reading of this, which takes place on the day of his inauguration, his attention is called to the following:

Instruction B *for the*
whole degree of Regent

The reader has seen (*ut supra*, art. xvi.) the Regent forewarned to pay a particular attention to this second part of the instructions. Let the reader also profit of the hint. He will see that many of the *arcana* of the Sect still remain to be revealed.

2d part of the instructions.

> I. The object of the Order being to render man more happy, virtue more attractive, and vice less powerful, it is necesssary that our brethren, the *teachers and governors of mankind*, should publicly assume an unimpeachable character. A Regent of Illuminism therefore will be the most perfect of men. He will be prudent, provident, ingenious, irreproachable, and of manners so urbane that his company shall be courted with avidity. He is to acquire the reputation of being enlightened, benevolent, honest, disinterested, and full of ardour for great and extraordinary enterprises, all contributing to the general good.

It would be useless to recall to the mind of my reader what is to be understood, in the language of Illuminism, by virtue, vice, or public good. He will therefore on reflection be the less surprised at perusing the following instructions framed for these *virtuous teachers and governors* of mankind.

II. The Regents are to study the means of ruling and governing without betraying any such intention.[2] Under the mask of humility, but of a real and candid humility, grounded on the persuasion of their own weakness, and on the conviction that their *whole strength rests on our union*, they must exercise an absolute and boundless dominion,[3] and must direct every thing toward the attainment of the views of the Order.

Let them avoid a pedantic reserve, at once disgusting and ridiculous in the eyes of the sage. Let them give the example of a respectful submission to the Superiors. Should they be possessed of the advantages of birth, it will be an additional reason for showing their obedience to a Superior born in a lower station of life— Let their conduct vary according to the persons with whom they have to deal. Let the Regent be the confidant of one, the father of another, the scholar of a third; very seldom a severe and inexorable Superior, and even on such occasions let him show with how much unwillingness he exercises such severity. He will say, for example, that he sincerely wishes the Order had given so disagreeable a commission to some other person; and that he is weary of acting the part of schoolmaster with a man who should long since have known how to conduct himself.

III. The grand object of our *sacred legions spread throughout the universe* being the triumph of virtue and of wisdom, every Regent

---

2   *Die Regenten sollen die kunst studieren zu herschen, ohne das ansehen davon zu haben.*

3   *Sollen sie unumschrankt regieren.*

must endeavour to establish *a certain equali-*
ty among men.—Let him take the part of those
who are too much debased, and humble the
proud. Let him never suffer the fool to lord it
too much over the man of wit, the wicked over
the good, the ignorant over the learned, nor the
weak over the strong, though the latter should
in reality be in the wrong.[4]

IV. The means of acquiring an ascendancy
over men are incalculable. Who could enumer-
ate them all? . . . They must vary with the disposition of the times. At one period it is a taste
for the marvellous and extraordinary that is to
be wrought upon. At another the lure of secret
societies is to be held out. *"For this reason it*
is very proper to make your inferiors believe,
without telling them the real state of the case,
that all other secret societies, particularly that
of Freemasonry, are secretly directed by us. Or
else, and it IS REALLY THE FACT IN SOME STATES,
THAT POTENT MONARCHS ARE GOVERNED BY OUR
ORDER. *When any thing remarkable or impor-*
tant comes to pass, hint that it originated with
our Order.—Should any person by his merit
acquire a great reputation, let it be generally
understood that he is one of us."

How smoothly flows this combination of artifice
from the pen of the Illuminizing Legislator! But I
hope that my reader will not expect to find a method in my translation, where the Legislator has dis-
dained method. It is easy to perceive, that to heap

---

4   *Er soli nicht leiden dass der dummere über den klügem—der*
     Schwachere über den starkem, auch wenn dieser unrecht ha-
     ben sollte, zu sehr den meister spiele.

artifice upon artifice is much more his object, than to give a studied connection to principles with which he supposes his adepts to be sufficiently impressed. Or may it not be said, that this disorder is the effect of studied art? But let us proceed and trace the steps of Weishaupt.

With no other object than to give your orders the appearance of coming from a mysterious hand, you may, for example, put a letter under the plate of an adept when dining at an inn, though it might have been a much less trouble to forward it to him at his own lodgings—You may attend large and commercial towns during the time of fairs in different characters, as *a Merchant, an Officer, an Abbé.* Every where you will personate an extraordinary man having important business on your hands.— But all this must be done with a great deal of art and caution, lest you should have the appearance of an adventurer. It is to be well understood, that these characters are not to be assumed in towns where you are likely to be discovered either by the Police or the standers-by.—At other times, you may write your orders with a chemical preparation of ink, which disappears after a certain time.

> V. A Regent is as much as possible to hide from his inferiors all his weaknesses, even his ill-health, or disgusts; at any rate, he is never to complain.
> VI. Here he repeats the instruction on the art of flattering and gaining over women to their cause, already transcribed, page 43.

Chapter XV

VII. You must also gain over to the Order the
COMMON PEOPLE. The great plan for succeeding in this is to *influence the Schools.* You may
also attempt it by liberalities, or by great show
and splendour; at other times by making yourself popular, and even tolerating, with an *air of
patience, prejudices which may hereafter be
gradually eradicated.*

VIII. When you have succeeded any where in
making yourself master of the public authority
and government, you will pretend not to have
the least power, for fear of awakening the attention of those who may oppose us. But, on the
contrary, when you find it impossible to succeed, you will assume the character of a person
who has every thing at his command. That will
make us both feared and sought after, and of
course will strengthen our party.

IX. All the ill success or disgusts which may
befall the Order are to be concealed with the utmost caution from the inferiors.

X. It is the duty of the Regents to supply the
wants of the Brethren, *and to procure the best
employments for them,* after having given the
proper intimation to the Superior.

XI. The Regents shall be particularly cautious and discreet in their discourse;—but shall
carefully avoid any thing denoting the least per-
plexity of mind—There are even some occasions
whereon an extensive genius is to be affected;
on others, they may pretend that their friendship has made them say a word too much; by
these means the secresy of the inferior is put to
the test. They may also spread certain reports
among our people, which may prepare them to
receive ideas which the Order wishes to infuse

into their minds. On all doubtful occasions, the Regent will consult his Superiors by means of a *Quibus Licet.*

XII. Whatever rank or station a Regent may hold in the Order, he will seldom answer the questions of the inferiors verbally, but generally in writing, that he may have time to reflect or even consult on the answers he should give.

XIII. The Regents will unceasingly attend to every thing relating to the grand interests of the Order, to the *operations of commerce,* or such things as may in any way contribute to augment the *power* of the Order. They will transmit all plans of that nature to the Provincial. Should it be a case requiring expedition, he will give him advice of it by some other channel than the *Quibus Licets,* which the Provincial has not the power of opening.

XIV. They will follow the same line of conduct with respect to every thing that tends to influence the Order in general; and find means of putting its united forces in motion at one and the same time.

XV. When an author sets forth principles true in themselves, *but which do not as yet suit our general plan of education for the world; or principles the publication of which is premature; every effort must be made to gain over the author; but should all our attempts fail, and we should be unable to entice him into the Order, let him be discredited by every possible means.*

XVI. *If a Regent should conceive hopes of succeeding in suppressing any religious hous-*

es, and of applying their revenues to our object, for example, *to the establishment of proper* COUNTRY SCHOOLS; he may depend on it, that such a project would be particularly grateful to the Superiors.

XVII. The Regents will also turn their attention toward a solid plan for establishing a fund to support the widows of the brethren.

XVIII. *One of our most important objects must be, to hinder the servile veneration of the people for Princes from being carried too far.* All such abject flattery tends only to make those men worse who are already for the most part of very common and weak understandings. You wil show an example of the proper conduct to be held in this respect. Shun all familiarity with them; behave to them politely, *but without constraint, that they may honour and fear you.* Write and speak of them as you would of other men, that they may be made to recollect that they are but men like other people, and that their authority is a thing purely conventional.[5]

XIX. When there happens to be a man of merit among our adepts but little known by or entirely unknown to the public, no pains are to be spared to acquire celebrity for him. *Let our disguised brethren* every where sound the trumpet of his praises, and force envy and party spirit to be silent.

XX. The essay of our principles and of our schools is most easily and most successfully made in small states. The inhabitants of capitals and commercial towns are too corrupt, too

5 *Eine unserer vornehmsten sorgen muss auch seyn, unter das volke sclavische fürsten verehrung nicht zu hoch steigen zu lassen,* &c. &c.

much a prey to their passions, and think themselves too much enlightened, to submit to our lessons.

XXI. It is useful to send visitors from time to time, or to give a Regent that is travelling the commission to visit the meetings, to ask for the minutes, and to call on the brethren in order to examine their papers or journals, and receive their complaints.—These Plenipotentiaries, presenting themselves in the name of the high Superiors, may correct many faults, and boldly suppress abuses which the Prefects had not the courage to reform, though ready to enforce the commands of the visitor.

XXII. If our Order cannot establish itself in any particular place with all the forms and regular progress of our degrees, *some other form may be assumed. Always have the object in view; that is the essential point. No matter what the cloak may be, provided you succeed; a cloak is however always necessary, for in secrecy our strength principally lies.*

XXIII. For this reason we should always conceal ourselves under the name of some other association. The *infeerior lodges of* FREEMASONRY *are the most convenient cloaks for our grand object, (das schickliche kleid für unsere höhere zwecke)* because the world is already familiarized with the idea that nothing of importance, or worthy of their attention can spring from Masonry.—The name of a literary society is also a proper mask for our first classes. Under such a mask, should our assemblies be discovered, we may confidently assert, that the reason of our holding secret assemblies was partly to give a greater interest and charm to our pursuits; partly to keep off the crowd, and not to expose ourselves to the bantering and jealousy of others; in short to hide the weakness of an association as yet but in its infancy.

XXIV. It is of the utmost importance for us to study the constitutions of other secret societies and to *govern* them. The Regent is even bound, after having obtained leave of his superiors, to gain admittance into those societies, but he must not undertake too many engagements. This is an additional reason why our Order should remain secret.

XXV. The higher degrees must always be hidden from the lower. *A person more willingly receives orders from a stranger than from men in whom he gradually discovers a multitude of defects.* By this precaution one may keep the inferiors in a more proper awe; for they naturally pay greater attention to their behaviour when they think themselves surrounded by persons who are observing them; at first, their virtue may be the effect of constraint, but custom will soon make it habitual.

XVI. Never lose sight of the military schools, of the academies, printing presses, libraries, cathedral chapters, or any public establishments that can influence education or government. Let our Regents perpetually attend to the various means, and form plans for making us masters of all these establishments.[6]

---

6   *Militair-schulen, academien, Buchdruckereyen, Buchladen,*

XXVII. In general, and independent of their particular employment, the grand object of our Regents must be an habitual and constant application to every thing which can in any way add to the perfection and to the power of our Order, that it may become for future ages the most perfect model of government that can enter the mind of man;

or, in other words, that it may be hereafter said, such was the famous association which, by perpetually perfecting its laws and governments, at length taught mankind to cast off every law and every government. It would be useless for me to think of adducing farther proofs to demomstrate that such is the real object of the pretended perfection of Illuminism. The mysteries of the Sect have been too clearly laid open for us to harbour the smallest doubt of their intention. But to acquire this perfection and power for the Sect, Weishaupt has modelled still farther laws for his Regents, according to the different offices they hold in the Hierarchy of the Order.[7]

Dom-capitel, und alles was ein einfluss auf bildung und regierung hat, muss nie aus den augen gelassen werden; und die Regenten sollen unaufhorlich plane entwerfen, wie man es anfangen konne, iiber dieselben gewalt zu bekommen.

7 For the whole of the Second Part of this Chapter see the *Instruction B for the Degree of Regent*, of which it is nearly a literal translation.

Continuation of the Instructions on the Government of the Illuminées.—Laws for the Local Superiors.

reat as the authority of the *Major Illuminées* over the Minerval Academies may appear at first sight, no person of the *preparatory class* is in fact entrusted with any real authority. Even the Scotch Knight in his *intermediate* class does not enjoy any. The Order recognizes as real Superiors none but those who have been initiated into the class of the Mysteries. Even in that class the adept must have attained the degree of Regent before he can be named Prefect for the Scotch Knights, or Dean of his district. Those are the first two offices which the Order considers as having any real authority over the Brethren.

Though the Code expressly declares, that each Superior shall find in his instructions the respective laws concerning his particular duty, it certainly contains none for the office of Dean. A single Chapter is indeed to be found in the Code on his election and consecration. On the first establishment of a new district he is elected by the Provincial; but on his deposition or death the Epopts assemble and choose a successor by the plurality of votes, the Provincial only having the right of confirming such an election. With regard to what the Code terms his *consecration* (*Weihung des decani*), it is generally performed by what is called a Plenipotentiary, and in a sort of barbarous Latin, extremely inelegant. Were not the impiety of it as abominable as the ceremonial is low, it might form an excellent scene for the theatres of Bartholomew fair. The Illuminizing Legislator, a very inferior copyist of Molière's *Malade Imaginaire*, ridicules St. Paul, Moses, and all religious ceremonies, as Molière did the quack disciples of Hippocrates. Little wit is required to scoff at religious rites, and yet our Legislator has only succeeded in being disgustingly impious. Such turpitude is not worthy of our notice, for none but Epopts can admire it; this nevertheless is all the information the Code can give us respecting the Dean.[1]

---

1   Should any adept wish for a specimen of this miserable farce, let him figure to himself an assembly of Epopts in their sacredotal habits. The Delegate opens the piece by Domine aperi os meum: The two Assistants repeat the same—*The Plenipotenti-*

ary Fili mi quid postulas? *The Delegate* Ut Deus et Superiores nostri concedant nobis Decanum hunc quern ad te duco.— *Plenip.* Habetis decretum?—Habemus—Legatur—Communi voto atque consensu superiorum elegimus nobis in Decanum Fratrem N. N. Presbiterum Nostrae Provincial, Majoris Ordinis verum atque prudentem hospitalem, moribus ornatum, sapientem, illuminatum et mansuetum, Deo et superioribus nostris per omnia placentemque ad Celsitudinis vestrae dignitatem adducere, quatenus autore Domino nobis velut idoneus Decanus prae-esse valeat ut prodesse, nosque sub ejus sapienti regimine in securitate ac quiete magnis scientiis aliisque operibus curare possimus—*Plenip.* Disposuisti domui tux?—*The Elect* Disposui—Nosti quanta sit Decani cura et qua poena infligantur infideles et delatores?—Duce me Domine— Ego auctoritate superiorum inductus firmiter sub interminatione anathematis, inhibeo tibi, ne quid de scientiis occultis, vel secreta tibi revelanda abducas, surripias, vel alicui profano communices. Si tu autem aliquid attentare praesumseris, maledictus eris in domo et extra domum, maledictus in civitate et in agro, maledictus vigilando et dormiendo, maledictus manducando et bibendo, maledictus ambulando et sedendo, maledicta erunt caro et ossa, et sanitatem non habebis a planta pedis usque ad verticem. Veniat tunc super te maledictio quam per Moysen in lege filio iniquitatis Dominus promisit. Deleatur nomen tuum in libro viventium, et cum justis non amplius scribatur, fiat pars et hereditas tua cum Cain fratricida, cum Dathan et Abiron, cum Anania et Saphira, cum Simone Mago et Juda proditore. Vide ergo ne quid feceris, quo anathema mereris.—*Here follow the imposition of hands, the exhortations, and the benedictions, all in Latin. The Officiator, extending his hands again on the head of the Elect, terminates the ceremony with the following words*: Sicut ros Hermon qui descendit in montem Sion, sic desecendat super te Dei summae sapientiae benedictio (*see the last works of Spartacus—Nachricht von Weihung eines Decani*).—What execrable impiety must the Sect have infused into its Epopts to expect that such an impious derision of the Scriptures and of the most sacred rites could give them pleasure? Let not the

The same cannot be said of the instructions for the *Prefects*. These Local Superiors may have as many as eight Lodges at a time under their command, partly Minerval, and partly Masonic. The Prefect is the first Regent within his prefecture, and has the direction of all that part of the Order stiled in the Code *the lower part of the edifice*. All the *Quibus Licets* of his district pass through his hands. He opens those of the Scotch Knights, and the Solis of the Novices and Minervals; but every thing else he transmits to the higher Superiors. When he founds new Lodges, or receives new Brethren, he gives the new *Geographical* names and *Characteristics*, which he selects from the list that he has received from the Provincial. He makes a general report to the Provincial of every thing that has happened within his Prefecture once a month; and every three months transmits the reversal letters, the tablets sent by the Scrutators with notes on their *political and moral* conduct, and an exact return of the state of the funds belonging to each Lodge. He decides on the promotion of the Brethren as far as Scotch Knight, but can confer the latter degree only with the consent of the Provincial.—He has the right once a year of commanding all the adepts under his direction to return whatever writings the Order may have entrusted them with—He returns them to those on whose fidelity

---

reader think that I have exaggerated this barbarous cant. The whole ceremony is a buffoonery of the lowest class. Impiety depraves every thing, even the taste for literature.

he has reason to rely, *but not to those whom he may have any reason to suspect, or who are intended to be dismissed.*[2]

The foundation of the Edifice rests solely on the vigilance, experience, and zeal of the Prefect.—And it was to the direction of their conduct in every part of the Government that Weishaupt dedicated his lessons under the following heads:—I. *Preparations.*—II. *Tuition of the Pupils.*—III. *Spirit or love of the Order*—IV. *Subordination.*—V. *Secrecy.*— Each of these articles contains a cloud of those artifices which the reader has seen interspersed in divers parts of the Code, but which now become the peculiar study of the Prefect. I shall only extract the most striking, or those on which the Legislator particularly insists; such, for example, as the following, to be found in the first pages of the head *Preparation.*

> Our strength chiefly consists in numbers; but much will also depend on the means employed to form the pupil—Young people are pliant and easily take the impression.—The Prefect will therefore spare no pains to gain possession of the *Schools* which lie within his district, and also *of their teachers.* He will find means of placing them under the tuition of members of our Order; for this is the true method of infusing our principles and of training our young men: it is thus that the most ingenious men are prepared to labour for us and are brought into

---

2   Instructions C for the Regents, and No. I—X.

discipline; and thus that the affection conceived by our young pupils for the Order will gain as deep root as do all other early impressions.

Under the same head are to be found instructions for the Prefect equally curious, on the propagation of the Order.

> When a new colony is to be founded, begin by choosing a bold and enterprizing adept entirely devoted to the Order. Send him some time beforehand to live on the spot where you intend making the new establishment.
>
> Before you proceed to people the extremities, begin by making your ground good at the centre.
>
> Your next object must be, to gain over such persons as are constant residents, as *Merchants* and *Canons*.
>
> Such missions should only be entrusted to *brethren of independent fortune,* and who would occasion no expence to the Order; for though all the brethren are entitled to succour when in real want, yet those of one province are as seldom as possible to be an expence to the neighbouring ones. Nor are the other districts by any means to be made acquainted with the weakness of the Order in yours. Beside, the funds must find a sufficiency to succour those of the Minerval school who may stand in need of it, that our promises in their case may be performed.

Chapter XVI

You will not seek to extend yourself till you have consolidated your establishment in the capital of your district.

You will seriously examine and cautiously select from the Brethren those who are the most able to undertake such a mission.—You will next consider whether it will be proper to begin your establishment by a *Minerval Church* or a Masonic Lodge.

Pay most particular attention to the man whom you place at the head of the new colony; observe whether he is courageous, zealous, prudent, exact, and punctual; whether fitted for the forming new adepts; whether he enjoys a good reputation or is much considered; whether he is a man of business and capable of a serious and constant application; in short, whether he has all the necessary qualifications for an undertaking of such high importance.

Consider also the locality. Is the place proposed near to or distant from the capital of your district?—Is it a dangerous or safe situation for such an undertaking?—Is it great or small, more or less populous?—By what means can you best succeed, and which can be easiest employed?—What time would be requisite for the perfecting of such an establishment?—-To what persons can you apply on first setting off?—If your first applications be ill made, all future attempts will be fruitless.—What pretence or what name is to be assumed?—How is the new colony to be subordinated or *co-ordinated?* that is to say, what Superiors shall it be under, and with what Lodges shall it correspond?

When you shall have acquired sufficient strength in your new colony, and particularly if our Brethren enjoy the first dignities of the state, if they may freely and openly show themselves formidable to their opponents, and make them feel the painful consequences of counteracting the views of the Order; if you have wherewith to satisfy the wants of the Brethren; if, so far from having to fear from the government, the Order directs those who hold the reins—Then be assured that we shall not be wanting in numbers or in the choice of adepts; we shall soon have more than we have occasion for. *I cannot too strongly recommend this method of proceeding.*

If it be necessary for us to be masters of the ordinary schools, of how much more importance will it be to gain over the *ecclesiastical seminaries and their superiors! With them, we gain over the chief part of the country; we acquire the support of the greatest enemies to innovation; and the grand point of all is, that through the clergy we become masters of the middle and lower classes of the people.*

But remember that great caution is necessary with the Ecclesiastics. These gentlemen are generally either too free or too scrupulous; and those who are too free have seldom any morals.

The legislator then proceeds to the exclusion of the

religious, and tells the Insinuator to avoid the Jesuits as he would the plague.

While perusing these laws, I suppose the reader makes nearly the same reflections which I am tempted every instant to commit to paper.—Should the following article ever meet the eye of a Prince, it will give him ample room for reflection.

> When the Prefect shall have gradually succeeded in placing the most zealous members of the Order in the councils and offices under the Prince, he will have arrived at the full extent of his commission. He will live done much more than if he had initiated the Prince himself.[3]

> In general, Princes are not to be admitted into the Order, and even those who are received are seldom to be permitted to rise above the degree of *Scotch Knight*.

After what has been seen of this degree and those that precede, it is rather extraordinary that Weishaupt should deign to grant admission to Princes; for he did not wait for this degree before he clearly insinuated his plans. Princes, at least, who had not surmised them before their admission to that degree must have been void of penetration indeed. What hopes then could the Legislator entertain of their not perceiving his plots against all

---

3   *Kann der Prafect die fürstlichen Dicasterien und Rathe nach und nach mit eifrigen ordens mitgliedem besetzen, so hat er alles gethan, was er thun konte. Es ist mehr, als wenn er den fürsten selbst aufgenommen hatte.*

legitimate authority? His confidential letters will explain the enigma:—"Brethren," he writes to his Areopagites,

> you will take care to have the following corrections made before you show the constitutions of our degrees to the Elector.—In the degree of *Minor Illuminée* in place of the words *imbecile Monks* say *imbecile men*—In the degree of *Major Illuminée* blot out the words *Priests and Princes are in our way.*—With respect to the degree of *Priest* show no part of it *excepting the discourse on sciences,* and read that over carefully lest any *allusion or reference to any other part of the degree should remain.*[4]

These corrections begin to clear the enigma; a more insidious expedient will veil his plots in complete darkness. "*I mean,*" says Weishaupt when speaking to the Areopagites of the inferior degrees, "*to revise the whole system.*" Then, attributing to the Jesuits his own immorality, he says, "I mean that it should be a complete Jesuitical piece; not a single word shall be found in it that can in any way be cavilled at by religious or political governments. Let us act with caution; do nothing without a reason; things must be prepared and brought on step by step."[5] The adept who has given us the most complete and candid account of the degrees of Illuminism assures us,

---

4   *Orig. Writ.,* vol. II., 2d Jan. 1785.
5   *Ibid.*—Weishaupt's let. 15th March, 1781.

that he had seen a discourse for the degree of
Epopt in which every thing respecting religion
and government was omitted.[6]

Here then we find Weishaupt not only correct-
ing but even forming fictitious degrees to dupe the
princely adept, and to persuade him that the dark
and mysterious recesses of the hireling crew have
been laid open to him, while the real adept smiles
at his credulity. Such artifice certainly aggravates
Weishaupt's criminality. But will that excuse the
princely adept? Notwithstanding the veil artfully
thrown over the impious and seditious principles
of the sect, did he not begin by swearing *obedience and protection* to the Order? His court soon
swarms with Illuminées; he thinks he reigns over
them, but is no more than their stately captive. And
should he fall their victim, will it not be said that
he met with his just fate? What strange madness
can induce Princes to inscribe their names on the
registers of secret societies! Have they not duties
to fulfill toward the public? On what right can their
oaths of submission and protection be grounded,
sworn in the recesses of secret Lodges, to men who
hide themselves from public view, when their labours, cares, and protecting power, are to extend
over the whole state and to all its citizens? On the
throne, or with pretensions to it, do they not de-
gradingly swear obedience and protection to Masters of Lodges! By what right will they promulgate
laws emanating from Lodges? When their subjects

6   *Geschichte der illumin*, Grad., page 66.

swore allegiance and fidelity to them, did those subjects expect to be governed by a slave, or be subjected to laws proclaimed indeed by their Prince, but dictated by some *Master Illuminée* or *Rosicrucian*? And ye, magistrates of the people, who are to sit in judgment over the mutual and disputed claims of the citizens in general, what confidence can be placed in you after you have sworn *obedience* and protection to this illuminizing Sect, even in actions just or *unjust*? Such reflections will rise refulgent from the page of history; and would to God that the Revolution had not already indelibly engraved them!

If ever self-love should have directed the actions of men, and supplied the place of nobler motives, the princely dupe will have found ample matter in the laws of Illuminism to stimulate his, when he but casts his eye on the following article contained in the instructions for the Prefects, or local Superiors, under the head *formation of pupils*:

> What will numbers avail us, if unity and similarity of sentiment do not prevail?—*No rank, no state of life, can dispense the brethren* from our labours or our trials. To accustom them to despise all distinctions, and to view the world and human nature in the grand scale, the Prefect shall carefully collect all the anecdotes he can, remarkable either for their generosity or meanness, not regarding to whom they relate, whether Princes or Citizens, rich or poor. He will transmit them to the Masters of the Min-

ervals; and these will expose them in a proper manner to their pupils. They will not forget to give the name of the Prince of great personage, though the trait should dishonour him; for,

says the Code, "every member must be made sensible, that we distribute impartial justice, and that among us the wicked man upon the throne is called a villain (*ein schurke heist*) just as freely, if not more so, than the criminal who is being led to the gallows."

Under the same head we may observe another article remarkable enough, on the means of rendering the language of the adepts more uniform when speaking before any of the Order, or of facts relating to it.

On these occasions the Prefect will take care secretly to instruct the *lower Superiors* in what stile they are to hold forth, what ideas to propagate, and in what manner they should make their pupils speak.

> Hence the pupils will constantly accord themselves in every thing, whether in language or action, with the Superiors, though their motives may be unknown to them. But these means we shall all tend toward the same object; the young adepts will accustom themselves to search and dive into the intentions of the Order; to refrain from acting; or to be silent on all doubtful occasions, till they have received the advice or orders of their Superior as to what they ought to do or say.

Under the head *Love or Spirit of the Order*, the Prefect is instructed, that such *Love or Spirit* is to be infused by descanting on the beauty and importance of the object of the Sect, the integrity of its members, the greatness and certainty of its means, the utility of the instruction imparted, and security promised to all its pupils by the Order.—This *Love* will always be proportionate to the certainty of *being happy while attached to the Order, and of finding real happiness in no other place*. To stimulate it, *he must always feed them with the hopes of new discoveries more and more important*; and, lest their zeal should diminish,

> *try to keep our pupils constantly occupied with objects relating to the Order; make it their favourite pursuit.*—See what the Roman Catholic Church does to make its religion familiar to its followers, how it keeps their attention incessantly toward it; model yourself by that.—It would be impossible to foresee all cases and lay down rules for them;—Let it then be the constant study of the Prefects and other Superiors to prepare themselves for unforeseen events— Let them propose and distribute prizes for the best compositions on such cases. Perpetual vigilance will render it impossible for the edifice not sooner or later to succeed, and to take a proper consistency according to the local circumstances. Exhort the Brethren to complacency, beneficence, and generosity toward each other *and toward the Order*.

Chapter XVI

The next article treats of *Obedience*. Here the Prefect is informed, that should he have been diligent and successful in impressing the young pupils with the grandeur of the views of the Sect, they will doubtless obey the Superiors with pleasure. How can they do otherwise than submit themselves to be conducted by Superiors who have so carefully guided them hitherto, who contributed so much to their present happiness, and who promise to perpetuate it in future? May the man who is not to be enticed into obedience by such advantages be rejected from among us; *let him be cast out from the society of the elect!* The spirit of obedience is to be more particularly infused by *example* and instruction—by the conviction, that to obey our Superiors is in fact only fulfilling our own inclination—by the gradual progress of the degrees—by the hopes of discovering more important truths—by fear properly managed—by honours, rewards, and distinctions granted to the docile—by contempt cast on the stubborn—by avoiding familiarity with the inferiors—by the exemplary punishment of the rebellious—by the selection of those whom we know to be devoted to us and ready to execute all our commands—by a particular attention to the *Quibus Licets* whereby we may see how far the Orders of the Superiors have been executed;—and by the punctuality of the intermediary Superiors in sending the *tablets* or reports respecting their inferiors. *The more particular those tablets are, the better they will be; for it is on them that all the operations of the Order are grounded.* It is by their means that the progress and number of the Brethren are to be known; that the strength or weakness of the machine, and the proportion and adhesion of all its parts are to be calculated, and that the promotion of the Brethren, the merits and demerits of the assemblies, of the Lodges, and of their Superiors, are to be judged.

When treating of *Secrecy*, "The Prefect is informed, that *this is the most essential article*; and it is on that account that even in countries where the Sect may have acquired sufficient power to throw off its mask, it is to remain veiled in darkness."

> The Prefect is always to hide with dexterity the real object of his views according to local circumstances. Let him agree with the Provincial on what shape he shall assume to conceal the Order.—As in the religious institutions of the Roman Church, where religion, alas! is but a pretext; exactly so, only *in a nobler manner, must we enwrap our Order in the forms of a mercantile society, or some other exterior of a similar nature.*

In vain would the reader ask me, whence the Illuminized Code had taken the idea of Religion being only a *pretext* for the religious institutions in the Catholic Church. It has not come to my knowledge, that the most barefaced Sophisters have ever advanced a calumny of this sort. I have seen the religious founders, such as St. Francis,

St. Benedict, or St. Basil, and other founders of orders, described by the Sophisters as superstitious enthusiasts. But even among the apostates who must have been acquainted with the Orders they had lived in, we have never heard one pretend that Religion was only a *pretext* either for the institution they abandoned, or for their ancient brethren. Did any of them ever assert, that ambition, avarice, or any pretext beside Religion, had given rise to the foundation of the Order of the Capuchins, Friars, Benedictines, or Carmelites, and of so many other convents destined for men or women? This, however, is not a calumny originating with Weishaupt; it is not to be found in his instructions sent to Knigge, and on which the latter formed the Code of Laws for the Regents and Local Superiors, though he subjoined many of his own ideas. Knigge was totally ignorant of every thing relating to religious Orders. Weishaupt was born a Roman Catholic, and might indeed, in his impiety, have repeated the ideas of many apostate Sophisters, or have left this strange comparison of his Illuminism with the religious institutes, since it was in the Code: but I should be truly surprized were I to find that it was a Calumny of his invention. He knew too well how much he stood in need of darkness to envelope his designs; and he also knew, that in the Roman Catholic Church no religious institute was adopted, until it had been made public and examined by the constituted authorities.

After this absurd calumny follows a recapitulation of every thing we have already exposed to our readers in the first Chapters of this Volume, on the necessity of hiding the proceedings and even the very existence of the Lodges. But I find the following additions in this place.

"Lest the number of the Brethren should expose them to discovery, by their assemblies being too numerous, the Prefect will take care that no more than ten members shall assemble in the same *Minerval* Church."

> Should any place contain a greater number of pupils, the Lodges must be multiplied, or different days of assembly must be assigned, that all may not meet at once; and should there be several Minerval Churches in the same town, the Prefect will take care that those of one Lodge shall know nothing of the others.

For the better direction of the lower part of the edifice, he will observe the following rules—He is to nominate the Magistrates of the Minervals; but the chief of these Magistrates can only be named with the consent of the Provincial. He will be responsible for those he names.—He will overlook the Masonic and Minerval Lodges, to see that every thing is regularly and punctually executed. He will not permit any discourses to be delivered there which may give any strong suspicions of what is contriving against Religion, the state, or morals.—He will suffer no Brother to be advanced to the higher de-

grees before he has acquired the requisite qualities and principles; on this point, says the Code, he
cannot carry his precautions, *anxiety*, and *scrupu-
losity* too far.

> It has already been stated in the rules, that
> persons not belonging to the Order may be
> received into the Masonic Lodges of Illumi-
> nism—The Prefect will carefully watch lest
> any of these strangers should take the lead in
> the Lodges.—They should as far as possible be
> honest men, sedate, and quiet; but by some
> means or other they should be made useful to
> the Order.—Without leave of the Provincial, the
> Prefect shall hold no correspondence on mat-
> ters relating to the Order with any person out
> of his province—as his peculiar object will be,
> to watch over and to instruct the Superiors of
> the Minerval and Masonic Lodges, he will have
> recourse to the Provincial in all doubtful cases
> of any importance.
>
> Let the Prefect make himself perfect master
> of these rules; let him follow them with preci-
> sion; let him always attend to the whole of the
> object; let him take care that each one may at-
> tend to his duty, *doing neither more nor less
> than the law require*s; and he will find in this
> instruction all that is necessary for the regula-
> tion of his conduct.

Such is the promise which terminates the laws
for the Prefect of Illuminism. The *five articles*
treated of in these regulations are prefaced by a
far more pompous promise: "If, it is said, we have

exactly foreseen every thing relating to these five articles, nothing will be impossible for us in any country under the Sun ."[7]

---

7   *Ist nun in diessen fünf stücken alles gehörig besorgt, so ist in iedem lande unter der sonne nichts unmöglich*—The whole of this Chapter is extracted from the Instructions C for the Prefect, from Page 145 to 166.

CHAPTER XVII.

Instructions for the Provincial.

By far the greater part of the code of laws which has just been laid before the reader as relating to the *Regents* and *Prefects* of the Illuminées, was originally written by Weishaupt for the instruction of his Provincials. This is evident from the first digest of these laws, as they appear in the second part of the second volume of the *Original Writings* of the Sect, from page 17 to 43. It is even one of those parts which Knigge looked upon as a master-piece of politics.[1] So replete with artifice did he think it, that he deemed it a pity to

---

1   See his *Last Observations*.

circumscribe the knowledge of it to the Provincials alone. The reader has seen what use he has made of them, thoroughly persuaded that the Regents in general, and particularly the Local Superiors, could greatly benefit the Order by attending to them. The Areopagites and General consented to these new dispositions; but the following part of this chapter remained appropriated to the Provincials.

> I. The Provincial shall make himself perfect master of the whole constitution of the Order.— The system of it should be as familiar to him as if he had invented it.

> II. As a guide for all his actions, he shall adopt the whole government and the instructions already laid down for the Regents and Local Superiors, not neglecting a single rule.

> III. The Provincial shall be chosen by the Regents of his Province, and be confirmed by the National Superior. . .[2] The high Superiors (the Areopage and General) have the power of deposing him.

> IV. He shall be a native of, or at least be thoroughly acquainted with the province under his inspection."

> V. He shall be engagted as little as possible in public concerns, or in any other enterprize, that he may devote all his time to the Order.

---

2   There is an omission in the copy from which these rules have been printed, which makes part of this article unintelligible.

Chapter XVII

VI. *He shall assume the character of a man retired from the world, and who only seeks rest.*

VII. He shall fix his residence as nearly as possible in the centre of his province, the better to watch over the different districts.

VIII. On his being named Provincial, he shall leave his former characteristic, and assume that which the high Superiors shall give him.—The same Superiors will send him the impression of the seal he is to bear, and he will wear it engraved on his ring.

IX. The archives of the province, which the Regents will have taken care to seal up and carry away on the demise of his predecessor, are to be entrusted to him on his nomination.

X. The Provincial will monthly transmit the general report of his province to the National Inspector immediately over him. As he himself only receives the reports of the Local Superiors a fortnight after the month is up, he will necessarily be always a month behind-hand, making, for example, the report of May about the end of June, and so on. This report will be subdivided into as many parts as he has Prefects under his inspection. He will carefully note every thing of consequence that has happened in any of the schools or lodges: also the names, ages, country, station in life, and the date of the reversal letters, of each new adept; the high Superiors wishing to have no further information concerning the new adepts until they come to the class of Regent, unless on some particular occasion.

XI. Beside this monthly report, he is to apply to the National Superior in all extraordinary cases which are not left to his decision. He is also to send in his personal tablets every three months; and he will undertake no political enterprize without having first consulted.

XII. He has nothing to do with the other Provincials. Let things go on well or ill in a neighbouring province, it is no business of his. If he wishes to ask any thing of the other Provincials, let him apply to the National Inspector.

XIII. If he has any complaint to make against the Inspector, he will direct his letter *Soli* or *Primo*.

XIV. All the Regents of the province are his counsellors; they are to second and help him in all his enterprizes. If it be convenient to him, he should have two of them near his person to serve him as secretaries.

XV. He confirms the nominations of all the Superiors of the inferior degrees. He also names the Prefects, but they must be approved by the Director, who can refuse his sanction.

XVI. He has a right to send the brethren *who are pensioned* by the Order, and to employ them in those parts of the province where he may think them most useful.

XVII and XVIII. He transmits the characteristics of the brethren and geographical names of the lodges to the Prefects, as he receives them from the high Superiors.

XIX. He is also to send the names of the excluded brethren, that an exact list may be preserved in all the assemblies.

XX. When he has any reprimand to make to a Brother, whom it may be dangerous to offend, he will assume an unknown hand, and the signature of *Basyle*. This name, which no member of the Order bears, is peculiarly preserved for that object.

XXI. He will sometimes write to the Inferior degrees; and on the proposition of the Epopts he will decide what books are to be put into the hands of the young adepts according to the degrees they are in.— He is as much as possible to promote libraries, cabinets of natural philosophy, *Musæums*, collections of manuscripts, &c. in the most convenient parts of his Province; these, it may easily be conceived, are only intended for the adepts.

XXII. The Provincial opens the letters of the Minor and Major Illuminées which are directed Soli. He also reads the *Quibus Licets* of the Epopts and *Primos* of the Novices; but can neither open the *Primo* of the Minerval, the *Soli* of the Knight, nor the *Quibus Licet* of the Regent."[3] This gradual power of opening the letters of the Brethren according to the degree

---

3　This article is extracted from the instructions for the Prefect; but, being directly addressed to the Provincial, I have placed it here.

they belong to, plainly indicates that some mark peculiar to each degree is made use of; but I have not been able to discover that mark. The reader will have observed, that all the letters, even the *Quibus Licets*, are opened by Brethren of a higher degree than that of the adept who writes; and consequently he can never know who it is that answers him, as the rules of this Hierarchy are only made known to the Brethren in proportion as they rise in dignity. The Provincial himself can only form a conjecture as to the persons who open his letters and those of the other Brethren which he is not permitted to open himself.

XXIII. He shall raise no Brother to the degree of Regent, without having first obtained the consent of the National Inspector.

XXIV. He is to inform the Dean of the branch of science which each new adept has made choice of on his admission into the Minerval Academy.

XXV. Lest any of the Archives should be mislaid, he will take care to form but one bundle of all the tablets, reversal letters, and other documents relating to the same adept.

XXVI. He will apply himself to procure as many co-operators as possible for the Order, in the scientific branches.

XXVII. He will transmit to the Deans all remarkable treatises or discourses, and every thing relative to the degree of Epopt; for example, the lives historical or characteristic, dissertations, &c.

XXVIII. If among the Epopts any men be found endowed with great talents, but little fitted for the political government of the Order, the Provincial must devise means of removing them from such functions.

XXIX. When the Chapters of the Scotch Knights are composed of more than twelve Knights, he will raise the ablest among them to the degree of Epopt.

XXX. In each Chapter he will have a confidential Epopt, who will be his *secret censor* or spy.

XXXI. The Provincial will receive his letters patent from the National Superior—When he issues those for the Chapters of the Scotch Knights, he will make use of the following formula: We of the Grand Lodge of the *Germanic Orient*, constituted Provincial and Master of the district of N N, make known that by these presents we give to the venerable Brother (here is the characteristic and true name of the new Venerable or Master) full powers to erect a secret Chapter of the *most holy* Scotch Masonry, and to propagate this *Royal Art* conformably to his instructions by the establishment of new Masonic Lodges of the three symbolic degrees—Given at the Directory of the District—

(L. S.)   SECRET PROVINCIAL
                  OF THE DIRECTORY.

without any further signature.

XXXII. To say every thing in a few words, the Provincial has the special charge of putting his province in a proper situation for attempting every thing for the general good, and for preventing all evil.—*Happy the state where our Order shall have acquired such power!* Nor will it prove a difficult task for the Provincial who shall implicitly follow the instructions of his high Superiors.—Seconded by so many able men *deeply versed in moral sciences*, submissive and secretly labouring like himself, there can be no noble enterprize which he may not undertake, nor evil design which he cannot avert—Therefore let there be no connivance at faults; no *Nepotism*, no private piques; no views but for the general good; no object, no motives but those of the Order. And let the Brethren rely upon us, that we shall never create any Provincials but such as are capable of fulfilling these duties; *but let it be also remembered, that we reserve in our hands all the means necessary for chastising the man who should presume to abuse the power he has received from us.*[4]

XXXIII. This power must never be employed but for the good of the Brethren. We should indeed help all whom we can help; but when the circumstances are similar, the members of our society are always to have the preference.— Particularly as to those whose fidelity is proof against all the powers of seduction. In their support let us be prodigal of our toils, our money, our honour, our goods, even our blood; and *let the least affront offered to any Illuminée be the general cause of the Order.*

Thus terminate the instructions for the Provincial. They forewarn us of the existence of a most tremendous power above him whence all the authority of the Order emanates; a power which reserves to itself the means of chastising whoever

---

4 See the Instruction D for the degree of Regent.

shall abuse that portion which it has entrusted to any of its adepts; that is to say, who shall not have made it subservient to the grand object and to all the plots of the Sect.—There are, in fact, three offices in the hierarchal Orders of Superiors above the Provincial. First, the *National Directors*, then the *Supreme Council* called the *Areopagites* by the Sect, the authority of which extends over the Iluminees of all nations; and that is presided over by the *General of the Order*. The following Chapter will give every light on these supreme Magistrates of Illuminism which the known Archives of the Sect can reflect.

Of the National Directors, of the Areopagites, and of the General of Illuminism.

I n the general plan of the Government of the Illuminées it is said, that every Brother shall receive particular instructions according to the rank he holds in the Hierarchy of the Order: Yet I have never been able to discover those intended for the use of the National Directors. This part of the Code is not to be found either in the *two volumes* so often quoted of the *Original Writings*, or in that of *Philo and Spartacus* which has thrown so much light on the mysteries. It does not appear, that any of the German writers who have been the best informed on, and the most strenuous opponents of, Illuminism have ever been able to discover them. For some time I even entertained doubts whether the *Superiors* called *National Directors,* and those styled *Inspectors,* were not of the same degree in the Hierarchy of the Sect.—They were certainly distinct employments in the year 1782; for Weishaupt's letters at that period mention Germany as divided into *three inspections,* each *Inspector* having several Provincials subordinate to him.[1] But, on the other side, the general account which the Order puts into the hands of its Regents, and the last works of Philo printed in 1788, mention no intermediate office between the *Provincials* and the *Nationals,* which latter are sometimes described as National *Superiors,* at others as *National Inspectors.* Their correspondence and subordination is direct from the Supreme Council.[2] It is therefore evident, that in the last digest of the Code the two offices of *National Inspector* and *Director* were united. But in vain would the Sect conceal the instructions which it has appropriated to the functions of these *National* Superiors. The denomination alone testifies the importance which attaches to their office; and if the precise nature of their duties be wanting, it is easy to supply the deficiency, by what has already escaped the vigilance of the Sect in the foregoing parts of the Code.

---

1   *Original Writings,* vol. II., let. 15, to Cato.

2   Directions System, no. 5, and Philo's *Endliche erklärung,* page 81.

Chapter XVIII

Let the reader recall to his mind what has been said in the Chapter on the *Epopts,* of the systems which they were to form in order to seize on the empire of the Sciences and direct them all toward the accomplishment of the plots of the Sect. In the same degree we have seen them annually assembling in each province, and compiling from their partial attacks every means that their inventions could furnish, insensibly to enslave the public opinion, and to eradicate from the minds of the people what the Sect is pleased to call religious prejudices. We have seen the class of Regents more particularly occupied in sapping the foundations of the throne, and in destroying that veneration in which nations held the persons and functions of their Sovereigns—Nay, there exists a particular law framed for the Epopts which has not yet been cited, and which must here be introduced. It is to be found *in the Second Volume of the Original Writings, second Section, intitled—Articles agreed upon by the Areopagites in Ardameth* 1151 (A.D. December 1781)—There under the article HIGH MYSTERIES, I read,

> If among our Epopts *any speculative geniuses* are to be found, they shall be admitted to the degree of *Mage.*—These adepts shall be employed in collecting and digesting all the grand philosophical systems, and will invent or compile for the people a system of religion which our Order means as soon as possible to give to the universe.[3]

---

3 *So werden die selben* Magi—*Diese sammeln und bringen die*

I do not forget that I am to treat of the *National Directors*; but am somewhat afraid that my readers may adduce this plan for giving a new religion to the whole universe, as invalidating their plot for the destruction of every religion. Let such readers, however, reflect on the religion which Weishaupt has himself laid down for his *Mages*. It is the rankest *Spinosism*, admitting of no God but the world itself; that is to say, absolute Atheism. Let them also remember, that one of the last secrets of the Grand Mysteries, is to reveal to the adepts that all religions are grounded on and are the invention of imposture. Nor is it by any means difficult to account for these two schemes of the Sect, the one for the creation of a new religion, the other for the destruction of all. These plans are to be successive in their operations.

Sentiments of Religion are too deeply engraven in the minds of the people for Weishaupt to flatter himself with suddenly eradicating it, or at least without substituting some capricious and sophisticated faith, which in reality would no more constitute a religion than the *Worship of Reason*, of which the French Revolution has given us an impure essay. The religion, therefore, to be invented by the Mages of Illuminism is no more than a

---

höhere philosophische systeme in ordnung, und bearbeiten ein volks-religion, welche der Orden demnächsten der welt geben will.—In the original, which is in Cato-Zwack's handwriting, the words *volks-religion* are in cypher, thus 20, 14, 2, 3, 18,—17, 8, 2, 4, 6, 4, 14, 13.

preparatory step that should destroy the religion of Christ throughout the universe. This advantage gained, it will remain no very difficult task to open the eyes of the whole world on the inanity and imposture of their own; and thus it will have served as a scaffolding which naturally disappears with the edifice that is to be pulled down. This religion to be invented may be considered as on a parallel with those new governments, those democracies, which are to amuse the people until the period shall come when their Illuminizing Equality and Liberty shall have taught them, that each one is essentially his own sovereign, that this sovereignty is an imprescriptible right inherent in each man, in direct opposition to democracy, and even to all property or social compact.

Such is the general tenour of the systems to be invented and prosecuted by the Sect, for attaining the grand object of these Conspirators. All the adepts which the Sect comprises under the denomination of *speculative geniuses* are perpetually labouring at these systems under the direction of the Provincials. But they are not the persons who complete the plans; they are only to present the first sketch, which each Provincial is obliged to transmit to the *National Directory*, there to undergo a further investigation and receive its final polish.[4] One of the first duties, therefore, of the *National Director* will be to collect all these anti-religious and anti-social systems, to pass judgment on them,

---

4   Instructions for the degree of Epopt, no. 12 and 14.

and to declare how far they can contribute towards the universal disorganization. But even these could not alone suffice for so great a work; they are surrounded by the Elect of the nation as the Provincial is by the Chosen of the provinces. This council of the Elect, after mature deliberation, declare which are the systems that are worthy of being adopted by the Order; and they will make all the additions and corrections that they may conceive conducive to the success of the general plan. Thus corrected and digested, these systems of impiety and disorganization are deposited in the *archives* of the Director, which now become *national*. It is to these that the Provincials have recourse in all their doubts, and hence flow all those lights which are to expand themselves throughout the nation:— it is hence also that the National Director[5] will take all the new regulations which he may judge necessary for the better combination and concordance of the efforts of the National Brethren.—But the Sect does not confine its views to one nation. It has formed within itself a supreme tribunal, which has subjected all nations to its inquisition. Composed

---

5   *Deswegen kommen jährlich ein mal alle Presbyter einer provinz auf der grossen Synode zusammen, machen ein grosses verzeichniss der in diesem jahr gesammlten beylagen an die National Direction wo selbst es in die haupt-katalog eingetragen, und damit ein schatz von kenntnissen formirt wird, woraus jeder befridigt werden kann: denn daraus werden die regel abstrahirt, und was noch fehlt, weitere beobachtungs aufgaben, wie schon ervahnt worden, aufgeschrieben um feste satze zu bekommen. Ibid.*, no. 15.

of *twelve Peers* or Fathers of the Order,[6] it is presided over by the General; and, under the name of Areopagites, it becomes the common centre of communication from the adepts of all nations, as the *National* is the centre of one particular nation, the *Provincial* of one province, the *Local Superior* of the lodges of his district, the *Minerval Master* of his academy, the *Venerable* of his Masonic Lodge; and, finally, as the *Insinuator* or *Recruiter* is of his novices or candidates. Thus, from the first step to the pinnacle of the Order, every thing is connected and gradually ascends by means of the *Quibus Licets, Solis* and *Primos*— Every thing that happens in each nation gradually ascends to the *National*, and from these *Directors* all is transmitted to the centre of all nations, to the supreme council of the Areopagites, and the General in chief, the universal Director of the Conspiracy.

The grand point, therefore, to be observed in the code concerning the National Director is, his direct correspondence with the Areopagites. It is evident from the terms expressed in the general plan of the government which the Sect reveals to its Regents. "In every nation there shall be a National Director associated and in direct communication with our Fathers, the first of whom holds the helm of the Order."[7] This accounts for the injunction given to the Provincial, to make frequent and exact returns to the National Director of every thing that may take

---

6   Philo's *Endliche erklarung*, page 119.

7   *Directions System*, no. 4.

place in his province; to have recourse to him on all doubtful occasions, or in cases of especial importance; and never to take any step in politics without having first consulted him.[8] This explains why the choice of those adepts which are to be advanced to the political degree of Regent, or to the Prefectships of districts,[9] is left to the option of the National, or even the nomination of the Provincials.[10] This informs us why all the *Quibus Licets* of the Regents are reserved to the Director, that is to say, that all the secrets of their political discoveries may more certainly reach the hands of him who is to leave no secret hidden from the Fathers of the Order.[11]

Such then are the rights of, such the laws for the National Inspector of Illuminism; and so great is the importance which the Sect attaches to this office. To him are forwarded all the secrets of the brethren spread throughout the provinces, the Courts, or towns; to him are sent all the projects, all the reports on the successes gained by, or dangers impending over the Order; on the progress of its plots; on employments, dignities, and power to be acquired for the adepts; on the candidates to be rejected, the enemies to be crushed, the councils and state offices of princes to be seized. To him, in short, are reported all the means which can retard or accelerate the fall of the Altar and of em-

---

8   *Ibid.*, no. 10 and 11.

9   *Ibid.*, no. 15 and 23.

10   *Ibid.*, no. 9.

11   *Ibid.*, no. 22.

pires, the disorganization of every church and state within his inspection.—It is by means of his direct correspondence, and that of his Co-nationals, that the discoveries of the Scrutators, the political plans of the Brethren, the speculations of the plodding *geniuses* of the Order, the plans proposed and debated in the councils of Princes, and every thing, in short, which can weaken or strengthen the opinion of the people; which is to be foreseen or hindered, to be anticipated or hastened in each town, court, or family, are concentrated, and subjected to the views of the supreme council of the Sect. Hence no sovereign, no minister of state, no father of a family, no man in the bonds of the most intimate friendship, can say, My secret is my own, it has not, it will not, come to the knowledge of the Areopagites. By means of these same National Directors too, we behold all the orders of the Illuminizing Peers gradually descending to the adepts of all nations, of all provinces, academies, and lodges, whether Minerval or Masonic; and immediately re-ascending through these same Nationals an exact statement to the Areopagites in what manner each command has been executed. It is by the Nationals too, that the supreme council is informed of the negligent Brethren who need to be stimulated, of the transgressors and stubborn adepts who deserve punishment, and stand in need of being reminded that they have sworn to submit both their lives and fortunes to the commands of the high Superiors (the unknown Fathers) of the Areopagites. In vain would the Sect strive to conceal the laws which the code lays down for these Inspectors. After what the reader has already seen of the laws of the Order, he must naturally conclude that such are evidently the mysteries comprehended in those words, *There shall be in each empire a National Director associated or in direct correspondence with the Fathers of the Order.*

With respet to the laws and interior economy of the councils, it is easy to be conceived, that the Sect has succeeded in encompassing them with impenetrable darkness. Some few rays of light, however, have been cast on it, and that by the Fathers themselves.

In the first place, we see *Philo*-Knigge, in his Apology, speaking as follows of these supreme magistrates of Illuminism:

> Their labours, with regard to the parts purely speculative, were to have in view the knowledge and the tradition of all the important, holy, and sublime discoveries to be made *in the religious* mysteries and in the higher philosophy. Twelve Areopagites only are to compose this tribunal; and one of them is to be the chief. When any one of the members dies, or retires, his successor is chosen from among the Regents.[12]

This general idea given by Knigge of the Supreme Council is indeed mysterious;—but he could scarcely be expected to *publish* more, knowing

---

12   *Last Observations of Philo*, page 115.

as he did the fate which awaits those who betray the secrets of the Sect. He has, however, at least said enough to give us clearly to understand, that all the religious and philosophical or rather impious and sophisticated speculations of the Epopts, perpetually perverting the sciences and operating the extinction of all religious ideas, are concentrated within the council of the Areopagites; we have seen them combining, digesting, approving, or rejecting *those plans of a new religion which the Mages* are directed to invent, and which the Sect *means incontinently to give to the world.*

In his familiar correspondence, Spartacus speaks more openly and with greater latitude to his beloved Cato. Therein it appears, that anti-religious systems do not alone employ the meditations of the Fathers; for, soon after having mentioned the object of those *Quibus Licets* in which the young adepts were to give an account of the prejudices they might have discovered in themselves, which of them predominated, and how far they had succeeded in destroying them, he proceeds to say, "It is by these means that I discover such of our Order as have the proper dispositions for adopting certain *special* doctrines, and more elevated, on governments and religious opinions."[13] He then continues,

---

13   *Aus diesen kann ich ersehen welche geneigt sind gewisse sonderbare staats lehren, weiters hinauf religions meynungen anzunehmen.*

> *The maxims and politics of the Order are completely explained in the end.* Here, in the Supreme Council, they project and examine the plans to be adopted for gradually enabling us to attack the enemy of reason and human nature *personally* (*auf den leib*). Here also the mode of introducing such plans into the Order is discussed, and it is decided to which brethren they are to be entrusted, and how far each one can be employed in their execution, in proportion to the insight given to him.[14]

The reader is already too well acquainted with the maxims and policy of Illuminism, not to join with me in saying, Here then is the grand object of this Supreme Council of the Sect! It is in that dark recess that all those artifices are devised for rendering the disorganizing systems of Equality and Liberty familiar to the Illuminizing adepts: There is exactly ascertained the proportion which each class of the Brethren can bear in this universal destruction of religion, empire, society, and property; there again is the day anxiously sought and the means prepared, for hereafter throwing off the mask, and attacking *personally* the defenders of religion, laws, and property, as so many en-

---

14 *Und am end folgt die totale einsicht in die Politic und maximen des Ordens. In diesen obersten Conseil, werden die project entworfen, wie den feinden der vernunft und Menschlichkeit nach und nach auf den leib zu gehen seye: Wie die sache unter den Ordens mitgliedern einzuleiten, wen es anzuvertauen? Wie ein jeder a proportione seiner einsicht kanne dazu gebraucht werden.—Original Writings*, letter to Cato -Zwack, 10th March, 1778.

emies to reason and humanity; there concentrate all the declarations, the reports, the plans of all the brethren dispersed throughout the universe, that the Sect may judge of its own strength, and compare it with that of the friends to the Altar and the Laws. To sum up all, it is there that the artifices and means are determined on, and the merits and powers of the higher adepts are investigated prior to their being entrusted with that part of the grand conspiracy to which their abilities are best adapted. Let the reader remember, that it is not a stranger to the Sect who has thus described the Areopage; it is the grand Legislator of Illuminism himself. Can we any longer stand in need of the regulations for this council? No; we well know what they must be; we know that impiety, and the most consummate arts in seduction and sedition, are to be their leading features; we further know, that its members must resemble Weishaupt himself, before they can be permitted to sit with him in council. What other bond of union do they need, beside the machination of the most hideous plots, the just or unjust means of forwarding the interests of the Sect as much as circumstances will permit, and the ensuring of success by the blackest and most profound artifices that depravity can invent? The fertile genius of the Legislator, however, would not commit the success of the least of his crimes to chance. He attempted to sketch a code of laws for his Areopagites, and for any future Spartacus that might succeed him. The code contains but a *sketch* of what he calls *laws ad interim*. It is to be found in the ninth section of the first volume of the *Original Writings*, and is addressed to the Areopagites. Many other passages of his letters relate to the same object.—I have transcribed the following articles:

> The Areopagites shall form the Supreme Council (literally, the Supreme College).—Their occupations shall relate to affairs of the greatest importance, and they shall pay little or no attention to such as are less essential.—They may *recruit*, it is true (*können sie zwar recroutiren*); that is to say, they may entice Candidates into the Order; but they must leave the care of their instruction to some intelligent adept. From time to time they will visit these Candidates, to inspire them with fresh ardour, to stimulate their zeal—They will be particularly careful in seeing that the progress and method of our Illuminees is every where uniform—They will more particularly watch over Athens (*Munich*, the principal Lodge after that of Ingolstadt, where Weishaupt resided at the time he wrote these instructions). They will make no reports concerning that Lodge to any body but Spartacus. They will send monthly a statement of all the principal events, *a sort of Gazette (Ein art, von Zeitung)*, to the Brethren (*Conscii*); that is to say, to those only who are initiated in the last secrets. But (continues Weishaupt) *nota bene*, this Gazette as yet has been no more than our common journal; the *Conscii* must compose one for the use of the Areopagites. These latter will labour at *projects, ameliorations*, and

other objects of a similar nature, which are to be made known to the *Conscii* by circular letters. They are the people who are to bear a part of the weight of the general correspondence— They are not allowed to open the letters of complaint (*die litteras gravatoriales*); that is to say, those containing any complaints against them. These are to be transmitted to the general, to Spartacus, as a sure means of informing him that they fulfil their duty. This instruction being only provisional, and relating solely to the Areopage, shall not be circulated; but the council will take a copy and send back the Original to Spartacus.[15]

The assembling of the council is to be regulated according to the feasts marked in the calendar of the Order. (*Nach dem calendario Illuminatorum an Ordens festen*)."But this was soon found to be insufficient, and Weishaupt exhorts his Areopagites to meet in their senate every post-day, and at the hour of the delivery of the letters.

Short as this sketch of a Code for the Areopagites may seem, it clearly denotes the essence of their functions, and shows how they are to act as a central point for the whole Sect. A grand question was still undecided when Spartacus gave these laws to the council; which was nothing less than, Whether Spartacus was to preserve a legislative and sovereign power over the Members of this Council, similar to that authority which they were

15 Extracts from the Instruction to Cato, Marius, and Scipio, *Original Writings*, vol.I., sect. ix.

to exercise over the rest of the Order?—Great Conspirators will seldom brook control even by their fellows. They will be equal among themselves and in their dens of conspiracy. *Spartacus*-Weishaupt was naturally of a despotic disposition. His Areopagites for a long time complained of it.[16] But he contended, that as founder, he had the indefeasible right of giving to the association those laws and regulations which he judged necesssary for its perpetuation. He soon, indeed, repented of the decision he had given against himself in favour of his Senate, "That the plurality of votes should dictate the eternal laws of the Sect" (*Lex semper valitura*)[17] Notwithstanding these complaints of the Areopagites, however, he speedily found means of re-instating himself in that authority, the privation of which only thwarted his artful conceptions, by subjecting them to the opinions of persons less consummate in the conspiring arts than their master. He sometimes submits to the justification of his conduct; but that is the very moment in which the reader should observe him artfully reclaiming all the rights and pretending to the exercise of unlimited despotism, though his cant appears to reject the very idea of it. Addressing his opponents in the shape of his pupils, he recalls to their minds the monstrous services he has rendered them in their youth, as so many benefactions of the most

---

16   Letters of Philo to Cato and *Last Observations of Philo*.

17   Letter of the 8th November, 1778.

tender friendship, and asks them "of what they can in their consciences complain?" "When (says he) did you ever observe harshness or haughtiness in my conduct, with respect to you? When did I ever assume the tone of Master? Is it not rather with an excess of confidence, of goodness, of openess with my friends, that I may be reproached?"—When in this manner Weishaupt has captivated his Areopagites, he comes to the point:

> Read then (he says) my letters over and over again. You will therein perceive that the grand object of our Society is not a thing of small consequence for me; that I know how to view it, and treat it also, in the most serious manner; that I have always aimed at the establishment of order, submission, discipline, and activity, as the sole means that can lead you to the grand object. In undertaking a work of such vast importance, was I not obliged by prayers, exhortations, and advice, to maintain and stimulate the ardour of my first, my dearest companions, on whom every thing depended?—If I wish to keep the supreme direction in my own hands, hear my reasons, which are most certainly of great weight:
>
> In the first place, I must necesssarily know with whom I have to deal, and must be ascertained of the fidelity of our people; and, to effectuate this, I am not to receive reports from a sixth hand, or perhaps one still more remote, on the execution of my plans, which have been approved of by the Elect of our Mysteries . . . *In the next place, am I not the Constructor of this grand Edifice? Is there no respect due to*

me? . . . . When my system shall be completed, will it not be necessary for me to inspect the
whole, and keep every man at his station? It is
a great and radical defect in a society, where a
Superior is dependent on the Inferiors, as it has
been attempted to render me.

But, to show you how much I value the friendship of my former friends, above all the authority I may exercise over others, I renounce all my
rights, all my authority. Accept my warmest ac-
knowledgements for all your past labours and
patience. I flatter myself they have been hurtful
to nobody, and that many have acquired from
me lights on secret societies which they would
not easily have found elsewhere. The purity of
my intentions is my consolation and my recompense. From this instant I betake myself to obscurity and repose, where I shall not meet with
zealous and envious opponents. There I shall be
my own master, and my own subject.[18]

The Illuminizing Despot thus artfully pleaded
his cause. The Areopagites were impatient of his
authority, but at the same time felt the want of so
disorganizing a genius; and that they might not be
deprived of its co-operation they reproached the
Legislator with the extinction of his zeal.—The fire,
however, was only hidden beneath the embers;
they once more submit to the yoke of their former
chief, who, inflamed with zeal, dictates the conditions on which alone he will deign to place himself once more at their head. Every thing is worthy

---

18   *Original Writings*, vol. I., sect. 49.

of being remarked in them. The haughty spirit in which they are conceived, the nature, object, and extent of the power he assumes over the Supreme Council and Elect of the Order, are all worthy of our attentive notice.

I begin (says he) by telling you before hand, that it may not any more be a subject of surprize, that I will be more severe than ever. I will not overlook a single fault, and shall in that respect be much more strict toward persons whom I know rather than toward those with whom I am not so familiar. My object and views require it. And to whom would you have me address myself, if not to the chiefs of the Order, since they alone are in direct correspondence with me? That things may succeed, it is necessary that we should be actuated but by one opinion, one sentiment, and be acquainted but with one language! And how can this be accomplished, if I cannot freely speak my mind to our people? I will then re-assume my post of General on the following conditions:

I. That you will execute neither more nor less than what I shall command. I shall expect it in future; at least, should any change be thought necessary, I am to receive previous notice of it.

II. I expect that every Saturday a proper report shall be sent to me of every thing that has taken place during the week, and that it shall be in the form of *Minutes* signed by all the Elect present.

III. That I shall be informed of all the Members that have been recruited, or persons that are to be recruited, with an outline of their

THE ANTISOCIAL CONSPIRACY

characters; and let some particulars concerning them be added when they are admitted.

IV. That the statutes of the class in which you labour be punctually observed, and that no dispensations be granted without previous investigation. For should each one take upon himself to make such changes as he pleased, where would be the unity of the Order.—What I exact from you, you shall exact from those that are subject to you. If there be no order and subordina- tion in the higher ranks, there will be none in the lower.[19]

It was on the 25th of May 1779, that Weishaupt dictated these laws to his Areopage. A fifth condition seems to have made them merely provisional, and to have entrusted the despotic power in Weishaupt's hand only until the order had acquired a proper consistency; but he took care not again to lose the newly-acquired supremacy; though the Areopagites still regretted the loss of their Aristocracy, and the being reduced to be the mere agents or prime ministers of the Spartacus of the Order. But let us attend to that Spartacus, who has always represented the most legitimate authority as an outrage on human nature. Let us hear him invoking Machiavel in support of that which he wishes to exercise over the Order. He pleads his own cause with Zwack, who is also jealous of his Master, by showing all the disorder it occasioned, by every body wishing to introduce his own ideas

---

19   *Original Writings*, vol. II., letters 49 and 50.

into the Order, and then quotes the following passages from Machiavel:

> It must be laid down as a general rule, that it seldom or never happens that any Government is either well-founded at first, or thoroughly reformed afterwards, *except the plan be laid and conducted by* ONE MAN ONLY, who has the sole power of giving all orders and making all laws that are necesary for its establishment. A prudent and virtuous Founder of a State, therefore, whose chief aim is to promote the welfare of many rather than to gratify his own ambition, to make provision for the good of his country, in preference to that of his heirs or successors, ought to endeavour by all means to get the supreme *authority wholly into his hands*: nor will a reasonable man ever condemn him for taking any measures (even the most extraordinary, if they are necessary) for that purpose: The *means* indeed *may seem culpable*, but the end will justify him if it be a good one;—for he only is blameable who uses violence to throw things into confusion and distraction; and not he who does it to etablish peace and good Order.

After this long quotation which Weishaupt has made from a French transation of Machiavel, *Chap. IX. Discourses upon the first Decad of Livy,* he continues in a sorrowful tone: "but I have not been able to obtain so favourable a decision. The Brethren have viewed that which is but a necessary law in the art of governing, in the light of ambition and a thirst of dominion."[20] In the midst of this contention for power, he felt himself so superior in the art of governing conspiring associations at least, that he did not hesitate at writing to his Areopagites, *As to politics and morality, Gentlemen, you must confess that you are as yet at a great distance behind me.*[21] He at length succeeded in persuading them, that it was necessary that the General of the Order should also, as president of the Areopagites holding the *helm of the Order*, be the absolute director.[22]

Weishaupt, who left nothing relating to the disorganizing arts in an imperfect state, must, no doubt, have composed instructions to guide his successors in the exercise of their supremacy, and to teach them how to make the same use of it which he intended. But the reader will easily conceive, that these never could have escaped the vigilance of the Sect, nor pierced the dark cloud with which it had enveloped itself. It may even be possible that Weishaupt had not sufficient confidence in his Areopagites to entrust them with the entire plan. Throughout the whole hierarchy of Illuminism the lower degree is entirely ignorant of the particular instructions of the superior degrees; and why should not Weishaupt, who wished to perpetuate his disorganizing genius in all the succeeding Generals, have followed the same plan?

20 *Original Writings*, vol. II., let. 2, to Cato.

21 *Ibid.,* let. 10.

22 General Plan of the Order, no. 5.

He undoubtedly dictated laws and rules for their conduct, gave them rights which were to maintain both themselves and their Areopagites in their hierarchical superiority, and second them in the pursuit of their grand object; and these were entitled Instructions for *the General of the Illuminées*. No historian can flatter himself with the discovery of such a code of artifice and cunning; the most unrelenting wickedness and hypocrisy had invented it; and genius alone can pretend to dive into such secrets. The historian can only pretend to collect those articles which are to be found in Weishaupt's familiar correspondence, or in other parts of the code or writings of the Sect. Were we to throw this compilation into the form of instructions, the following might be nearly the result of our research.

I. The General shall be chosen by the twelve Peers of the Areopage, on the plurality of votes.[23]

II. The Areopagites can only elect one of the members of their senate for General; (*ein aus ihrher mitte gewähltes oberhaupt*);[24] that is to say, a man who has sufficiently distinguished himself among the Regents to be admitted among the twelve supreme adepts of Illuminism, and who has afterwards made himself so eminent in their council, that he is judged to be the first Illuminée in the world.

---

23 *Last Observations of Philo*, page. 119.
24 *Ibid.*

III. The adept is supposed to possess qualities requisite for a General in consequence of those he may have evinced before he was called to the Supreme Council. As he is to preside over the whole Order, he must (more than any body else) be impressed with the principles of the founder, and be divested of all religious, political, or national prejudices. The grand object of the Order must be more particularly inculcated into him, namely, that of teaching the whole universe to set aside all government, laws, and altars; and he must perpetually attend to the grand interests of human nature. His zeal is to be stimulated at the sight of every man who is subjected to any authority. It is to reinstate the inhabitants of the earth in their original Equality and Liberty that he is constituted General of all the Illuminées that are or will be spread over the world during his reign, all labouring at the accomplishment of the grand revolution of the *Man- King*.[25]

IV. The General shall have immediately under him the twelve Peers of the Supreme Council, and the various agents and secretaries which he shall judge necesssary to second him in the exercise of his functions.[26]

V. The better to secure himself from the notice of the civil and ecclesiastical powers, he may assume, after the example of the founder, some pub-

---

25   See the Mysteries.

26   See above.

lic office under the very Powers the annihilation of which is to be his sole object. But he will be only known to the Areopagites and to his agents and secretaries in his quality of General.[27] The better to conceal the residence of the General, the town where he has fixed will have three names. The common name known to all; the geographical one peculiar to the Order; and a third known only to the Areopagites and the *Conscii* or Elect.[28]

VI. Our success greatly depending on the moral conduct of the Areopagites, the General will pay particular attention to prevent all public scandals which might hurt the reputation of the Order. He will represent to them in the strongest colours how much bad example will contribute to alienate from the Order the kinds of persons who might otherwise prove its most useful members.[29]

VII. The better to preserve that respect which virtue commands from inferiors, the General will assume the character of austere morals. That he may always have the grand object present to his mind, and be wholly occupied with the duties he has to fulfil; let him never lose sight of that great maxim so frequently inculcated in his letters by the founder, as the leading feature to which he owed all his successes. *Multum sudavit et alsit, abstinuit venere et vino. He neither feared heat nor cold; he abstained from wine and women,* that he might

---

27 *Orig. Writ.,* Spartacus' letters, *passim, et supra.*

28 *Orig. Writ.,* vol. I, sect. 3.

29 *Ib.,* vol. II., let 9 & 10.

always be master of his secret, always be master of himself, and prepared for all exigencies where the interests of the Order might require it.[30]

VIII. The General shall be the central point for the Areopagites, as the latter are for the whole body of Illuminées. That is to say, each Areopagite holding correspondence with the National Inspectors is to make a report of all the *Quibus Licets* sent, and of all the secrets discovered by the corresponding Inspector; the secrets thus flowing from all parts will ultimately settle under the eye of the General.[31]

IX. The functions of the General, and the success of his dispositions, greatly depending on the information he receives by means of this correspondence, he will distribute it among his Areopagites, assigning to each that of a particular nation whose Inspector is to transmit all his reports to him.[32]

X. The principal heads of this correspondence shall be—1st, The number of the brethren in general, that the force of the Sect may be ascertained in each nation.—2dly, Those brethren who distinguish themselves the most by their zeal and intelligence—3dly, Those adepts who hold important offices about the Court, in the Church, Armies, or Magistracy: also what kinds of services might be expected from or prescribed to them in the grand revolution which our Order was preparing for hu-

---

30   *Ibid.*, vol. I., let 16, &c.

31   *Vide supra.*

32   *Ibid.*, vol. II., let 6, 13, &c.

man nature.—4thly, The general progress which our maxims and our doctrine were making in the public opinion; how far nations were prepared for the grand revolution; what strength and means of defence still remained in the hands of the civil and ecclesistical powers; what persons were to be placed or displaced; what engines were to be played off, to hasten and secure the success of our revolution; and the means necessary to bind the hands of those who might resist.[33]

XI. If from this correspondence he should judge it necesssary to dismiss any of the brethren from the Order, (and all the rights recognized by the adepts as inherent in the Order, particularly that of *Life and Death* being in the hands of the General) he will have to decide what further punishment is to follow the ejectment: whether the culprit is to be declared infamous throughout all the lodges of the Order, or whether the pain of death is to be pronounced against him.[34]

XII. The General, after having chastised the imprudent, cowardly, and treacherous adepts, will turn his attention toward the discovery of those brethren who may be best fitted for seconding his views in each empire. Without making himself known to them, he will establish a line of communication between them. He will himself prepare the links of this immense chain after the manner

---

33 See the different degrees and the views with which the *Quibus Licets* and tablets, &c. &c. are written.

34 *Orig. Writ.*, vol. II., let 8, *et supra*, Oath of the Novice.

laid down by our founder as the grand means of governing, from his mysterious centre, all the diverging ramifications of the Sect to the extremities of the earth; as a means of vivifying invisible armies in an instant, of putting them in motion, of directing their course, and of irretrievably executing the most astonishing revolutions, even before the very Potentates whose thrones are overturned have had time to surmise their danger.

XIII. The use of the chain is obvious and easy. To touch the fist link is all that is required. A single stroke of a pen is the grand spring that imparts motion to the whole. But the success depends on the choice of the time. In his hidden abode the General shall medidate the means, and catch the propitious moment. The signal of universal revolution shall not be given till a time when the combined force and instantaneous efforts of the brethren shall be irresistible.

The illuminizing General who shall have managed this chain with the greatest art, who shall have spread it both far and near, who shall have imparted to it a sufficient power of action to bear away and overturn at a single effort every throne and every altar, all political and religious institutions, and shall strew the earth with the ruins of empires—He will be the creator of the *Man-King, sole king, sole sovereign* of his actions as of his thoughts. To that General is reserved the glory of consummating the grand revolution which has so long been the ultimate object of our mysteries.

Chapter XVIII

Whatever proofs I may have adduced, that must naturally lead my readers to such a conclusion, it may nevertheless be an object of surprise to them to see that Weishaupt had really planned this long chain of subterraneous communications, by which himself and his successors were empowered invisbly to actuate thousand of legions, which instantaneously, on a day prescribed, might burst into existence armed with pikes and torches, and all the horrid implements of universal revolution. Let my readers then cast their eyes on this *series of progression*, which Weishaupt has with his own hand traced in his letters first to *Cato*-Zwack and afterwards to *Celsus*-Baader. The explanations are his own, and let them be particularly attended to.

> For the present, direct nobody to me but *Cortez*, that I may have some leisure to digest my speculations, and determine each one's place; for every thing depends on that. My operations with you shall be directed by the following table:

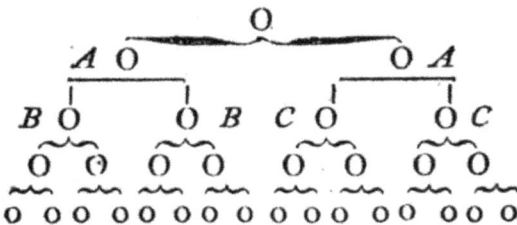

> Immediately under me I have two adepts, into whom I infuse my whole spirit; each of these

corresponds with two others, and so on. By this
method, and in the simplest way possible, I can
inflame and put in motion thousands of men at
once. It is by such means that orders are to be
transmitted and political operations carried on.[35]

A few days after he writes to *Celsus*-Baader, and
tells him,

I have sent to Cato a table (*schema*) showing
how one may *methodically* and without much
trouble *arrange a great multitude of men in
the finest order possible*. He will probably have
shown it to you; if he has not, ask for it. Here is
the figure (*then follows the figure*).

The spirit of the first, of the most ardent, of
the most profound adept daily and incessantly
comunicates itself to the two A, A; by the one
to B, B; by the other to C, C: B B and C C com-

35 I here feel it incumbent on me to insert the original text, to
show that I do not exaggerate Weishaupt's meaning. The following are the terms in which he writes to Cato:—"An mich
selbst aber verveisen sie dermalen noch keinen unmittelbar
als den *Cortez*, bis ich schreibe, damit ich indessen speculiren,
und die leute geschickt rangieren kann; den davon hangt alles ab. Ich werde in dieser figur mit ihnen operiren." (*Here
stands the figure already inserted above: The Letters ABC
allude to the explanation given in the Letter to Celsus*). "Ich
habe zwey unmittelbar unter mir welchen ich meinen ganzen
geist einhauche, und von diesen zweyen hat wieder jeder zwey
andere, und so fort. Auf diese art kann ich auf die einfachste
art tausend menschen in bewegung und flammen setzen. Auf
eben diese art muss man die *ordres* erheilen, und im poli-
tischen opieren." *Original Writings*, vol. II., let 8, to Cato, of
the 16th February 1782. It may be remarked that Weishaupt's
style is none of the purest.

Chapter XVIII

municate it to the eight following; these to the
next sixteen, from thence to the thirty-two and
so downwards. I have written a long explanation of it all to Cato. In a word, *every man has
his Aide-Major, by whose means he immediately acts on all the others. The whole force
first issues from the center and then flows back
again to it.* Each one subjects, as it were, to his
own person, *two men whom he searches to the
bottom, whom he observes,* disposes, inflames,
and drills, as it were, like recruits, that they may
hereafter exercise and fire with the whole regiment. The same plan may be followed throughout all the degrees.[36]

---

36 The original text of this letter is to be found in the Original
   Letters, vol.II. Let 13, to *Celsus* without any date. It is as follows: "*Ich habe an Cato ein schema geschickt, wie man pl-
   anmassig eine grosse menge menschen in der schonsten ordnung . . . abrichten kann . . . Es ist diese forme.*"
   "*Der geist des ersten, wärmsten, und einsichtsvollesten
   communicirt sich unaufhorlich und täglich an A A—A an B
   B: und das andere an C C—B B, und C C communiciren sich
   auf die namliche art an die unteren 8. Diese an die weitere
   16, und 16 an 32, und so weiter. An Cato hab ich es weitläu-
   figer geschrieben: Kurz! Jeder hat zwey flügel adjutanten,
   wodurch er mittelbar in all übrige wirkt. Im centra geht alle
   kraft aus, und vereignigt sich auch wiëder darinn. Jeder
   sucht sich in gewisser subordination zwey männer aus, die
   er ganz studiert, beobachtet, abrichtet, anfeuert, und so zu
   sagen, wie recrouten abrichtet, damit sie dereinst mit dem
   ganzen regiment abfeuem und exerciren können. Das kann
   man durch alle grade so einrichten.*"
   I do not find the long explanation mentioned as sent to Cato
   by Weishaupt, nor do I remember to have seen it. It would
   most certainly be curious, and we should see in a clearer light
   how he was to infuse his spirit into and fire the minds of thousands of men; but still these two letters are proofs more than

This is not a document which, like many others, flowed unintentionally from Weishaupt's pen, and which he left his disciples to collect, in order to form the political Code—*Give me leisure to digest my speculations, and to determine each one's place—It is by such means that orders are to be transmitted, and political operations carried on.* These words evidently demonstrate, that it is not a provisional law which he is about to pronounce, but a premeditated one, that is to last till that fatal period when whole legions, fired with his spirit, are to be led to that terrible exercise for which he had so long been drilling them; that time so expressly foretold by Weishaupt and his Hierophants, when they were to *tie hands*, to *subjugate, fire on, and vandalize* the whole universe.

When this fatal law shall be fulfilled, then will the last Spartacus sally forth from his baleful den, and triumphantly claim the sanguinary palm of murder and destruction from the Old Man of the Mountain, who would scarcely have been worthy of being his precursor. The earth loaded with the ruins of laws and empires; mortals blaspheming their God; nations lamenting over their conflagrating towns, their palaces, public monuments, and arts, and even their cottages, all overthrown; society weeping over its laws;—such shall be the sight which the last Spartacus will contemplate with joy, when he shall exultingly exclaim, "At length, my

---

sufficient for our purpose.

Brethren, the long-wished for day is come; let us celebrate the name, and dedicate this day as sacred to the memory of Weishaupt, our founder. We have consummated his grand mysteries; no laws shall exist, but those of his Order. Should nations be ever tempted *to return to their wickedness,* (to laws and society) this code, which has once destroyed their bonds, may do it again."

Will not hell vomit forth its legions to applaud this last Spartacus, to contemplate in amazement this work of the Aluminizing Code?—Will not Satan exclaim, "Here then are men as I wished them. I drove them from Eden; Weishaupt has driven them to the forests. I taught them to offend their God; he has made them reject their God entirely. I had left the earth to repay them for the sweat of their brow; he has stricken it with sterility; for it will be in vain for them to pretend to till and sow that which they shall not reap. I left them in their inequality of riches; but he has swept all away; he has destroyed the very idea of property; he has transformed mankind into brigands. Their virtues, happiness, and greatness under the protecting laws of society or of their country, was an object of jealousy to me; but he has cursed their laws and their country, and has reduced them to the stupid pride and ignorance of the roaming, savage, and vagabond clans. In tempting them to sin, I could not deprive them of repentance and the hope of pardon; but Weishaupt has taught them to scoff at crime and despise repentance. Villany without remorse, and hopeless misfortune, are all that he has left to the miserable inhabitants of the earth!

Meanwhile, before Satan shall exultingly enjoy this triumphant spetacle, which the Illuminizing Code is preparing, let us examine how far success has hitherto attended on its footsteps?—What share has it borne in that revolution which has already desolated so many countries and menaces so many others.—How it engendered that disastrous monster called *Jacobin*, raging uncontrouled, and almost unopposed, in these days of horror and devastation—In short, what effects this Code of the Illuminées has produced, and what effects it may produce.—This will be the object of the *historical part* of the Sect, and of the IVth and last volume of these Memoirs.

END OF THE THIRD PART.

Notes Concerning Some of the Passages Contained in the First Two Volumes.

he public has felt convinced how nearly it is concerned in the conspiracies which for the subject of these Memoirs; and to this circumstance it is, that I am indebted for the great success they have met with, and the sale of an entire Edition of 1000 Copies before the Third Volume was sent to press.[1] By such an extraordinary mark of public approbation, I am naturally excited to vindicate these Memoirs from any aspersions

---

1   The English Edition has found nearly a similar demand, though the translation was only undertaken after the French Original had been some time published.

that might in the slightest manner impugn their authenticity. Not indeed that any such danger is to be apprehended from a letter send to the Editors of the *British Critic*,[2] and which its author only chooses to sign with the initials D. J. I am not, however, the less obliged to the anonymous writer; for, by treating what I have said concerning Voltaire's death as calumny and vulgar report (though I had affected nothing but what was grounded on juridical minutes deposited at Paris in the hands of Mons. Momet, Notary Public, and on the testimony of the celebrated Mr. Tronchin), he affords me the opportunity of laying before the public the following letter from M. De Luc, a name that needs no observation from me to enhance the value of its testimony.

Letter from M. DE LUC *on the Death of Voltaire.*

Sir,

Your *Memoirs illustrating the History of Jacobinism* having been the other day the subject of conversation, it was objected, that the description of Voltaire (so prominent a feature in your Work) was so very dissimilar to that given by the other historians of his life, that persons at a distance from the source of information were at a loss what judgment to form. The dif-

---

2   *British Critic: A New Review*, was a conservative, high-church quarterly journal, founded in 1793 and instigated by the British reaction against the French Revolution. —Ed.

ference between your account of his death, and
that which appears in a *Life of Voltaire* translated from the French by Mr. Monke, and published in London in 1787, was particularly noticed, and incited me to consult that work. The
Translator describes himself as *a young naval
officer, who, while at Paris, wished to employ
his recess from professional duty, both to his
improvement and advantage.* Nothing but
the youth of Mr. Monke, and his want of experience, can excuse his undertaking; for, to let
his countrymen benefit by the proficiency he
was making at Paris, he diffused among them,
through the medium of this translation, all that
poison which was then so insidiously emitted,
to produce an effect now but too well known,
and which I hope does not at this day contemplate without horror.

I will make no observations *on this Life of
Voltaire*; you know from what source it came,[3]
and how little capable it was of seducing any but
heedless youths who, without any knowledge
of the age they lived in, were still susceptible
of a sort of admiration for everything that was
great, though in vice and villainy. As one of the
artifices of impiety is to represent its champions
calmly breathing their last in the bed of honour,
I feel it incumbent on me to confirm what you
have said on one of those circumstances of the
death of Voltaire, which is so closely connected
with all the rest.

Being at Paris in 1781, I was often in company with one of those persons whose testimony

3   I have seen this life of Voltaire. Mr de Villette was the author of
it; and Mr. Monke might just as well have exercised his talents
in translating Condorcet.

you invoke on public reports, I mean Mr. Tronchin. He was an old acquaintance of Voltaire's at Geneva, whence he came to Paris in quality of first physician to the father of the late Duke of Orléans. He was called in during Voltaire's last sickness; and I have heard him repeat all those circumstances on which Paris and the whole world were at that time full of conversation, respecting the horrid state of this impious man's soul at the approach of death. Mr. Tronchin (even as physician) did every thing in his power to calm him; for the agitation he was in was so violent, that no remedies could take effect. But he could not succeed; and, unable to endure the horror he felt at the peculiar nature of his frantic rage, he abandoned him.

So violent at state in an exhausted frame could not be of long duration. Stupor, the forerunner of dissolution, must naturally succeed, as it generally does after any violent agitations generated by pain; and it is this latter state which in Voltaire has been decorated by the appellation of *calm*. Mr. Tronchin wished to discredit this error; and with that laudable view, as an eye witness, he immediately published in all companies the real facts, and precisely as you have stated them. This he did to furnish a dreadful lesson to those who calculate being able in a death-bed to investigate the dispositions most proper to appear in before the judgment-seat of the Almighty. At that period, not only the state of the body, but the condition of the soul, may frustrate their hopes of making so awful an investigation; for *justice* and sanctity as well as goodness are attributes of God; and he sometimes, as a wholesome admonition to mankind, permits the punishments denounced against the impious man to begin even in this life by the tortures of remorse.

But this inaccuracy respecting the death of Voltaire is not the only one with which the aforenamed author might be upbraided. He has supressed many well-known circumstances relating to his first disposition to return to the church, and his consequent declarations, which you have given on well-authenticated records, all anterior to that anguish of mind which his co-operators have wished to supress, and of which they themselves were too probably the cause. They surrounded him, and thus cut him off from that which alone could restore tranquillity to his soul, by employing the few moments he still had to live in making what reparations he could for the evil he had done. But this artifice could not deceive those who were better acquainted with Voltaire's character; for, not to notice the acts of hypocrisy which earthly considerations frequently made him commit, those of which the sudden fear of a future state have made him guilty are also known. I will give you an example of one, which was related to me at Gottinguen in December 1776 by Mr. Dieze, second librarian of that University; and you may, Sir, make what use of it you please.

During Voltaire's residence in Saxony, where Mr Dieze served him as secretary, he fell dangerously ill. As soon as he was apprized of his situation he sent for a priest, confessed to him, and begged to receive the sacrament, which he actually did receive, showing all the exterior signs of repentance, which lasted as long as his danger; but as soon as that was over, he affected to laugh at what he called his *littleness*, and, turning to Mr. Dieze, "My friend (said he) you have seen the *weakness of the man.*"

It is also to *human weakness* that the sectaries of his impiety have attributed the paroxysms of fear in him and some others of his accomplices. Sickness, say they, weakens the mind as well as the body, and often produces pusillanimity.—These symptoms of conversion in the wicked at the approach of death are, undoubtedly, signs of a great *weakness*; but to what is it to be attributed? is it to their understanding? certainly not; for it is in that awful moment that everything vanishes which had clouded it during their life. That *weakness*, therefore, is to be wholly attributed to their internal *conviction* that they have sinned.

Led away by vanity, or some other vicious passion, those men aspire at creating a Sect: ignorance and the passions of other men second their undertaking. Inebriated with their triumph, they persuade themselves that they are capable of giving laws to the whole world: they boldly make the attempt, and the hood-winked crowd become their followers. Having attained the zenith of happiness for the proud and vain glorious soul, they abandon themselves to all the wantonness of imagination and desire. The world then, in their eyes, becomes a vast field of new enjoyments, the legitimacy of which has no other standard but their own inclinations; and the fumes of an incense lavished on them by those whom they have taught to scoff like themselves at every law, perpetuates their delirium. But when sickness has dispersed the flattering cohort, has blasted their pleasures, and all hopes of new triumphs; when they feel themselves advancing, abandoned and naked, toward that awful *eternity* on which they have taken upon themselves to decide, not only for themselves but for all those who have been led away in the whirlwind of their fictions.—If in this terrible moment, when pride has lost its support, they come to reflect on the arguments on which they grounded their attack against the universal belief of a *Revelation* which was to serve man as a positive and universal rule in matters of faith—the weakness then of their arguments (which they dare no longer attire in the garb od sophistry) stares them in the face; and nothing but the total extinction of their feelings can quell the terrors of a conscience which tells them that they are about to appear before the tribunal of the Author of that same *Revelation*.

It is to point out this real *weakness* of the anti-christian chiefs that we must labour through their whole history, for the benefit of those who, without any further examination (and persuaded that these opinions are grounded on deep research) become their dupes and disciples: It is, I say, incumbent on us to show that those men had not, any more than their sectaries, any real *conviction*, and that their obstinacy in their opinions solely proceeded from the narcotic fumes of the incense of their admirers. For this purpose it is my intention shortly to give to the public, in confirmation of what you have said of Voltaire, all that my former acquaintance with him has brought to my knowledge. The times in which we live make it the duty of every man who has had a nearer view of the plots laid by the Sect against Revelation to unfold all the circumstances of them, which are as shameful from

their voluntary ignorance, as from their atrocity; and it is this sentiment, Sir, which makes me
partake in common with all true friends to humanity, of that admiration and gratitude which
are due to you for your generous exertions in
this charitable career.

I remain, Sir, Your's, &c. &c.

De Luc.

Windsor, the 23d Oct. 1797.

After such a testimony, let People talk of Voltaire dying with the calmness of a Hero.

II.

In the Second Volume, there is a passage of a different nature, (page 438), but which has given rise
to objections far better grounded. It relates to Mr.
Sinetty's arrival at Lisle as deputy for the Grand
Orient of Paris. I know not by what mistake he was
said to be an officer of cavalry, when in reality he
was an officer of infantry. As to *the fact related*, it
is of little importance in which he served; but the
mistake might inculpate two other officers of the
same name who served in the cavalry, and whose
loyalty and attachment to their King could never be affected by the Jacobin Missionary bearing
the same name. This mistake, however, has given
rise to much research. Mr. Le Comte de Martange,

(whom I mentioned as being in the regiment of La Sarre in 1776, and who has long since been a general officer), was applied to, and in the first answer he returned appeared to have mistaken the sense of my Memoirs (indeed he only knew them by public report at that time), thinking that I had charged the Military Lodge of Lisle with having contrived and set on foot the Jacobin Conspiracy. The reader will easily conceive how he must have treated such an assertion; but so far was I from hinting at any such thing, that I said the officers of the regiment of La Sarre had taken this emissary for an *enthusiast* and a *madman*, who on his side soon found that the officers were *Masons of his stamp.* The Count also says, that he never was acquainted with any other Sinetty than the officer of cavalry whose character is universally and deservedly esteemed by every body. Though it may be very possible for the Count to have lost all memory of a person whom he had only seen twenty years ago for a few hours, nevertheless this is the only expression that seems to denote that he was not present at the scene I have mentioned. I am intitled however to say, that the Count has since written a second letter, in which he says that he has *read my Memoirs,* and that he has there found such a concatenation of demonstrations as tempts him to think that the person who gave me the information might have been mistaken only as to some names or particular circumstances. In short, as an ultimate proof I will adduce the candour with which the person who thought himself most interested in getting the denial of the fact ascertained declared that he was perfectly convinced of the truth of it. Thus, should I lose the testimony of a witness whom I had cited, I shall have replaced it by the verdict of an impartial judge. The fact is, however, that I had taken too many precautions to have been misinformed on a fact with which I had long since been acquainted, but which I would print only on the testimony of an eye witness.

III.

I must farther inform my readers, that frequent errors have been committed in the press among the key figures in the quotations; and in Voltaire's Letters some Readers may be misled by the variety of Editions. But I again repeat, that not a single quotation has been made which is not to be found in the works quoted; and a general *Errata* shall be given at the end of the Fourth Volume, in which the Dates shall be added to the Letters.

Index.

I

T